D0744564

THE CHINESE MACHIAVELLI

3,000 YEARS OF CHINESE STATECRAFT

by Dennis and Ching Ping Bloodworth

HEIRS APPARENT

THE CHINESE MACHIAVELLI

by Dennis Bloodworth

THE CHINESE LOOKING GLASS

AN EYE FOR THE DRAGON

ANY NUMBER CAN PLAY

THE CHINESE MACHIAVELLI

3,000 YEARS OF CHINESE STATECRAFT

Dennis & Ching Ping Bloodworth

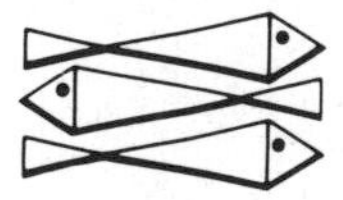

FARRAR, STRAUS AND GIROUX
New York

First printing, 1976
Printed in the United States of America
Designed by Marion Hess

Library of Congress Cataloging in Publication Data

Bloodworth, Dennis.
The Chinese Machiavelli.

Bibliography: p.
Includes index.
1. China—Politics and government. I. Bloodworth, Ching Ping, joint author. II. Title.
DS740.B52 1976 320.9'51 75-42143

Acknowledgments

Our warmest thanks are reserved for Dr. John C. S. Hall, now at the Australian National University, Canberra, to whom we are indebted for his excellent direct translation of Ching Ping's original Chinese draft and for his pertinent queries and suggestions. However, it must be emphasized that many of the quotations the book contains were added when the final, expanded manuscript was developed from that draft, and since they were translated and often condensed by the authors themselves (when not taken from other sources), Dr. Hall is not responsible for them.

Our principal sources are Chinese (see page 335), but we are indebted to the English translations of the *Chuang Tzu, Mo Tzu, Hsun Tzu,* and *Han Fei Tzu* by Burton Watson (Columbia University Press) for quotations on pages 27–28, 29–31, 36–37, 39–40, 68–69, 76, 88; to *Three Ways of Thought in Ancient China* and *The Way and Its Power* by Arthur Waley (George Allen and Unwin) for quotations on pages 44–46 and 88; and to *A History of China* by Wolfram Eberhard (Routledge and Kegan Paul) and *Revolution in China* by C. P. Fitzgerald (Cresset Press) for quotations on pages 196 and 288, respectively.

We have drawn in particular on translations of *The Art of War* by Samuel B. Griffith (Clarendon Press), *The Romance of the Three Kingdoms* by C. H. Brewitt-Taylor (Charles E. Tuttle), and the *Records of the Grand Historian of China* by

Burton Watson (Columbia University Press). The majority of references to Machiavelli and Clausewitz in Chapter 31 have been taken from *Machiavelli: The Discourses*, edited by Bernard Crick; *Machiavelli: The Prince*, translated by George Bull; and *Clausewitz: On War*, edited by Anatol Rapoport (all Penguin Books). To all of these our grateful acknowledgments are due. We would like to thank the editors of *The Observer* for permission to use material earlier published in *The Observer* magazine.

We also want to thank Dominic Chen Bloodworth for systematically checking the translation, Sheila Colton for reading and analyzing the finished English-language manuscript so painstakingly, and Edward de Souza for typing and correcting it with such care.

IN MEMORY OF
Liang Shu-hsiung, known as Liang Hsin-ch'ang
(1878–1931)

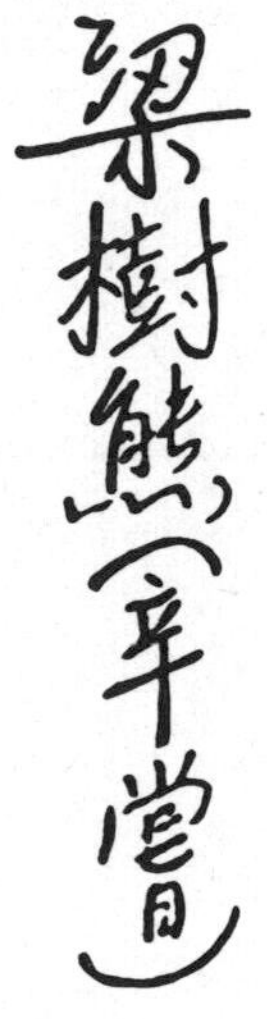

Contents

PART THREE: RULING

PART FOUR: ANALYZING

Maps

Legend

Niccolò Machiavelli was the very devil, men have said. But this book is not about some rival prince of darkness in Peking, nor does it set out to damn the Chinese for a race of unscrupulous schemers. The title sprang to mind because the name Machiavelli marvelously evokes the whole world of statecraft that he described, the policies of princes and the maneuvers of generals observed across the two thousand years of history that separate Cyrus from Cesare Borgia. And it is the Chinese equivalent of that world, observed for the most part across the twenty-five hundred years that separate Confucius from Mao Tsetung, that is our subject.

China has emerged from the wings to play her role downstage among the great powers whose shifting relationships shape our destinies, and she plays it according to her own peculiar conventions. For this reason, questions about the principles and motives and aims that dictate her diplomatic, political, and military strategy bubble up in the Western mind almost weekly. How could the Chinese welcome the arch-imperialist Richard Nixon in Peking while simultaneously fulminating against "American aggression" in Vietnam? Why did they quarrel with socialist Moscow and make up to capitalist Washington? Why do they consistently refuse to regard China as a superpower at all? Why do their leaders give ground here only to be incomprehensibly stubborn there? Who is outsmarting whom? And why are they Communist anyway?

In *The Chinese Machiavelli* we have tried to switch on the past to illumine the present, to trace through millennia of moral wrangling and military adventure and the use and misuse of power—through all the thinking, fighting, and ruling of the centuries—the hard-won lessons that have given the Chinese political animal his instincts and may explain China's moves on the chessboard today.

Unlike my earlier book *The Chinese Looking Glass* (which it inevitably overlaps, for a nation has only one past), *The Chinese Machiavelli* is solely a study of the Chinese power game and is written within the framework of a chronological history. Its gallery of thinkers and princelings, despots and empresses, warlords and bandits succeed each other in their proper order, but the teachings of the sages and the antics of the foolish are recounted only insofar as they are directly related to the theme.

Our "Machiavelli," therefore, is not one Chinese but the sum of all Chinese and their experience, assembled from the identikit of Chinese history, as Machiavelli himself drew the features of "Machiavellianism" from men and events in ancient Greece and Rome and Renaissance Italy. And the Florentine inevitably raised the same fundamental problems that his composite Chinese namesake faced, for his pragmatic and objective writings had a universality of their own. He urged princes to realize that they must be ready to do evil in order to safeguard the state, and that sometimes by doing good they might endanger it. But he did not imply that the evil then became good, and the good evil. A man had to make peace between his private conscience and political expediency, for both had quite separate claims on him.

This is humanity's eternal dilemma, and it throws a huge, distorted shadow across the canvas of Chinese history in the shape of an unending conflict between the "weak" Confucians who preached morality and manners within a feudal hierarchy and the Legalists who preached despotism and the iron rule of law in the interests of a single strong and stable state. By 1974 the debate had been translated into Communist dialectic but was far from over, it seemed, for the leader-

MODERN CHINA

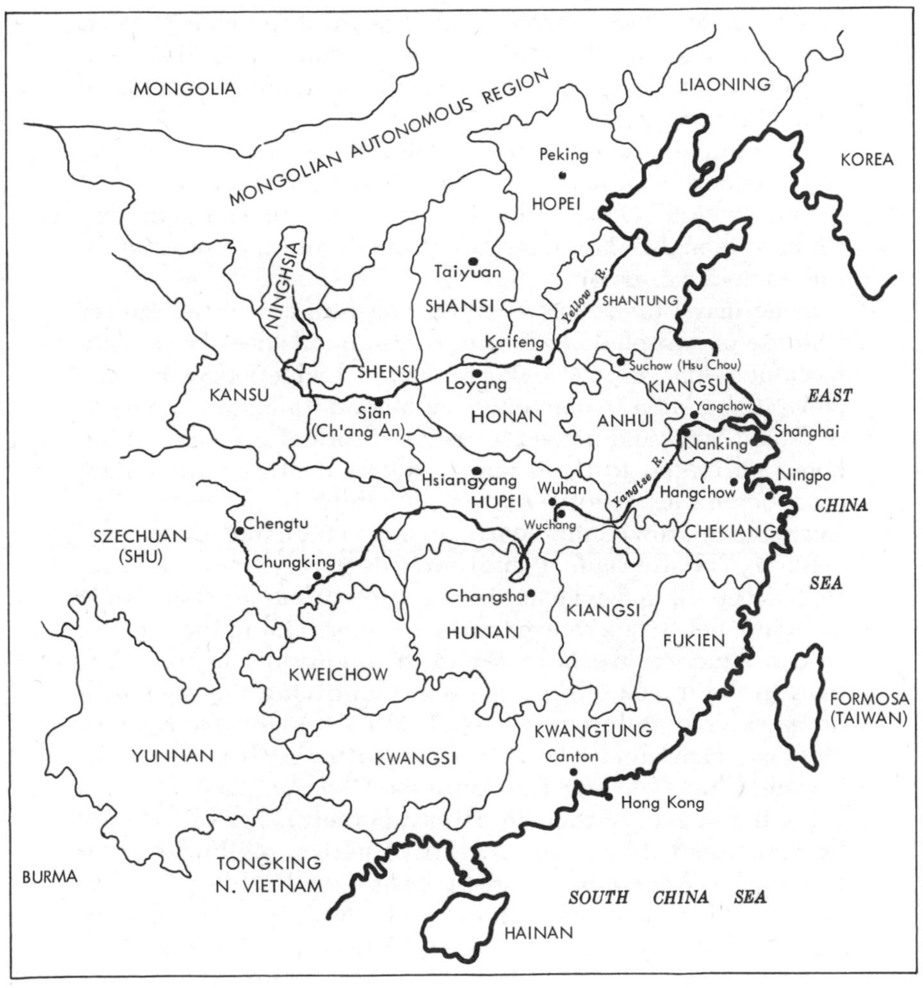

ship in Peking had launched a nationwide campaign calling on the millions to condemn Confucius as a trickster whose "righteousness" was merely a device to perpetuate slavery, and to praise the Legalists whose ruthlessness had subsequently enabled them to forge the warring kingdoms of China into one great empire.

The campaign once more revealed the compulsive preoccupation of the Chinese with their own past, and proved that to burrow into Chinese history for clues to contemporary Chinese thought—including the Thought of Mao—was no futile academic exercise.

Some may protest that a dismaying number of the earlier Chinese philosophers and kings and generals are of necessity mock-ups—images that emerge from a hodgepodge of facts, fable, fragmentary memories, fifth-hand quotations, misinterpreted texts, and blatant forgeries. More often than not the books attributed to them were written centuries after they died, beginning with the *Kuan Tzu,* which is associated with Kuan Chung, the central figure in our first chapter.

But as Voltaire said, all ancient history is no more than accepted fiction, and when it is the known legend that molds mankind, not the unknown truth, we must deal in the legend. In consequence, we have set down traditional history as it lives in the minds of the Chinese, identifying the man with his work—the philosopher Mo Ti (Mo Tzu) with the *Book of Mo Tzu,* Han Fei (Han Fei Tzu) with the *Han Fei Tzu,* Chuang Chou (Chuang Tzu) with the *Chuang Tzu.**

For the sake of further simplicity, emperors are called only by their reign titles. Conventional English spelling has replaced the Wade-Giles system where applicable (Taiping, not T'ai P'ing), and the umlaut has been dropped as largely unnecessary. Liu Shao-ch'i is described as "President" to avoid confusion with "Chairman" Mao. Quotations have been abbreviated and sometimes paraphrased to make them

* "Tzu" in this context may be translated as "Master." Thus the man's name is Mo Ti, he is commonly referred to as Mo Tzu, and the work attributed to him is called the *Book of Mo Tzu,* usually contracted to the *Mo Tzu* (*Han Fei Tzu, Chuang Tzu,* etc.).

clearer. Certain titles and terms—China, Korea, Manchuria, Taoism—have been used for periods before they existed. The number of Chinese names in the text itself has been kept as small as possible, and most explanatory notes put at the end of it for the sake of smooth narrative. This is first and foremost a book for the ordinary reader.

It is an amoral book, for we have tried to emulate the open-minded analytical spirit of Machiavelli, so rare in an age corrupted by "involvement." We have accordingly discussed—and illustrated with often bloodthirsty historical episodes—the merits and demerits in Chinese eyes of such matters as murder, terrorism, treachery, deceit, clemency, courage, and loyalty without concern for conscience, Christian or Communist.

China has been the subject of much fine scholarship to which we acknowledge our debt with deep gratitude, for we are not sinologists, and we have drawn upon it, not added to it. Nevertheless, the academic field has been muddied by certain self-styled scholars who assume that a strong political bias is a substitute for knowledge, and a Ph.D. a substitute for understanding. Since our object is not to give a slanted Western view, as seen from academic left or right, but a straight Chinese look at the Chinese, full face, we would therefore like to add what follows, by way of reference:

Liang Hsin-ch'ang, to whom this book is dedicated, was not only a scholar held in high regard, but a Chinese, and not only a Chinese scholar, but a revolutionary. Although he came of a wealthy family of Confucian officials, he plunged into the revolutionary movement against the ruling Ch'ing Dynasty while still a student, and when older spent much of his family fortune in rallying the masses of six counties in Kwangtung Province behind Dr. Sun Yat-sen, who was to become founder and President of the Chinese Republic.

Arrested while raising support in the French possession of Kuangchouwan, Liang was flung into jail in Hanoi as a dangerous radical and held for three years—one of which he passed in solitary confinement in a windowless cell. The counterrevolutionary authorities in Canton asked the French to hand him over for execution, but Sun Yat-sen was able to intercede with Paris on his behalf and he was eventually released.

When Sun Yat-sen became "Generalissimo" of the new revolutionary government in Canton, he made Liang Hsin-ch'ang his senior personal secretary,* but in 1925 Dr. Sun died, Chiang Kai-shek succeeded him as leader of the Kuomintang (the Chinese Nationalist Party), and revolutionary ideals soon gave way to autocratic military rule. The last years of Dr. Liang were filled with disillusion, and he died in his turn in 1931.

While Sun Yat-sen was still alive, however, Liang Hsin-ch'ang sent his eldest son to the newly opened Whampoa Military Academy, where Chiang Kai-shek was the Commandant, Chou En-lai was Director of the Political Department, and Mao Tsetung lectured on the peasant movement. The son became a Nationalist general, fought successfully against both the Japanese and the Communists, and is now living in retirement in Taiwan.

On the other hand, Liang's elder daughter was a Communist who had studied medicine in Germany, and who remained behind when Mao Tsetung overran China in 1949 in order to serve the new People's Republic as a doctor. Accused of "revisionism" six years later, she took her own life. Meanwhile the younger daughter, won over by intellectuals who believed in a socialist "third force" for China, left the country to join them and taught in Hong Kong.

A republican revolutionary, a Nationalist general, a Communist doctor, a socialist teacher—despite their differences, they were Chinese before all else. Their common "political" heritage went back beyond the legends of the Hsia Dynasty. And one of them—the younger daughter—is my wife and the co-author of this book: Ching Ping.

D.B.

* The Chief of Secretariat was Hsu Ch'ien.

Whoever considers the past and the present will readily observe that all cities and all peoples are and ever have been animated by the same desires and the same passions; so that it is easy, by diligent study of the past, to foresee what is likely to happen in the future of any republic . . .

Niccolò Machiavelli, *The Discourses*

PART ONE

THINKING

1

Curtain Raiser

When does the history of good and evil, of the compassion and scheming and cheating and butchery that separate man from the lesser brutes, really begin? A Christian might say with Cain, if Cain ever lived. A Chinese might say with the Emperor Fu Hsi, had he not had the tail of a serpent. Or perhaps with the foundation of the house of Hsia in 1990 B.C. But the Hsia Dynasty, although dignified by traditional dates, has not left a scrap of evidence that it ever existed before it yielded to the first king of the house of Shang in 1557 B.C.

The culture that gave us gunpowder and roses, silk, paper, porcelain, and peaches is therefore not even old by the severe standards of the Mediterranean—Cheops built his pyramid more than twenty centuries before the Shang Dynasty was founded. But the evidence of a far more antique civilization is nonetheless there, and it is enough to see the intricately wrought Shang bronzes to know that this culture did not spring fully grown from a field sown with no more than dragons' teeth. In the bend of the Yellow River where the story of the Chinese began, society had been developing for several thousand years.

The ancients were to call China "Serica," for the "Seres" were weaving silk a full millennium before Christ was born. They were casting elegant polychrome pots, carving ivory and jade, using brush and ink to write on bamboo strips. The rites during which the king—man's intermediary between

Heaven and Earth—plowed a ceremonial furrow to open the spring sowing season were still performed by the Manchu Emperors of the Ch'ing Dynasty, which fell in 1912.

But if polychrome pots are not legend, they are also not political history, and it was only in the eighth century B.C. that both Rome and China suddenly came alive for posterity. The Chou Dynasty had succeeded the Shang, written records had succeeded mere myth, barbarians had seized the Chou capital seventeen years before the founding of Rome in 753 B.C., and China—the Middle Kingdom—was entering upon the uneasy period of weakness and division thereafter known as "Spring and Autumn."

The central authority of the dynasty was progressively sapped, and the realm split into fifteen rival feudal states fringed and patched with many more minor fiefs, so that the map looked like the motley of papal Italy familiar to Machiavelli. Few paid more than lip service to their royal pope, the Chou "Son of Heaven," and with his frightened formal consent the bigger states rose in succession to establish their hegemony over the rich Central Plain that was the heart of "All under Heaven." The curtain had risen on flesh-and-blood princes and the men who were to play Plato and Plotinus, Caesar and Clausewitz, Machiavelli and Metternich and Dr. Henry Kissinger in China's long and violent history.

It had also risen on a drama played according to an overriding geopolitical convention that never changed. The inner states of pure Chinese culture were ringed by barbarous or semi-barbarous neighbors who were quick to take advantage of their quarrels or their lack of loyalty to the king, and the more thoughtful ministers therefore exhorted their overlords above all to close ranks around their sovereign against all outsiders—even when they despised him. The first man known to have enunciated this basic principle, which was to hold together a united empire as diverse in its origins as a divided Europe, was a certain Kuan Chung, who was born in the seventh century before Christ. Few in the West have heard of him, but his faint shadow suggests the shape of all that is to follow from Confucius to Mao.

Kuan Chung was chief minister of Ch'i,* a feudal state on the lower reaches of the Yellow River rich in salt and silkworms. It was all the richer for the sage Kuan Chung, who employed officials to supervise the separation of the salt and the casting of iron into agricultural implements, who coined copper currency to control prices, estimated the land tax according to the fertility of each plot, and did all in his power to quicken the economy. For "only when clothing and food are adequate," he said, "can men know glory and shame." Want was a valid excuse for waywardness and treachery. Honesty and loyalty demanded a full stomach.

Kuan Chung's words have been passed down the line for twenty-five centuries, in which the more acute political strategists have learned to placate the lean and hungry—or exploit their desperation. And these have included both the go-slow "revisionists" of Communist China, who angered Chairman Mao Tsetung by arguing that the millions should be given rice before revolution, and Chairman Mao himself, who first used their wretchedness to rouse them.

Kuan Chung set out to harmonize the needs of the economy with the needs of defense. He divided the state into twenty-one districts, in all of which men tilled the land. But whereas in six they were farmer-craftsmen who fashioned tools and weapons and did not fight, in fifteen they were farmer-soldiers who were mobilized in time of war. "Taking the army from the peasants" dodged the expense of feeding and housing regular troops, there was always an adequate supply of men, and when the battle was over they laid down their arms, picked up their hoes, and became farmers once more. Mao put this economical principle into practice during his struggle against the Chinese Nationalist Kuomintang (KMT) under Chiang Kai-shek, when his guerrilla armies, as he ordered, "came from the people, and went back to the people," and it is perpetuated in the vast peasant militia of China today.

It was when the Duke of Ch'i, contemptuous of his own

* See map of the Spring and Autumn Period.

monarch, proposed to launch a little seasonal aggression against the neighboring fiefs in order to enhance his personal power, that Kuan Chung urged upon him his overriding duty to defend the realm by "respecting the king and repelling the barbarian." He pointed out that when the feudal states feuded, the first thing that happened was that the more uncouth tribal fiefs on their fringes rose against them, and what made the duke's proposal even more reprehensible was the disagreeable fact that at least two of those fiefs were stronger than Ch'i itself. The royal house of Chou might have fallen into decay, but the king was still the king, the lord of All under Heaven, and if the great Duke of Ch'i would stop playing the bully and behave like a loyal vassal, the other feudal states of the Middle Kingdom would accept his leadership and unite behind him against the woolier tribes threatening its periphery.

The duke relented, and an agreement was reached among most of the states whereby they made common cause and the stronger swore to defend their weaker partners. However, some of the feudal lords stayed aloof, and the Duke of Ch'i, now determined to impose peace and harmony, began by sending troops to seize a border town from the recalcitrant Duke of Lu. After consulting his advisers, the Duke of Lu decided not to try to win the lost territory back by force of arms, but to join the grand alliance if the Duke of Ch'i would recall his army. In the winter of 682 B.C., accordingly, the Duke of Lu traveled in state to Ch'i for the oath-taking ceremony, and a dramatic episode ensued.

It was a solemn and magnificent occasion. Kuan Chung had ordered the construction of a seven-tiered dais, each tier of which was guarded by tall soldiers bearing yellow banners. Below this were the cavalry of Ch'i, so thickly massed that their horses covered every inch of the ground, and only the dukes of the two states and a handful of accompanying officials were allowed on the dais to sign the treaty. After the two lords had exchanged courtesies, a grand dignitary of Ch'i bearing a brass bowl brimming with bull's blood enjoined them to smear their mouths with it in order to seal the alliance, as was customary.

THE SPRING AND AUTUMN PERIOD

722 - 481 B.C.

The eastern states

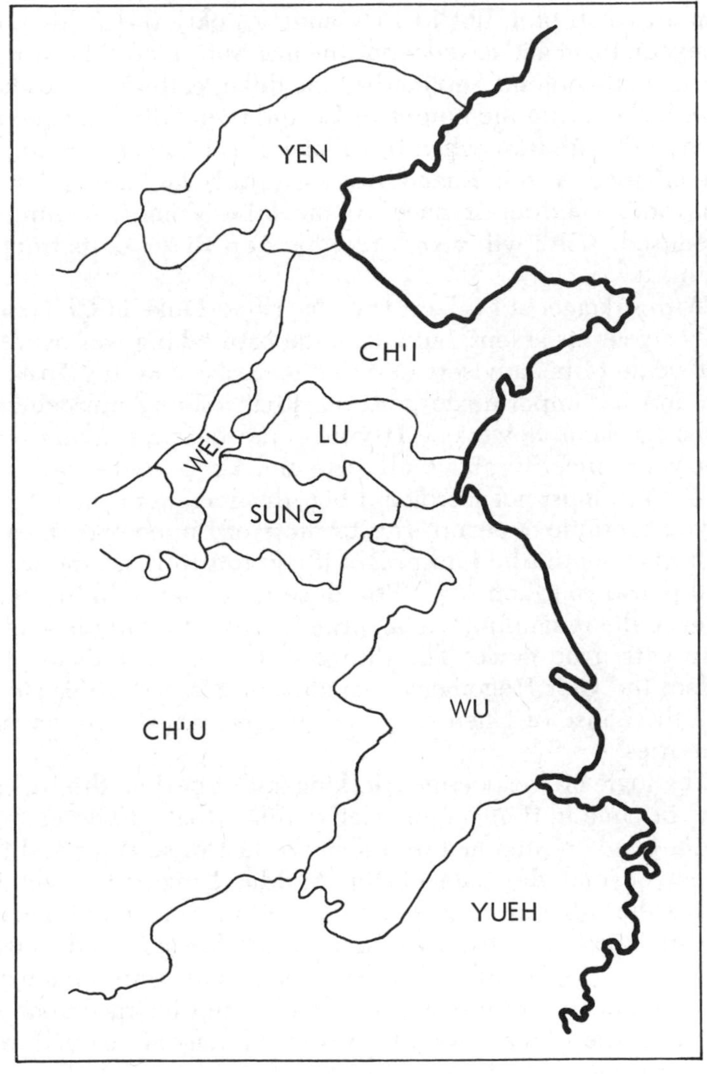

At that moment a high-ranking general of Lu named Ts'ao Mo suddenly drew a dagger from his ceremonial dress and grasped the Duke of Ch'i with his other hand as if he were about to stab him, but Kuan Chung quickly thrust his body between them and asked what the man intended. The would-be assassin violently upbraided the duke, calling him a cheat who had overrun the border of Lu and then failed to keep his word and withdraw when the Duke of Lu had agreed to join the alliance. At this Kuan Chung carefully laid a map before him and, yielding at once to the other's angry argument, promised: "Ch'i will recognize the Wen River as its frontier with Lu."

With a dagger at his face, the chagrined Duke of Ch'i could only signal his assent, but when the oath taking was over, he and some of his advisers decided to assassinate the Duke of Lu and his importunate general. Kuan Chung immediately opposed them, however. "If you would be master, you must put your sincerity above all else and keep your word," he said. "You must not sacrifice a big advantage for a small gain. If you continue to occupy the territory of Lu, no one on earth will trust you in the future. But if you return it, all the world will praise your honesty." The duke gave way, and in consequence the remaining feudal princes submitted to his leadership with good grace. The dangers of disunity and invasion faded, the Ch'i Hegemony lasted from 685 B.C. to 643 B.C., and the house of Chou survived (if precariously) for several centuries.

The logic of "respecting the king and repelling the barbarian" became in time an instinctive reflex that still served the Chinese when Mao had replaced the last royal ruler and the threat beyond the pale of the Middle Kingdom might lie across the Siberian border, or the Yellow Sea, or the Pacific Ocean. Those who expect China to sacrifice a big advantage by breaking her word for the sake of a small gain, moreover, will wait in vain. For in the stubborn, retentive race memory of the Chinese, the catch phrases of the past are carved as if in stone.

2

Tall Man from Lu

"Had it not been for Kuan Chung," said the prestigious Master K'ung a century later, "we would still be wearing our hair long and folding our clothes to the left" (having been conquered by benighted tribes with these deplorably un-Chinese habits).

Confucius, as the Western world was to call Master K'ung, may have been fussy about points of dress and etiquette from the first just because he was "without rank and in humble circumstances." According to one authority,[1] he was a village bastard and an outcast, the fruit of an overimpetuous union unblessed by customary wedding ritual who was an object of mockery to all those around his mother until, unable to bear the sneering any longer, she fled with him to the capital.

But the stark poverty of information about K'ung Ch'iu the man offered an irresistible temptation to those who fashioned "Confucius" the myth, so that even his antecedents are in dispute. All that is known is that he was born in the small state of Lu in about 551 B.C., supposedly the offspring of minor aristocracy who had come down in the world. His father died when he was a child, and he and his elder brother had to make their own way. Sensitive, perceptive, he grew up in a harsh, chaotic age that tempered his convictions in its fire—his rejection of all that was eccentric and oppressive, his reverence for harmony and order.

He did not study under any particular teacher, for none accepted him, but picked up his education working as a petty official—he was at one point a "keeper of stores," at another responsible for the pasturing of oxen and sheep. But he was profoundly inquisitive and eager for knowledge, he gathered around himself other young men anxious to learn, and from this relationship grew a school in which he was the Master and his closest students his disciples.

For Confucius had a message to impart, a message of a happy society founded on benevolent government, and he wished not only to preach it but to practice it. Although many of his pupils rose to positions of authority, however, Confucius was never to take high office in Lu himself, and when nearly sixty, disappointed and aging, he set out in search of an honest ruler who would employ his talents elsewhere. He wandered for more than ten years through the states of the Middle Kingdom without finding one, and returned to Lu to discover that one of his own disciples had become a powerful counselor, only to betray his principles. He went back to teaching, and died without complaint, the bare tale of his life the biography of a pathetic failure.

Why did the keenest young men of his day sit at his feet? Their record of him in the *Analects* * answers the question, for it brings him to life—bold, poised, stimulating, human, and wholesome. He came to be known as the "Tall Man," for he was an exceptionally big fellow with a composed, deceptively deferential air which concealed a talent for plain speaking ("I hate your glib-tongued people"). He dressed neatly in a long, broad gown with wide sleeves, wore a sash at the waist, and a high hat. "When at his leisure, his manner was easy and his expression cheerful . . . he was mild yet firm, dignified but not fierce, respectful yet relaxed." He described himself as one "who in his enthusiasm for learning forgets to eat, who in his enjoyment of it forgets to worry, and who does not notice that old age approaches," for "with only coarse rice to eat, with plain water to drink, and a bent arm

* The "Four Books" of Confucian commentaries on the teachings of the Classics (see page 11) are the *Analects,* the *Great Learning,* the *Doctrine of the Mean,* and the *Book of Mencius.*

for a pillow, I still find joy. Riches and honors gained through unrighteousness are to me as drifting clouds."

But "if the Master was in the company of one who sang well, he would ask him to sing again and join in himself," and he was so enchanted when he heard the ancient Shao music in Ch'i that he "forgot to taste meat for three months." He could play the lute and drink and joke with the best, he was an archer, he bred dogs, "he fished, but not with a net; he shot, but not at sitting birds." As for his attitude toward youth: "I have never refused to teach anyone, even he who came on foot with nothing to offer but a bundle of dried meat. . . . A young man must be treated with respect. How do we know that in the future he will not be equal to what we are now? It is the man who has reached the age of forty or fifty without being heard of who is not worthy of regard."

What did he teach? At first the inner meaning of the learning he transmitted may elude us. For texts, we are told, he used the five Classics, but their titles do not all suggest serious philosophical study—the *Book of Odes,* the *Book of Rites,* the *Book of Changes* (an antique work of divination), the *Book of History,* the *Spring and Autumn Annals.* Turn to the first page of the first Book and we find:

> A pair of water fowl call "kuan kuan"
> On a small island on the river.
> O demure and lovely girl,
> How the young knight seeks to wed her . . .
> Loved even in dreams . . .
> Sought but not found . . .
> Sleepless he longs for her,
> Turning and turning until morning light.

For the *Book of Odes* is an anthology of three hundred poems and folk songs supposedly assembled by Confucius himself from every state.

> There is a young girl bewitched by Spring,
> And a young lad to lead her astray,
> A young girl like carved jade.
> Gently, gently, she says,

Do not touch my kerchief,
Do not make my dog bark.

Master K'ung was not bigoted or puritanical or cantankerous as later generations were to imagine the "Confucius" fabricated by the Confucians, but an open-minded man who took pleasure in life as in learning, a thinker with a keen sense of balance whose object was not to kill natural appetites but to curb excess, to urge moderation upon others, not misery.

The *Odes* had a deeper significance, however. They provided educated men with a conventional code that saved faces and preserved tempers. They could be quoted as allusive impersonal statements to cajole, caution, reprove, or even threaten, and in their diplomatic encounters princes and counselors would exchange classical tags in place of blunt speech—"If you do not study the *Odes* you will have nothing to talk with," warned Confucius. Many of the songs were political in content, but even love poems could echo a universal truth from another era whose message might otherwise have to be expressed in a direct "Do not dare violate my borders, or else . . ." ("Gently, gently . . . do not touch my kerchief, do not make my dog bark"). They muffled the jarring clash of dispute, replacing rough reality with smooth verbal ritual.

And ritual was the intricate mechanism that actuated Confucian morality. It is related that even as a boy Confucius watched the sacrifices being performed in the ancestral temple of the ruling house of Lu, and on returning home solemnly imitated them. Carefully setting out bowls and dishes in their appointed places on a small table, he practiced the formal movements, following the prescribed sequence of steps for advancing and withdrawing, kneeling and worshipping. It was for him the most intoxicating of games. It was also to become the foundation for his philosophy, and thus of the spiritual cast of China for more than two thousand years.

At the core of the Master's teaching lay *Li*. *Li* may be translated as "rites" or "propriety" with equal inadequacy, but it was the basis for the harmonious feudal society that was his forlorn dream. For while not all, perhaps, were born virtuous, manners makyth man, and even the base could acquire virtue by honoring in their daily lives a ritualistic code of correct behavior until it became instinctive, ruling every waking moment and every personal relationship.

Li regulated the conduct between son and father, student and teacher, vassal and king, and it cut both ways: "The duke must fully observe the proprieties toward his ministers, and his ministers must be completely loyal to the duke." "Since you govern, why must you take life?" Confucius once admonished an aristocrat. "If you work for their benefit, the people will live in concord and be content. Those who are above are like the wind, those who are below are like the grass. When the wind blows on the grass, the grass will bend before the wind."

Ritual also regulated the conduct between Heaven and Earth, and notably the royal sacrifices made by the Son of Heaven to ensure good crops. It provided the guidelines for the true Way, and to discard it was to lose all moral direction. If the times were evil, it was because the ruler was not observing *Li.* He had angered Heaven, and he had failed to set his own subjects a *proper* example. But since *Li* had been inherited from the sage-kings of the long past, the remedy for the sovereign was to emulate the ancients, his subjects would then emulate the sovereign, and there would be peace and plenty. The key to the Confucian Utopia, therefore, was to be found in the study of the Classics, from which alone *Li* and the antique precepts of humanity and righteousness that informed it could be learned.

"Use poetry to arouse the good in men. Use ritual to give it form. Use music to set it in harmonious motion," said Confucius, for whom music was essential to the process of purifying men's minds. It was to music that solemn rites were performed, and music that set the mood for good intention to be translated into devout action. "The ways of music and government are directly related," notes the *Book of Rites.* The

Chinese were convinced that a monarch might promote virtue among his people with the right repertoire, that his rule could be judged by the music played in his country.

Music remains part of the politesse of Chinese diplomatic ritual, so that when the British Foreign Secretary visited China in 1972, he was not only greeted with "God Save the Queen," but tempted to dance in the Great Hall of the People to the strains of "The Eton Boating Song" (another Anglo-Saxon dignitary was treated to "How Much Is That Doggie in the Window?" played by a crack orchestra of the People's Liberation Army).

The traditional Chinese view that music is political explained the acrimonious debate between moderates and Maoists on "things foreign"—the violent condemnation of Beethoven as "bourgeois" in 1974, and of Western classical music as "capitalist art" sinfully short on "class content," an "absurd" addiction that was only to be found in China among those afflicted with a "slave mentality." Yet when the Maoists lashed out at a Beethoven sonata for its lack of social significance, they were perilously close to their hoary old enemy. Confucius had protested: "Ritual, ritual! Does it mean no more than the dress to be worn, the gifts of jade to be sent? Music, music! Does it mean no more than the striking of bells and drums? If men do not understand the principle of virtue, what use is ritual? What use is music?"

For if to the Chinese Communists ritual and music are not mere mummery and melody but a means of serving the proletariat and inspiring revolutionary ardor, to Confucius they were a means of inspiring man's humanity for man. "If you govern the people by laws and control them with punishments," Confucius said, "they will try to keep out of trouble but will have no sense of shame. If you govern them with virtue and control them with *Li*, they will have a sense of shame and correct themselves." But like music, *Li* was hollow if performed without feeling. "At funerals it is better that the mourners feel sorrow than that they pay minute attention to ceremonial detail." Going through the motions was not enough.

A Confucian gentleman was unruffled and tolerant, swift to forgive the faults of those around him and just as swift to admit and remedy his own, deeply conscious of his duty to the community, and ready to assume the burdens it imposed. If a ruler, he was magnanimous; if a minister, faithful; as a father, kind; as a son, filial; as a brother, affectionate; as a husband, loving; as a friend, loyal. It is easy to understand why disciples of the Master imbued with these precepts of rectitude and fealty, versed in the intricate ritual of the times, learned in history, and nimble in quoting aptly from the *Book of Odes,* could win positions of trust. They would not cheat or murder their lord and they would be more than a diplomatic match for the counselors of his rivals. But then why did Confucius himself fail to find a patron?

Like all who call for a little more social justice, he was regarded by many as distinctly odd, even dangerous. When accused of burying his talent for government as a man might store away beautiful jade instead of selling it, Confucius retorted, "I am waiting for my price." He was not going to connive at the abuses of the corrupt and murderous parasites who for the most part ruled the states of the Middle Kingdom in his day, and instead of feeding them the sycophantic flattery they expected, he more often than not gave them the sharp edge of his tongue if granted an audience. "Even gamblers do something, and are therefore better than these idlers," he once remarked. When one noble asked him how to govern his state, Confucius replied that he should first learn to govern himself, and when the other complained that his subjects were inveterate thieves, the Master riposted, "If you did not covet what is not yours, they would not steal even if you paid them for doing so."

Disgusted by the miseries and brutalities of his day, Confucius yearned to reform the known world. He did not seek to overthrow the feudal hierarchy, but if the hereditary aristocracy would not study the ancients and mend their ways, then they must be guided by counselors like his own disciples who had absorbed the wisdom of the Classics, who were ruled by *Li,* who would be loyal not to princes but principles, and who would not just echo their master, but *tell* him. The people should be governed not by noblemen but by noble men.

Confucius therefore embarked on "the rectification of names," since it was essential to ensure that the title and the reality were one—it was already painfully clear that the chaotic condition of the Middle Kingdom arose from the failure of dukes to behave like dukes, and ministers like ministers. States should be run strictly in accordance with universal standards of what was "true" and what was "false," Confucius insisted. A cruel and immoral duke must automatically forfeit his revered status as duke, and if his subjects rose in rebellion and murdered him, their conduct was not contrary to the Will of Heaven. Loyalty to the ruler meant, in effect, loyalty to the principle of "the ruler" as patron and protector of the common people. If he ceased to correspond to the principle, he must lose that loyalty. Questioned about the killing of a royal tyrant, the Confucian philosopher Mencius merely replied, "Assassination? I have only heard that a fellow called Chou was put to death."

From this sprang the sacred right of the people to overthrow a bad king, whose downfall would in itself prove that the celestial sanction known as the "Mandate of Heaven" had been withdrawn from him.[2] The prerogative was to be evoked time and again down the long centuries of Chinese history until the Cultural Revolution of the mid-1960's, when Chairman Mao urged upon his militant Red Guards their "right to rebel" against the "revisionist" hierarchy headed by President Liu Shao-ch'i.

The rectification of names is also an enduring tradition, and it is because the Chinese are sticklers for precision that in their politics and public affairs they appear to be such consummate semantical jugglers. For the Maoists, a war started by Communist revolutionaries is a "just war" of liberation, but one started by capitalists is "a war of aggression." When Confucius spoke of the "people" he meant all of them, but when Chairman Mao spoke of "serving the people" he meant only the proletariat. When Confucius conceived world concord as the ultimate extension of family love and loyalty ("Within the four seas, all men are brothers"), he quite naturally visualized a feudal China ruled by men of virtue in which even the old and sick and weak would be cherished. When Communists speak of world peace, they quite naturally mean a world in which the last lonely voice of capitalist protest has been silenced. If anyone misunderstands the expression, it is his own fault.

Confucius may be seen as an ancestral image of the Chinese sense of social harmony, of the correct form and meticulous wording that characterize Chinese diplomacy today and make every action and syllable significant, and of the durable instinct that nevertheless puts customary *Li* before codified law. But Confucius has contributed more than that to the make-up of the Chinese Machiavelli.

The Master was a skilled bowman who emphasized that accuracy was more important than strength, and although he did not teach archery or charioteering, he discoursed on both, and he encouraged his students to learn them. They were polite accomplishments of the times, and the Chinese have long believed that the superior man should be versatile—Chairman Mao himself is an ideologist, a strategist, a writer, a poet, and a calligrapher. Moreover, in the days of Confucius the chariot was a vehicle for traveling and hunting, and the bow a weapon of the chase. The *Book of Rites* mentions five ways of driving, and lays down what to do when crossing wild regions, when following game, or when passing through a crowded city. For each occasion the *Li* was different, and only women and old men were allowed to sit. But that was not all.

As Confucius well knew, there were no women and old men aboard when a duke rode onto some field of doom with one man on his left carrying his bow and arrows and another on his right carrying his spears and lances. The chariot was above all the battle car of the aristocrat, supreme in war. It was highly maneuverable in many parts of the populous Central Plain between the Yellow River and the Yangtse River which was the key to military mastery of the Middle Kingdom. And the bow brought down more than deer.

The *Book of History* stresses the duty of the ruler to protect the lives and ensure the security of his people, and Confucius was a strong advocate of military readiness. The state should maintain an army capable of repelling barbarian invasion even when all was quiet, he asserted, for "when a gentleman is safe, he does not forget danger; while living, he does not forget death; while enjoying order, he does not forget chaos." The Master deplored unprovoked aggression, and said that if he were in the wrong, he would fear the puniest of opponents. But he added that if he believed he was in the right, he would "go forward even against thousands and tens of thousands," and when a vile but powerful usurper murdered the Duke of Ch'i in 481 B.C., Confucius urged the Duke of Lu to attack him: "Half the people are against him, and if we add the army of Lu to half the army of Ch'i, we can prevail." But the duke and his lords, conscious of the weakness of Lu, did not move.

This is the only authenticated incident of its kind, however, and it was not enough for the chroniclers who were to convert the teacher into a legendary hero (or for the Communists who then converted the legendary hero into a fabulous monster). From their hands he emerged as a descendant of the royal house, even of mythical emperors. The *Spring and Autumn Annals* that he was reputed to have edited, a dry-as-dust account of the period of decay before his birth, "struck terror into disloyal ministers and unfilial sons," and when he himself became a minister in Lu, he had men executed just for designing eccentric clothes.

Not surprisingly, he was given a martial background. His father was alleged to have been an army officer whose great courage and strength were widely acclaimed. Seeing the Lu vanguard cut off behind the closed gates of a city on one occasion, he broke the gates open with his bare hands, and on another threw back an invading army from Ch'i with two other officers and only three hundred men.

Ch'i was nevertheless to remain a menace to Lu. By the time Confucius was fifty-one, the same source [3] narrates, China was sinking ever deeper into confusion, the stronger feudal states harried the weak, "the pike swallowed the minnow," and he himself was made acting chief minister * by the Duke of Lu, for counselors of sagacity were much in demand. At this a minister of the Duke of Ch'i, whose armies had earlier filched three towns from Lu, pointed out that the capable Confucius was becoming dangerously powerful. The Duke of Ch'i therefore invited the Duke of Lu to a friendly meeting, but as his master was about to set off, Confucius warned him: "I have heard that in peace men should prepare for war, and in war they should prepare for peace. In the old days a lord never left his territory without his army."

The duke agreed to take a strong escort, and it was as well that he did. For once he and the lord of Ch'i were seated together, an official obtained permission for dancers to perform, and immediately a horde of yelling men brandishing flags and shields and spears milled around the distinguished visitor in order to terrify and possibly assassinate him. Confucius, confident of the armed soldiers behind him, roared out: "The dukes of our two states are meeting in friendship, what is the meaning of this barbaric exhibition?" and ordered the sinister chorus away. The performance was nonetheless repeated, whereupon Confucius peremptorily demanded that the "entertainers" be beheaded.

The crestfallen Duke of Ch'i, aware that his image as the most prestigious lord in the region was in danger of being shattered by the formidable man from Lu, chastised his minister for advocating barbarian methods when dealing with smaller states. Taking a leaf out of the book of Lu, where by contrast "they use the way of gentlemen to guide their prince," he gave back the seized cities—just as his ancestor had been obliged to return lands stolen from Lu by the words of Kuan Chung: "If you would be master, you must put your

* The term "chief minister" has been used throughout this book in preference to "prime minister," with its more universal modern connotations, or other alternatives.

sincerity above all else . . . If you continue to occupy the territory of Lu, no one on earth will trust you in the future. But if you return it, all the world will praise your honesty."

The legendary "Confucius" had scored a greater victory than he would have realized even had he existed—for the real Master K'ung. Because although the real Master was never acting chief minister of Lu and was not present on this dramatic occasion at all, it was his faith in historical example that the anecdote vindicated in the eyes of posterity. For more than two thousand years the Chinese have been quick to quote the lessons of the often imaginary past in any given situation, and the precept that "the pen and the sword must be mutually exploited," that ideally all peaceful discussion must be supported by a convincing military potential, has dictated Chinese diplomacy. Communist leaders in Peking therefore appreciated the implications behind the comment of Dr. Kissinger: "It is not easy to achieve through negotiations what has not been achieved on the battlefield." It sounded like another classical tag.

The Chinese preferred to join the United Nations only after they had developed nuclear weapons, and they developed those weapons not for aggressive war, but for aggressive peace—for they would rather talk from strength than fight from strength. Not that the two are mutually exclusive. The principle of simultaneously negotiating and fighting practiced by North Vietnam before the Paris Agreement of 1973 is fundamentally Chinese, and encapsulated neatly in the four-character phrase "*t'an t'an ta ta.*" It is seen in its most subtle form when Peking exchanges ambassadors with a "capitalist" government while discreetly arming and training guerrillas to overthrow it in a "people's war of liberation," the logic of this deceit being that it is the Chinese state that establishes diplomatic relations with the foreign capital, but the Chinese Communist Party that supports its enemies in the jungle.

However, for the Master, as for Mao Tsetung, the strength from which the game is to be played comes above all from the internal stability of the state itself. The ancient chronicler of "Confucius" recounts that in his mid-fifties he found himself unhappily administering a country in which "pork sellers stopped raising prices, and no one picked up anything lost in the road," but the nobility had become frivolous and disloyal. Matters came to a head when the Duke of Ch'i took revenge on him by sending eighty beautiful girls and sixty pairs of dappled horses as a gift to the Duke of Lu, and for three days that bemused aristocrat shrugged off public affairs and failed in the proper performance of the sacrifices to Heaven and Earth.

"Confucius" thereupon left Lu because he was disgusted by all this irresponsible profligacy—whereas Master K'ung left Lu because the only position of eminence he had been awarded seems to have been a sinecure designed to keep him out of hearing. Either way, it was then that the sage began his wanderings around the struggling, stricken Middle Kingdom, vainly preaching his creed of *"T'ien hsia wei kung"*—All under Heaven is for the commonweal, the people must come first, the ruler must extend his virtue to all in order to be trusted by all.

He saw a handful of aristocrats living in luxury, fields submerged under public highways, the wretched poor without homes, warmth, or food. He pleaded for a fair distribution of the very real riches enjoyed by the very few, "for if wealth is collected the people will be scattered," he said, "but if the wealth is scattered the people will be collected." His "socialist" comment was to be echoed by Dr. Sun Yat-sen, the President of the Chinese Republic proclaimed in 1912, but it has not endeared Confucius to the Maoists, who divided up the land among the impoverished peasants only to concentrate it again under the control of the state or the commune.

Confucius and Mao Tsetung nonetheless agree that "the world belongs to all," although one preaches kindness and the other preaches class war and collectivization. Both stress that strong diplomacy must be backed by strong forces, and strong forces spring only from a society in which contented citizens put a willing hand to plow or sword. Soldiers must be impressed with the justice of their cause, Confucius teaches—"to lead to war people who have not been educated is to throw them away." Mao, who believes that an indoctrinated army clad in its own Communist convictions must be victorious when pitted against mere military machinery, would concur. "You may take the commanders from their armies," the Master said, "but you cannot take the will from an ordinary man." "If we insisted on leading the masses to do anything against their will, we would certainly fail," warns Mao.

In consequence, Chinese, whether Confucian or Communist, tend to punish only where persuasion is useless. Legend has it that the humanitarian "Confucius" did not hesitate to order the summary decapitation of the more obdurate enemies of his duke when necessary. The often ruthless Mao ("Revolution is not a dinner party"), on the other hand, created a socialist state in which ideological non-persons like counterrevolutionaries may receive equally short shrift, but recalcitrants among the "people" who err and stray from the Marxist-Leninist path are not shot or sent to the salt mines. They are set on by earnest Maoists who argue and "reason" with them endlessly, wrestling with the deviationist devil in them until their souls are saved and they can become useful and respectable members of the Communist community.

The Chinese prefer brainwashing to bullets, the threat smoothly disguised as a political innuendo in a love song from the *Book of Odes,* the heavily armed escort in the wings at a friendly conference to ensure that the conference remains friendly—and the duke gets his way. There was only one Master K'ung, but China has inherited the wisdom of two—Confucius and "Confucius."

3

Little Jesus, Big Marx

He was a huge swarthy fellow from the north, his tough body battered by winds and rain, his face grimy the whole year round. In summer he was clad in a robe of coarse hemp, in winter a curious garment confectioned from odd bits of leather. He wore straw sandals, ate thin gruel boiled up from shoots and leaves, beans and other simple vegetables, and altogether he cut a very different figure from Confucius. But it was said that if "Confucius had no time to warm the mat he sat on, Mo Tzu had no time to blacken his chimney with smoke," for both worked untiringly at the business of spreading their respective doctrines.

Mo Ti, it is believed, was born in the Master's native state of Lu eleven years after K'ung's death, but may only have died himself in 376 B.C. at the ripe age of ninety-two. By the time he was gray, the flimsy unity of All under Heaven had frayed further, and the Chou sovereign was no more than an impotent chess king on a board fought over by greedy feudal overlords. For while far to the west the city-states of Greece were soon to be plunged into the Peloponnesian Wars, the Middle Kingdom had already been plunged into an era of fratricidal bloodshed known to history as the Warring States. One drama was dominated by the names of Sparta, Athens, Thebes; the other by the names of Ch'i, Ch'u, and Ch'in.*

* See map of the Warring States.

It was nonetheless an age in which great civilizations began to touch fingertips. The Persians were masters of all from Egypt to the Indus, and through intermediaries there filtered into China new ideas—the Egyptian coffin, the ox-drawn plow, and later the horse archer in boots and breeches. And while in a contentious Greece Socrates, Plato, and Aristotle sought to expand men's minds, in the warring states of China another golden shower of philosophers—the "Hundred Schools" that ranged from Confucius to the Taoists—illumined the fifth and fourth centuries before Christ.

Mo Tzu—Master Mo—was himself raised on the teachings of the Sage, but his was no Confucian "school for gentlemen," for he denounced the rituals on which Master K'ung had set such store as luxuries the ordinary folk could not afford. And among those luxuries were the "propriety," the "human-heartedness," and the "righteousness" that Confucius had insisted each man must cultivate from within. As Kuan Chung had said, the hungry could not know shame. For them, these spiritual self-disciplines were far more difficult to observe than Mo Tzu's own doctrine of a discipline imposed from without: Be righteous—*or else!* Righteousness was the Will of Heaven, warned Mo Tzu. The unrighteous who sowed death, poverty, and war would therefore reap a divine tempest, for they were defying that Will.

Mo Tzu has been called "a little Jesus" because he preached universal love—but he added that rulers should "enforce it among the people by laws and coercion," and he foreshadowed more than the Thoughts of Christ. He organized his disciples into an ascetic, strictly ordered, quasi-religious community which long outlasted him and whose successive leaders wielded absolute authority. The Grand Master, as he was called, controlled all thought and action, and all members of his company were force-fed with the spirit of self-sacrifice. They were taught not only to despise wealth, to prize righteousness, and to help each other in adversity, but also to put the community before the individual,

THE WARRING STATES
481 - 221 B.C.
(c. 350)

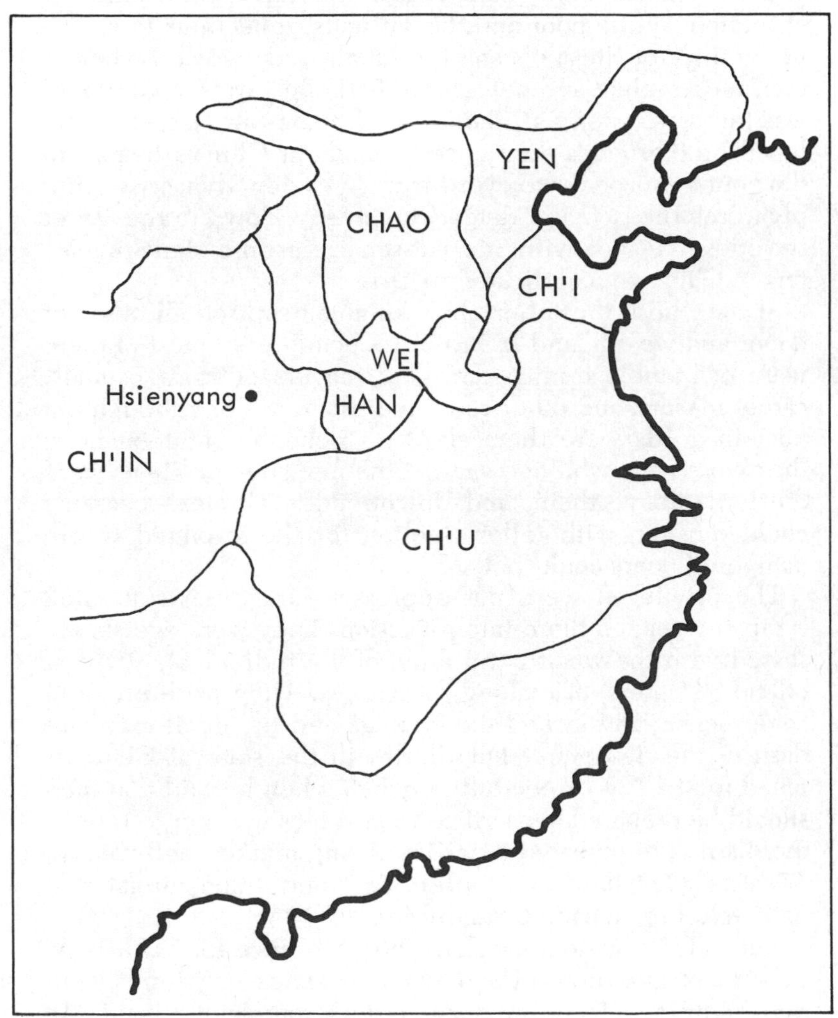

to work hard, go without, suffer discomfort, and face all dangers for the sake of the common people.

Mo Tzu was the forerunner of the gallant and beloved vagabonds who for more than two millennia were wandering champions of the poor and the virtuous, reflections in a Chinese mirror of Europe's shining knight-errants even when at their most violent and vulgar. Similarly, his Moist community was the prototype of all the mystic freemasonries and arcane blood brotherhoods that arose throughout China's history to fling out a usurper or to overthrow a decadent dynasty or simply to rob the rich and defend the needy, down to the secret societies in league with Sun Yat-sen against the Manchu masters of China who abdicated in 1912.

At their best, these horseless knights despised all offers of honor and wealth, and in Mo Tzu's community most of them were of humble origin—farmers, weavers of straw sandals, carpet makers, and other cottage craftsmen. For although the poor in goods were themselves no richer in righteousness, they were not cushioned against the raw edge of life as were the lords above them, and downtrodden Chinese peasants could quicken with fellow feeling for the wronged where pampered peers could not.

The privileged were not oppressed, and their soft salon sympathy goaded them into no action. They were egoists obsessed with the wealth and fame of the individual, afraid of offending others, of making difficulties. They were prone to compromise, and lacked the courage and the devil-may-care dash of the desperate. Dignitaries in the state of Ch'u listened to Mo Tzu respectfully enough when he said that men should be prepared to sacrifice themselves in order to relieve the distress of others—but not with any marked enthusiasm. "That is what the lower orders do," one grand minister finally told him, a trifle disdainfully.

Nor did the aristocracy share his reverence for hard work. Labor, not fate, determined whether states or people were rich or poor, safe or in peril, orderly or chaotic, said Mo Tzu—the labor of masses of men. He himself was a skilled craftsman and the implements he made were always strictly utilitarian, for he was a stern judge of cost-effectiveness. When Kung-shu Pan, the patron saint of all Chinese carpenters and a contemporary living in Lu, built a wooden bird which flew up into the heavens and did not come down for three days (so it is said), Mo Tzu was unimpressed. "It is not as good as the linchpin I whittled down to three inches yet which could take a weight of more than a ton," he scoffed. "Whatever you make, it is excellent if it serves man, but a poor thing if man has no use for it." Even the output of essential handicrafts should be limited to the demand for them.

Mo Tzu roundly condemned the gracious living and dying required of men by Confucian *Li* as inadmissible frivolity and a waste of the people's labor. Rich ceremonial burials, heavily ornamented coffins, embroidered shrouds, and the prescribed period of three years of mourning were abominations: "A coffin three inches thick is sufficient to bury a rotting body, three pieces of cloth are enough to cover a stinking corpse." Music? "Making music is wrong!" he thundered. Music did not feed or clothe the people. As for all other embellishments and adornments and luxuries—clothing was for keeping men warm, houses were for shelter, weapons for defense, boats and carts for transport, and "whatever is merely decorative and does not serve these ends should be avoided."

Mo Tzu lived in an age of almost insane internecine butchery, and he himself saw ruthless armies invading a weak state, devastating the crops, wrecking towns, burning ancestral temples and slaughtering cattle, cutting down the more stubborn defenders and dragging all captives off to be slaves. It inspired him to denounce military aggression more fiercely than any other act.

"If someone kills one man, he is condemned as unrighteous and must pay for his crime with his own life," he said. "According to this reasoning, if someone kills ten men, he is ten times as unrighteous, and if he kills a hundred, a hundred times as unrighteous. Yet when it comes to the even greater unrighteousness of assaulting other states, men do not know how to condemn it. On the contrary, they praise it and call it righteous and make a record of their wars to be handed down to posterity." And that is like calling a little black, black, but a lot of black, white, Mo Tzu added.

If Confucius was no purblind pacifist, however, neither was Mo Tzu. He was not only a strong advocate of an alert, well-prepared, and skilled defense as the best insurance against attack, but trained his own students as a free-lance fighting fraternity to provide that defense where it was most needed—on one occasion 180 of them died to the last man in a beleaguered client city, their discipline not permitting them to yield and still live.

So when he heard that Kung-shu Pan the carpenter had built a "cloud ladder" to enable troops from the powerful state of Ch'u to scale the walls of the capital of Sung, he sent three hundred of his followers to help man the threatened city, and at the same time packed a few dry rations and set off on a ten-day walk to Ch'u in order to dissuade the duke from invading his neighbor at all. While supporting the weak with arms, he proposed to subdue the strong with arguments.

The thongs of his straw sandals snapped several times on the way, his feet became callused and blistered, and when he passed through Sung he found it in an equally lamentable condition. Food and war had earlier taken their toll, and his disciples were shoring up the dilapidated walls of the old capital, which presented a melancholy picture of poverty and neglect. As if in sympathy, his sandals disintegrated, and he was obliged to bind his feet with the strips of cloth in which his food was wrapped.

In Ch'u, on the other hand, the streets were broad and bustling, the houses intact, the shops full of fine goods, the people lively, and Mo Tzu was received in some state by the duke.

"There's a man who does not want for a canopied carriage, gilded and decorated, but thinks to steal his neighbor's broken-down cart," Mo Tzu told him. "He does not want for elegant clothes, but thinks to steal his neighbor's rough old rags. He does not want for rice and meat, but thinks to steal his neighbor's gruel. Now what kind of a man is that?"

"He must be a kleptomaniac," the duke promptly replied.

"Right," said Mo Tzu. "Now the territory of Ch'u extends over five thousand *li*,* while that of Sung covers a mere five hundred. This is greater than the difference between a carriage and a broken-down cart. In Ch'u there are rare animals like the rhinoceros and stag, as well as a great variety and abundance of fish, while Sung does not even have wild hares or bream. This is like the difference between rice with meat and gruel. Ch'u has forests of tall pines and cedars, while Sung does not grow a single precious tree. This is like the difference between elegant clothes and rough old rags. So in my opinion if Your Highness attacks Sung . . ." Where was the difference between stealing goods and stealing states?

The duke concurred, but, tempted by his possession of Kung-shu Pan's cloud ladder, decided to invade just the same. Preceding the war-game analysts of today by some twenty-three centuries, therefore, Mo Tzu engaged Kung-shu Pan in a mock battle for the Sung capital, using his belt to represent the walls and two sets of wooden sticks the attacking and defending troops. Kung-shu Pan mounted nine separate assaults against the city, but he was beaten off with heavy losses each time and finally found himself left with no sticks at all, while Mo Tzu still had all his pieces in play.

The Duke of Ch'u dropped his obnoxious project, but when the Duke of Sung tried to confer a fief upon Mo Tzu, he refused it and went on his way to Lu. He wanted no reward, he said. He had simply acted in accordance with his desire to "promote what was of benefit to the world, and rid it of harm."

He nonetheless quoted this phrase on other occasions to justify more than defensive action. It was precisely his desire to "rid the world of harm" that had prompted the ancient sage-king Yu to lead the other lords against the ruler of the Miao people, Mo Tzu protested when questioned about that dubious act of aggression. The three Miao tribes were in disorder and Heaven had decreed their destruction. Heaven

* One *li* is approximately one third of a mile.

had also granted two other sage-kings sanction to overthrow tyrants whose evil had caught up with them. As careful about his terminology as Confucius, Mo Tzu silenced skeptics by saying, "You have failed to understand that what these men did was not to 'attack' but to 'punish.'" That was rectifying names with a vengeance.

He went even further when he struck out at the Confucian concept of clemency. The Master had said that a gentleman should not pursue a beaten enemy or shower him with arrows, but let him flee. Mo Tzu contended that this was a contradiction in terms. If the enemy was a benevolent ruler himself and so deserving of such leniency, no gentleman should have been fighting him in the first place. And if he was a tyrant, yet not chased and duly slain, "then the evil and disorderly will still live, and the world will not be rid of harm. Nothing could be more unrighteous."

Mo Tzu also charged the Confucians with an almost blasphemous fatalism. "Failure and success, rewards and punishments, all are fixed," many of them sighed, according to the *Book of Mo Tzu*. "Man's wisdom and strength can do nothing." Heresy, said the Grand Master. Just as ministers were above the people and rewarded or punished them, and the king was above the ministers and rewarded or punished them, so Heaven was above the king and rewarded or punished him and all beneath him. Furthermore, he added, not only Heaven but ghosts and spirits on earth had the power to favor the worthy who obeyed the divine Will that they live and work in peace, and to wreak vengeance on the wicked who flouted it. But since each man was free to choose whether he would be worthy or wicked, his destiny was in his own hands.

Confucius himself would not have concurred, for he declined to discuss Heaven or the occult, and saw all morality purely in terms of the social contract. "How should you deal with ghosts and spirits? You have not managed to deal with human affairs properly yet," he once retorted to an inquiring disciple. And from this attitude springs the easy atheism of the Chinese intellectual, Confucian or Communist, who can be relied upon to conduct himself without concern for a hypothetical god allergic to the smell of sin and sitting in judgment on "good" and "bad."

But with their fatalism and arrogance and contempt for the problems of the poor, the Confucians had become a corrupting influence, Mo Tzu fumed. "They act like beggars, scoff food like hamsters, ogle like he-goats, and waddle about like castrated pigs." Small wonder that after the second century before Christ, when Confucianism was established as the single official ideology of the Chinese Empire, Moism would sink into obscurity as a dangerous deviation.

It did not sink without trace, however. For Liang Ch'i-ch'ao, the modern Chinese philosopher who called Mo Tzu "a little Jesus," also called him "a big Marx," and if he was anathema to the Confucians, he was ancestral to the Communists. Mo Tzu was a champion of the have-not millions, an exponent of the value of labor and of the need to promote men to positions of power solely on the strength of their virtue. Government was no easy matter, and choosing the righteous for responsible posts (not just relatives or rich friends) was as sensible as "moistening the hand before touching what is hot" or employing a skilled tailor to cut a suit of clothes. Whether they were of humble or exalted origin was of no consequence, and peasants and lowly craftsmen should be able to rise to the top.

Mo Tzu was the advocate of a hierarchical system strikingly reminiscent of the computer-like Communist principle of "democratic centralism," whereby the masses feed the data from below to those above, and those above then feed their decisions to those below. "Upon hearing of good or evil," he said, "each shall report to his superior. What the superior then thinks right, all shall think right; what the superior thinks wrong, all shall think wrong. If the superior falls into error, his subordinates shall remonstrate with him; if his subordinates do good, the superior shall recommend them. One must identify oneself with one's superior and avoid forming cliques at lower levels."

In the ideal state the process continued up to the king,

"and what the king held to be right, all held to be right. Thus the world was properly ordered *because the ruler was able to unify the standards of judgment throughout his realm.*" In Maoist as against Moist terms: "Do not hesitate to expose the faults of superiors, avoid splitting tactics and the forming of local cliques, and carry out the instructions of the Central Committee of the Chinese Communist Party under the leadership of Chairman Mao." For the Moists as for the Maoists these "democratic" devices justified the absolute authority that the ruler and those around him should wield.

Mo Tzu's company of poor and righteous men was the first of a long line of roughshod revolutionary bands, of which the red guerrilla army of Mao Tsetung that assembled in the mountains to challenge Chiang Kai-shek in 1927 was the last. Mo Tzu had condoned "just wars" like the long Communist insurrection that followed, and his double standards were adopted by Mao: "We Communists oppose all unjust wars that impede progress, but we do not oppose just wars. We actively participate in them."

The Grand Master's vehement denunciation of elaborate Confucian burial and marriage rites must win the approval of the Maoists, who advocate cremation but praise customs like those practiced in Yenan, where peasants bury the dead in their own fields without tombstones so that the land may be plowed and the corpses fertilize the crops. The costly, arranged nuptials of the past are also of the past. At the beginning of 1972 the Peking *People's Daily* pointed out that the ideal New Communist Girl makes up her own mind to wed, requires no go-between, chooses her own mate, wants no presents of money, has no dowry, and needs no one to give her away. On the day she marries she takes with her only the *Works* of Chairman Mao and the tools of her trade (perhaps nothing more than a bamboo carrying pole) and goes to her husband's house, where photographs of the happy couple are pasted into a certificate inscribed with eight large characters reading: "Diligent and Frugal Household Management and Planned Parenthood." Relatives and friends are entertained with tea and some cheap crystallized fruits, and on the following morning husband and wife go off to work as usual.

When Mo Tzu denounced filial piety and the clannish system of allegiances in China, and demanded not only undiscriminating universal love but also the sacrifice of the individual for the good of his homespun community, he was again anticipating Mao Tsetung. The Communists have spurned family loyalty as feudalistic and one of the "poisonous elements" of Confucianism. The collective must come first, they insist, and against a backcloth of communal fields and communal piggeries, communal crèches and communal political study, private enterprise and even private feelings must yield to the demands of the Party and of the "production brigade."

Communist cadres are urged to suppress personal affection and to cultivate a higher "Party nature." "The life of anyone who joins the Party belongs to the Party. If a member is obliged to die to fulfill his duty, he must observe Party discipline and lay down his life of his own accord," wrote the former President Liu Shao-ch'i. Did the Grand Master of the Moists claim that he could "order the faithful to enter a fire or walk on sword blades"? During the Great Cultural Revolution of the 1960's fanatical young Red Guards boasted that for Chairman Mao they would "climb a mountain of swords or cross a sea of fire."

It might nonetheless be thought that the insistence of Mo Tzu on the Will of Heaven would jar on sensitive Maoist ears. Universal love is dictated by the Will of Heaven, the righteous who should be promoted irrespective of their origins are righteous because they obey the Will of Heaven, and the king is the king because it is the Will of Heaven—for if the king picks his ministers, it must be Heaven that picks the king.

Furthermore, it is the Will of Heaven that identifies a "just war" as a "just war," and not simply another deplorable exercise in naked aggression. When the ancient sage-kings launched their righteous campaigns, terrible portents worthy of the Three Witches in *Macbeth* revealed that their despicable adversaries were being "punished," not "attacked." The sun rose at night and for three days it rained blood. Hot and cold became confused, and cranes shrieked for ten nights and more. A woman turned into a man, and flesh fell from the skies.

Mo Tzu may appear to stand exposed as a peddler of pernicious feudal superstition, but he adds: "To me the Will of Heaven is like a compass to a wheelwright or a square to a carpenter who use them as measures, saying, 'What fits these is right; what does not fit them is wrong.' " If we substitute for the compass and square the dialectic of Marx, the Thought of Mao, and the theory of historical materialism, it becomes evident that for the Maoist these in their turn provide fixed measures that decide who shall rule, who is "righteous," and which wars are "just." The general principle is the same.

A philosophical specter for century after century, Mo Tzu has nonetheless always been present in the Chinese makeup, to be glimpsed in grim peasant rebellions and among the zealous brethren of secret societies. His spirit is alive today and influencing China's destiny at home and abroad—the spirit of the dogmatic Chinese do-gooder whose mission is to impose peace and love on all men, whether they want them or not, in accordance with a Will of Heaven worked out by himself.

4

The Straw Dogs

Nothing may seem more remote from the surly fire-and-brimstone admonitions of Mo Tzu than the elusive cloudmanship of Lao Tzu. But then who was Lao Tzu? His short, solitary work—the *Tao Te Ching*—begins:

> The Way that can be told is not the true Way;
> The names that can be named are not the true names.

And these obscurities apply to no one better than to the "Old Master" himself.

His birthplace is identified with one man, his job with another. He is said to have met Confucius, yet to have been made archivist of the royal domain of Chou a century after Confucius died.[1] Some say he did indeed live for two hundred years (before he rode through a pass in the Great Wall on a green ox, mounted the wind, and disappeared westward to become an Immortal). But the *Tao Te Ching* was compiled another century after that.

Lao Tzu had a Confucian regard for integrity and impartiality and for harmonious relations between man and his world, and he reserved a Confucian sorrow for those who coveted riches and were greedy for power. Yet whether Lao Tzu rode the wind or not, the two sages certainly ended by galloping off in opposite directions to father two interwarring, interwoven doctrines.

The Old Master was reputedly from south of the Yellow River, and he seems to have inherited the ingenious if easy-going and dreamy nature of the "southerner." But he did not inherit his craftiness, and he lacked the bustling energy of Confucius. His appearance was somewhat doltish—he was thick-lipped and gap-toothed, he had pendulous ears and protruding eyes, a broad forehead and a square block of a jaw. And on the face of it he had little to offer the Machiavellis of the Middle Kingdom.

For him *Tao*, "the Way," was the nature of a soulless, spontaneously evolving cosmos in which all happened of itself—like a tree growing without trying—as the opposing yet complementary impulses of *yang* and *yin* (light and dark, sun and moon, male and female, etc.) interacted *ad infinitum*, creating and destroying. Man should therefore eat when hungry, sleep when tired, do what must be done and no more, and above all conform to the current of this flowing universe of space and time, allowing himself to be swept along by the constant change.

Lao Tzu himself led a secluded life and preached "non-being" and "non-action." Men were wrongheadedly prejudiced in favor of "being," he protested, just because they could see and touch it. They forgot that something came from nothing, not the other way around, that it was useless to put thirty spokes in a wheel if no empty space was left in the center for the axle, and equally useless to build a house if no empty space was left in the walls for a door.

Just as an excess of positive "being" could impair rather than enhance, so could an excess of positive "action" distort the normal evolution of the cosmos. Man must know when to stop, for only if all avoided the cardinal transgression of unnatural striving would there be no strife. The Taoist sage understood that if he did not strain after success he would suffer no failures, that since material enjoyment would never satisfy man but simply multiply his problems, he should be modest in all things.

Lao Tzu's ideal state was "a small country of few inhabitants, whose plentiful implements, boats, carriages, and weapons are all in readiness but never used. There is no war and there is no writing, for events are recorded by knotting ropes. The people are content with their food, clothing, and houses, and because distances are short one can hear the cocks crowing and the dogs barking in the next settlement, yet people grow old and die without visiting it."

It is not surprising, therefore, to find Lao Tzu's more lively and loquacious follower Chuang Chou snapping his fingers at the world and valuing nothing but his freedom to "come and go alone, with the spirits of Heaven and Earth"—at least in his apocryphal guise as "Chuang Tzu," Master Chuang.

A native of Sung during the fourth century before Christ, as far as is known, Chuang Tzu has been described as a scholar of wide learning, the scion of an aristocratic family that had fallen on hard times in hard times. He was not without connections, presumably, but he despised ambitious busybodies and court climbers, and although he once served as a minor official in charge of the Sung lacquer-tree gardens, he resigned in order to teach and write. Thereafter he lived in a hut in a tumbledown alley, making his own straw sandals and sometimes borrowing to stave off starvation. His neck was scrawny and his face cadaverous, and he wore a patched gown of coarse linen, but he carried his poverty with an air, even in the presence of the duke.

For Chuang Tzu all opposites were the two faces of the same spinning coin inscribed with *yang* on one side, *yin* on the other, so that life and death themselves "were no more disconcerting than the passage of night and day." Who knew which was better, anyway? Death might be like the draining of a sore, the bursting of a boil.

Accordingly, he did not grieve when his wife died, but began beating a tub and singing, and when seriously ill himself, he said of his own burial: "Heaven and Earth shall be my inner and outer coffins. The sun, moon, and stars shall be my pearls, gems, and jade. All things shall be my food. What need have I of a grandiose funeral? You are afraid that the crows will eat me, so you want me buried under the ground where the ants will get me. Isn't that a trifle unfair?"

What applied to life and death, to crows and ants, applied to everything. In a universe that was all of a piece, only man tried to distinguish between good and bad, joy and sorrow, justice and injustice, nobility and meanness, whereas "acceptable and unacceptable are on a single string." All were manifestations of the Way, and therefore all were equal. Judgment was a mere matter of perspective, and consequently valueless. From one viewpoint Heaven and Earth were "tiny specks in the universe," while from another the tip of a hair was "a range of mountains." A wooden beam was a boon to a man who wanted to batter down a wall, but useless to one who wanted to plug a small hole, a thoroughbred was a godsend to the man in a hurry, but no good to a rat catcher.

It followed that there was for Chuang Tzu no such thing as truth: "Mankind eats beef and mutton. The deer crops grass. The centipede likes snake. The horned owl delights in rats. Of these four animals, which knows the true diet?" The "true" of the Confucians was the "false" of the Moists. Words, therefore, had no fixed meaning.

Chuang Tzu was walking in the hills with his students when he came upon an enormous tree. Its leaves and branches flourished, but the woodcutters had passed it by. "The timber is no good, so it is useless," one of them explained. That evening a friend ordered his servant to kill a goose in Chuang Tzu's honor. "One goose can call, the other cannot," said the boy. "Which shall I kill?" The host told him to kill the one that could not.

On the following day the students remarked: "The tree was spared because it was 'useless,' but the goose that could call was spared because it was 'useful.' Should we be 'useless' or 'useful'?"

"Adopt a position between the two, and avoid disaster," the Master replied. "Like the divine dragon, concealed and secret, change according to the season, but do not become involved."

Chuang Tzu recommended withdrawal from the world, for as he saw it the leaders of his day flagrantly flouted the *Tao*.

They adopted artificial moral standards by which they arbitrarily ruled what was good and what was bad, from these they drew up legal codes according to which they rewarded and punished, and the codes in turn became the basis for the final man-made monster, the government through which they ordered the lives of others.

While the Confucians spoke of duty and decency, the Taoists insisted that all social organization was ruinous. "The more laws there are, the more robbers and thieves there will be," Lao Tzu said. The more government there was, the more greed and ambition and corruption it engendered. While the four feet of the horse were natural to it, the man on its back was not. All Taoists admired the ancient sage who had allegedly rushed off to wash the filthy words out of his ears after an emperor had asked him to assume power in his place.

It is related that when the Duke of Ch'u sent envoys to Sung to invite Chuang Tzu to become his chief minister, they found him among the river reeds, small yet ethereal, fishing with a faraway look in his eyes. On hearing their message he did not turn away from his rod but said: "I have heard that there is a sacred turtle in Ch'u that died three thousand years ago. The duke keeps it in a casket wrapped in cloth and has placed it in a temple. May I inquire whether the sacred turtle wanted to be dead and to have its bones venerated by man? Or was its intention to stay alive and crawl around in the mud, dragging its tail?"

"Naturally, it hoped to crawl around in the mud, dragging its tail," replied the envoys.

"Go home," said Chuang Tzu. "I also want to crawl around in the mud, dragging my tail."

An appetite for power and riches was not only irrelevant in the cosmos of the Taoists; it was distressing and positively dangerous. "People find no rest because of four desires," remarked even a hedonist among them, "long life, reputation, high office, and possessions. Whoever has these four desires goes in terror of spirits, other men, authority, and punishment." All should cultivate a "clear and elevated" outlook even while they scrambled for wealth and fame, realizing that these were nothing more than a wisp of cloud passing across the eye.

Another Taoist expressed alarm because while on the road to Ch'i he "ate at ten inns and was served first in five of them." Keep down, said the sages. It is the big tree that attracts the gale, and the fat pig the butcher. Since universal destiny is worked out by alternating impulses of *yang* and *yin*, what rises must fall.

"Once a sword is honed to its sharpest, it will begin to lose its edge," said Lao Tzu. "When your hall is filled with gold and jade, it will no longer be safe." Poverty is the heir of riches, suffering the heir of happiness, and neither one nor the other can be avoided. Everything must revert. The sage, therefore, is indifferent to gain and loss, and it is safest to be neither "useless" nor "useful."

Weakness? But weakness beats strength, protest the Taoists. The most perfect exponent of non-action is water; "nothing under Heaven is softer than water, yet nothing can better prevail over the hard." When you beat it with a sword, it suffers no harm, but when it falls in torrents it shakes hills and valleys, bursting through dikes and flooding the plains. When it collects it is without limit, when it is a mere trickle it will filter into every crack. Man should flow with the *Tao* as water flows down the mountain, yielding to every rock, yet wearing everything in its path away.

Between them the Confucians and the Taoists engendered in the Chinese a spirit that accepted their conflicting philosophies as complementary *yang* and *yin* and absorbed both, so that behind the soldier and schemer has always been a get-away-from-it-all dreamer, and behind poverty of means has often lain peace of mind.

The Sung Dynasty poet Lin Pu built a grass hut on a small hill beside the West Lake and there he dwelled in seclusion, planting the hillside with plum trees. All his life he was unmarried and alone, but accompanied by wild cranes and drunk on the joy of clear winds and the bright moon reflected in the lake. He did not go to a city for twenty years, but composed tranquil verse of extraordinary beauty that drove away workaday cares. People went in awe of him, and wistfully called him the great hermit with the "plum-tree wife and crane children."

Throughout history cultured Chinese have delighted in going into retreat, living among hills and mountain streams and cascades, gazing at clouds, drifting in boats on lakes and rivers, picking flowers, breeding fish, and listening to the birds. It has been a Taoist escape from the *Tao* itself—from the blind fate that made them moneygrubbing merchants or power-hungry politicians and generals whose very avarice and ambition had not been theirs to choose or refuse in the first place. For as Lao Tzu had said:

> Heaven and Earth are ruthless,
> They treat all things like sacrificial straw dogs.

Trapped in the same shapeless but inexorable drama, each man had to perform according to an unseen script, ad-libbing his way through life and fatalistically accepting every twist of the plot. If he was up today, he could be down tomorrow, and therefore the more he could efface himself, the less he risked.

Perhaps the most popular curtainless curtain raiser throughout the history of the Chinese theater has been "Wu Sung Kills the Tiger," an episode from the great bandit saga *Water Margin.*[2] On stage there is an earsplitting banging of gongs and drums, while the hero and the beast follow their carefully rehearsed roles, the tiger rearing and leaping and lashing out with its claws and Wu Sung swinging his club, until the final blow is struck and the brute falls dead, right on time. However, if the actor playing Wu Sung has obstinately refused to seal the bargain by giving the traditional tip beforehand, the tiger will not breathe his last on schedule, but drag the fight out and leave Wu Sung buffeted and exhausted before he succumbs.

So when you play Wu Sung, the Taoists counsel, do not be arrogant or mean, for although you are the hero, your success depends on the tiger. If the tiger refuses to die, you will not look brave, but foolish. And if the tiger agrees to die, it will be because you have come to terms with him. Do not forget, moreover, that since custom demands that in time you relinquish one role for the other, you may be playing Wu Sung today, but tomorrow it will be you who plays the tiger. And as the actors are interchangeable, the audience beyond your vision feels neither joy for one, nor grief for the other.

Taoist flexibility is a device for surviving in an ever-changing world, as a boxer survives by rolling with the punches, and China is still an ever-changing world in which a cadre will be broken if he proves too brittle. In 1958 Chairman Mao launched the "Great Leap Forward," whereby China was to overtake British coal and steel production within fifteen years, and at the same time grouped the peasant millions into the supercollectives he called people's communes. The Leap turned into a stumble, farm output fell heavily, industry was dislocated, and many provinces suffered three years of misery and near famine. Mao resigned as President of the Republic, and Liu Shao-ch'i took his place.

Mao was discontented with the more pragmatic, less radical policies of Liu, however, and in 1965 lit the fuse of his "Great Cultural Revolution," in which Liu was disgraced and sacked and the whole Communist Party hierarchy smashed. For this political massacre Mao relied for military support on Marshal Lin Piao, the Minister of Defense. Lin became Mao's "closest comrade-in-arms," and in April 1969 his name was inscribed in a new draft constitution as the Chairman's heir-designate.

Fate and his own failings were nonetheless working against Lin Piao, and two years later he was dead and damned by those who had only yesterday hailed him as their future chief. By 1972 the generals and administrators in the Communist bureaucracy who had been humiliated and pitched out of office five years before were back in their commands and corridors of power, while the left-wing Red Guards who had earlier scarified them so vindictively were down on the farms, shoveling muck with the peasants.

In this tragicomedy the supreme exponent of the suppleness that ensures survival was the Prime Minister, Chou En-lai. Chou was not a fanatic, but a realist and a diplomat. He had an abundance of political wisdom and the experience of a lifetime devoted to the craft of revolution. He laid no plans that were radical or risky. He was pliant, tactful, sincere, and charming in his manner. He was the most excellent of men, yet he did not dwell on his merits.

By the early 1970's he was also the most powerful of men, yet he did not abuse his power. He did not make it obvious that he had restored order to China after the tumultuous Cultural Revolution instigated by Mao had reduced the Republic to near anarchy, for that would have antagonized the Chairman. And for every move he contemplated, he first sought Mao's approval, leaving him persuaded that he was personally directing his Prime Minister's program. In consequence China's abrasive militancy in foreign affairs faded, to be replaced without pain by the "smiling diplomacy" of a statesman who knew the virtue of water, as Lao Tzu had first perceived it.

Basically the so-called "power struggle" in Peking was—as it has always been—a give-and-take trial of strength over policy between pragmatic "moderates" and militant "Maoists" whose main differences were about the pace and path that China should adopt in her progress toward the ideal classless society. Otherwise, since all those involved were Chinese and Communist and revolutionary, they all wanted the same thing in the end.

It was not a struggle, therefore, but an interplay between *yin* and *yang*, and it is symbolical that it should have taken place within one party, whereas in the West it could have involved any number from two to twenty. For while the West has always seen the universe divided into clashing forces (beginning with Greek philosophy and an anthropomorphic Jewish god), to China it is the "great unity." And while the West found it disconcerting and ominous that Chinese foreign policy constantly corkscrewed, moving from left to right, frowns to smiles, mayhem to moderation and back again, to the Chinese the fluctuation was natural—and the thread still led straight upward.

Under the guidance of Chou En-lai, China's foreign policy developed an aqueous, all-pervasive quality that contrasted strikingly with the "solid" stands taken in less perceptive countries. But no Chinese believed that when it reached its apogee, the policy would not again "revert," and all undoubtedly took that factor into their calculations—including Chou En-lai.

The Taoist instinct is itself subject to *yin* and *yang*, however, and beautiful resignation in the face of inhuman destiny can sometimes become ugly conniving at only too human tyranny when seen in the eldritch light of political realities. Do not be stiff-necked when confronted with injustice, warned Lao Tzu. Give way. "Those who stand forward and clamor for justice will only be visited with greater injustice." Retreat now in order to advance later.

"Do not deviate from your orders," said Chuang Tzu. "Resign yourself to what cannot be avoided." Deeply imbued with Taoism, the Chinese millions bowed before oppressive and irrational rule for century after century until life became unbearable, it was too late for reform, and there was no alternative but bloody revolution.

However, there is far more in this quietist philosophy to tempt the tyrant than admonitions to all men to suffer in silence now, since things must change for the better once they cannot change for the worse. Later, self-styled Taoists of the Yin-Yang school postulated that the imperial dynasties supplanted each other as inevitably as the "five elements" which in each case controlled their destinies (metal cuts wood, fire melts metal, water quenches fire, earth tames water, wood overcomes earth). At any given moment, therefore, the ruler was the only possible ruler and all protest was useless.

Moreover, as Chuang Tzu implied, a sovereign cannot be labeled "noble" or "mean," and he should not himself chase after favorable repute by honoring conventional concepts of good and bad. If he aspires to emulate the Taoist sage, he may read in the *Tao Te Ching* that not only Heaven and Earth, but

> The Sage is ruthless.
> He treats the people like sacrificial straw dogs.

The people themselves should cultivate simplicity and cherish "few desires." They should be "without knowledge" and avoid being misled by their own intelligence. So:

> He empties their hearts
> And fills their stomachs,
> Weakens their will
> And strengthens their sinews.

In short, he opposes all ambition, learning, even thinking—in others.

And of course all moral codes are unnatural. Using Confucius as his butt, Lao Tzu scoffed at ethics founded on the legendary heroes (and villains) of the Good Old Days: "The ancients are long dead and even their bones have decayed. To put excessive trust in words that have survived them is futile. If you can rid yourself of your apparent pride in your own cleverness, you may become a gentleman . . . but if you lecture a tyrant on benevolence and righteousness, measures and standards, you are simply exploiting other men's shortcomings to parade your own excellence."

In the state of the Taoist sage, the whole dictionary of customary virtue and vice must be flung away, since there is no *yang* without *yin*, no good without evil, and anyway men should discard "duty," "humanity," "benevolence," and "righteousness," for these only stand out in times of strife. If there is harmony in every family, there are no "kind fathers" or "dutiful sons," and only when the country is dark with disorder do we hear of "loyal servants." Exceptional virtue should not be praised, because virtue should not be exceptional. Cut out all this sanctimonious terminology, say the Taoists, and people may learn to love one another again.

It may be objected that these teachings have been carefully

culled from their contexts to delight the despotic and to distort the quietist intent behind them. But that is precisely what the despotic did to Taoism themselves, lured on by the mystical omnipotence that it ascribed to the sage, and the promise of immortality that its later hierophants held out. "The soaring dragon rides the winds and mounts the mists, trailing in the vault of Heaven, but if the clouds scatter and the mists dissolve, he will lose the 'power' on which he ascended . . ." It reads like more Taoist daydreaming, but it was written by a Legalist, an advocate of cold-blooded autocratic rule based on a draconian system of prompt rewards and hideous punishments, whose ugly philosophy lies across the history of China like a well-worn garrote.

The primrose path from Taoism to Legalism was laid by scholars at the Chi-hsia Academy [3] who claimed that only a savage penal code that suppressed all desires and excesses could lead men to a life of innocent non-action, and so enable the ruler himself to rule without ruling. And it was the great Legalist Han Fei who then took the absolute metaphysical power of the Taoist sage and transferred it to the absolute monarch. Like the sage, his king was above right and wrong; as the embodiment of cosmic destiny, he treated men like "straw dogs," defining the law and then leaving it to operate of itself through minions who were permitted no more discretion than machines. Had Confucius insisted that all men should practice *Li* until it became second nature? The Legalist ruler would rigorously apply his law until all men instinctively conformed to it and, in so doing, conformed to the *Tao* itself. For by definition his law was a reflection of cosmic law, and his "right" and "wrong" a reflection of cosmic "right" and "wrong."

Lao Tzu had long since mounted the wind and ridden off westward toward immortality. He could not, therefore, turn in his grave, let alone stop the rot.

5

Government by Goodness

The rest of humanity had proved mortal enough, and in a brutal era the Taoists seemed justified in deriding organized society, and the Confucians in thinking that yesterday held the key to the problems of tomorrow. By the fourth century before Christ the codes of loyalty and chivalry still honored by the best men during the Spring and Autumn era had been contemptuously cast aside and the feudal system was collapsing into geopolitical rubble, treacherously mined from beneath. The cry "Respect the king and repel the barbarian" could now be met with the cynical retort "Which king?"—for not only was the Chou Dynasty ruler confined to a small royal domain, but every duke was styling himself monarch of his own feudal state.

Big fleas have little fleas upon their backs to bite 'em, however, and these pretentious princelings were in turn plagued by the ambitious aristocratic families within their realms which increasingly challenged their authority. Even before the turn of the century, the feudal state of Tsin had been split into Han, Wei, and Chao by powerful upstarts whom the impotent Chou "Son of Heaven" had no choice but to confirm in their synthetic new fiefs.

This period of the Warring States, marked by the savage scramble for supremacy of the seven great dominions of Ch'i, Ch'u, Ch'in, Yen, Han, Wei, and Chao, was nonetheless no scramble among savages. The overlords were already arming their soldiers with the trigger-operated crossbow that Europe was to use for the first time only a thousand years later, and in their feudal capitals craftsmen were working in lacquer and gold filigree, and silver inlay on bronze. The Chinese were living according to written law and a year of 365 and a quarter days—and eating with chopsticks rather than fingers.

The Duke of Wei may have been an upstart but his rule was benevolent, even progressive, for it was marked by much civilized reform. Although he made himself master of the Central Plain, he did not do so by leading his own armies into a series of haphazard exercises in massacre or chivalry after the manner of his warlike forebears. He employed a brilliant strategist under whose leadership the well-disciplined troops of Wei economically defeated Ch'i and Yen and also inflicted stinging reverses on Ch'in and Ch'u. Some years after this man died, the King of Ch'i hired an equally able professional, and it was the turn of Wei to be overrun.[1]

The Chinese had come a long way, war was no longer a game, and it was characteristic of that age of incessant violence that the feudal lords should eagerly hire the free-lance philosophers and soldiers of fortune who traveled around the devastated Middle Kingdom, offering their formulas for victory to this prince and that. Often the sons of aristocratic families dispossessed when the seven larger fiefs had engulfed the smaller, these roving advisers were heard with attention and treated with respect by their new masters until they failed, when they might be boiled or chopped in two. And they included a very special breed—the *yu shui*, or "wandering persuaders."

The persuaders were men with an acute understanding of "international" affairs, masters of devious argument and diplomatic finesse, ingenious, daring, and dependent for their lives on their ability to weave the military and political threads of power into whole cloth. They overlapped—but were not identical—with the peripatetic magi, sages of the "Hundred Schools" with theories on everything from astronomy to the art of government, of whom Confucius had perhaps been the first, and Mencius [2] was now the most illustrious Confucian.

The distinction was lost on most of the lords, however, and when the King of Ch'i consulted Mencius, it was primarily to discuss his own private problem with him, which was how he could imitate the dictators of the past who had hacked their way to hegemony over the other feudal states. But he drew small comfort from the words of the philosopher-errant, for Mencius was a man who believed above all in goodness, even in the fourth century before Christ. And where a king was concerned, goodness did not consist in bludgeoning the neighbors into submission, or in measuring the virtue of all acts in terms of gain. As he told another monarch, "If you start asking how you can profit your realm, your officers will soon be asking how they can profit their families, and your subjects how they can profit themselves, and while all those above and below are struggling for profit, your kingdom will fall."

There was only one way whereby the ruler of Ch'i could unify the Middle Kingdom under his dominion, said Mencius, and that was by practicing compassion and righteousness, for then he would earn the trust of All under Heaven. Men would respond, because they were born good. It was the rough passage through life that stripped their souls of grace, just as the vandalism of acquisitive woodcutters could turn a green and shady hill into a gaunt, naked rock.

But until there was a benevolent government that gave the people a settled livelihood, only the educated and affluent could afford principles, Mencius continued, echoing Kuan Chung. To drive men to crime through need and neglect and then to punish them for it was to trap them in a net, like animals. Once a good king made sure that they had the means to support their families even in lean years, on the other hand, they in turn would be good. And of the factors that won wars, "Heaven's weather is not equal to Earth's terrain, and Earth's terrain not equal to Man's concord."

The sharpest weapon of the overlord, therefore, should be the welfare of his people. Taxes, the conscription of labor, and cruel punishments should be reduced or abolished altogether. "Let each family have five *mou* * of mulberry trees, so that all over fifty may have silk clothes. Let them have time to look after chickens, pigs, and dogs, and men over seventy will have enough meat. Give them a hundred *mou* for crops and time to till them, and the eight households will never starve. And if schools are built to teach the young their duty to their elders, then the old will not have to bear heavy burdens on their backs."

Village cooperation has a confused but venerable history among the Chinese, and when their present leaders first parceled out land among the peasants and organized them into small "mutual-aid teams" before thrusting them into the deep end of the Communist collective system, they were introducing nothing unfamiliar. Mencius, who is believed to have lived from 386 to 312 B.C., tried to revive a pattern of farming already semi-legendary in his day, whereby eight peasant families were given eight plots of land around a ninth. All eight families would pool their labor to cultivate the ninth communal plot and surrender the yield in full payment of their taxes, instead of being obliged to submit a fixed tribute in kind from their own fields, even in times of flood, drought, and famine.

The sage had a nose for social injustice and the sharp contradictions between class and class that in theory would do him credit in an age of concerned persons and Communist doctrine, and he did not mince his words for the mighty. "There is plump meat in your kitchens," he told the Duke of Wei (by then "King Hui"), "and the horses in your stables are well fed and sturdy. But hunger shows on the faces of your people, and outside the city lie the corpses of those who have starved to death. This is tantamount to feeding animals off human beings."

His realistic sense of equity did not save him from calumny, however. In 1973 the Department of Philosophy at the University of Peking accused him of siding with the ex-

* One *mou* is approximately one sixth of an acre or one fifteenth of a hectare today.

tortionate aristocracy and binding the farmer to the land so that he could not rebel. For Mencius had in fact said nothing to win the approval of the Maoists. He had not cried out for social revolution, but urged that villagers should be given "a full belly and clothes to wear." And this reformist heresy simply encouraged them in what was ultimately to prove the most stubborn of all conspiracies against Communism—a conspiracy of peasant pragmatism that was to well up in the faces of the Maoists from more than two thousand years down the shaft of Chinese history.

Communist attempts in 1958 to establish totally collectivized people's communes, and to introduce other measures on the farm calculated to rid the rustic masses of their lust for private gain, private land, and private lives, soon met with mute but consistent sabotage. The regime was obliged to modify the commune system drastically and to allow the farmers to run their own thriving "capitalist" businesses on the side, to cultivate their own plots, raise their own pigs and poultry, and sell their produce on a legalized local free market whose official "rectified" name was a "peasant fair."

Furthermore, Mencius saw men divided into two castes—those who ruled and were fed, those who fed and were ruled—and to the class-conscious who believe in a classless society he cut a poor figure beside successors of Mo Tzu, who believed that the same men could "plow the land with one hand and govern the state with the other." But against this proposition he developed his own effective argument.

Did a farmer who grew rice in order to eat also make his own clothes and cooking pots and iron tools? No, came the reply, that would interfere with the plowing and sowing, so he exchanged grain for them. But why did he not work as his own potter and smith, instead of imposing on others? Well, if he did so, he would have no time to till the soil, would he?

"Exactly. Then how is it possible for a man who governs a kingdom to plow the fields on one hand and look after the state on the other?" Mencius asked triumphantly. "Some exert their minds in the management of public affairs, others exert their strength in plowing the fields. All must divide up the work and cooperate. Each must keep to his station . . . otherwise would not the whole of society fall into chaos?"

Despite the long "democratic" tradition of the Chinese mandarinate, a civil service theoretically open to all, this famous argument helped to pin men's minds to the Confucian pattern of authority for two millennia of empire. The Maoists found themselves fighting against it in the 1970's when they sent professors and students down to the farm to "learn from the peasants," gave preference to youngsters of proletarian origin when awarding places in Chinese universities, and called on the masses to participate in the administration. The ingredients did not dissolve. Most peasants could not see themselves among those who "labor with their minds," most intellectuals agreed with them, and the leadership remained thick with militants of petit-bourgeois origin, as it had been since the beginning of the Communist revolution half a century before.

Mencius was no saint anyway. He wore no coarse robe of hemp like Mo Tzu, but drove around in a carriage in style, and showed a talent for being venomously inaccurate about those with whom he disagreed. For him Mo Tzu was a menace who wanted to "abolish fatherhood" because he advocated universal love without preference for parents, and the Taoists were menaces who wanted to "abolish princehood" because they did not believe in government. By disparaging duty and goodness, moreover, they were (like King Hui) "feeding wild beasts off human beings."

Nor did Mencius divorce his humanitarian homilies entirely from the secret ambitions of the powerful. His "goodness" was always geared to greatness, and he was not above a little gentle casuistry. When the King of Ch'i overran Sung, Mencius implied that his unprovoked and inexcusable assault on the smaller state had nonetheless been a "just war" because its king had obviously sealed his own fate by failing to govern righteously. Had he done so, Mencius argued speciously, "All within the four seas would look toward him and want him and no other for their lord. Then what would Sung need to fear from mighty Ch'i and Ch'u?" In fact, the King of

Sung was not as black as he had been painted, but the victim of a vicious smear campaign deliberately mounted to justify his extermination.

When Ch'i went on to annex Yen in 314 B.C., Mencius condoned this reprehensible move in turn as "punishment" and not "aggression," echoing both Confucius and Mo Tzu. The King of Ch'i then piously asserted that as the opposing forces had been evenly matched it was self-evident that his victory had indeed been the "Will of Heaven," and that he would have been flouting it had he not ordered the onslaught in the first place. Among Chinese, success sanctifies the act. Only failure condemns.

It must nevertheless be added that Mencius had already warned his covetous patron that all his schemes for widening his realm through war were as futile as "trying to get fish from trees," and after the conquest of Yen he told the king, "You have doubled your territories without practicing good government, and you will surely have All under Heaven against you."

In spite of his occasional ambiguities and his quasi-military aphorisms, therefore, the overlords turned rather toward those with less tame and tiresome formulas for achieving the straightforward objectives they had each set themselves—riches, land, power, and dominion within the four seas—and notably toward the school founded by "Master Ghost Valley."

6

The Day of the Kissingers

It is said that this Kuei Ku-tzu was a Taoist mystic, a recluse who lived in solitude beside a deep, limpid stream in a remote fold of the Central Plain known as Ghost Valley. But his disciples were "persuaders" of incisive political intellect, prized for the clarity and impartiality with which they would put the case for and against this or that plan—only to annihilate the subsequent arguments of those who did not choose the course they had privately favored from the outset. And the most formidable among them were Su Ch'in and Chang I, whose minds dueled with each other across the entire chessboard of China in the second half of the fourth century before Christ.

Now, as a sound Confucian, Mencius upheld the principle that the *hsien*, the true sage-adviser, was above even the king he advised, so that it was the king who should seek him out if he wished to beg for his services, not the sage who should go cap in hand to the king. He did not regard persuaders as sages, however, and he once scoffed at the suggestion that even these two outstanding pupils of Master Ghost Valley were "superior men" worthy of a ruler's respect. Nonetheless, the inquirer who had made the suggestion was right when he said of one of them: "If he but utters an angry word, all the princes tremble." Which could the United States more easily afford to lose, observers were asking in 1974—President Richard Nixon or Dr. Henry Kissinger?

When Su Ch'in and Chang I first crossed swords, Ch'in was the strongest of the Warring States, and was regarded with apprehension by men who feared that its masters were set upon "swallowing up All under Heaven." Of the other big fiefs only Ch'i and Ch'u could still put up a stiff fight against these "tigers and wolves." Mencius himself had already had to caution one weak prince against progressively yielding more and more land to a threatening enemy ("What gives the people their food should not be allowed to encompass their ruin"), but appeasement and procrastination were now in the air, and the classical Chinese counsel against trying to buy peace—"It is like using wood to smother a fire"—dates from this period.

Su Ch'in therefore embarked upon an ambitious project for forging a collective security pact against Ch'in among the other six states of the Middle Kingdom, and his first move was to go to the ruler of Yen, who was even then trying to ingratiate himself with Ch'in. Pointing out that Yen was prosperous and at peace, he went on: "And why is this, do you think? It is because Chao forms a buffer against Ch'in in the south. If the armies of Ch'in want to attack Yen, they must cross Chao, and even if they were to take your capital, Yen would be difficult to garrison as it is remote and the road is long. Therefore as far as Yen is concerned, Ch'in is helpless.

"But it is not the same with Chao. If Chao attacks Yen, then in ten days the Chao armies could be in your capital. Now, you make no contact with Chao under your nose, but you are on the contrary joining up with Ch'in, which is a thousand *li* away. Yet if only you would befriend Chao, Ch'in would be even less able to harm Yen and you would have won a diplomatic victory."

The King of Yen concurred, and sent Su Ch'in to Chao, where he emphasized that the combined armies of the six rulers would be far larger than those of Ch'in, and if they fought side by side, they must prevail. All talk of placating Ch'in by ceding territory should be ignored, for there need be no fear of invasion if only the states would agree to form a "vertical alliance" among themselves (so called because they were strung in a double line from north to south).

Traveling on to Han as the envoy of Chao, Su Ch'in accused the king of cringing before Ch'in in a ridiculous fashion which would only prompt his acquisitive neighbor to demand more of his territory and cities every year, until there was nothing left. To the King of Wei he compared groveling to Ch'in with losing a war without striking a blow, and insinuated that those officials who urged him to bend before these semi-barbarians were taking bribes from them.

Having lined up four rulers successfully, Su Ch'in sought an audience with the King of Ch'i. Unlike the states on Ch'in's border, he argued almost contemptuously, Ch'i was distant and powerful. Yet the king bowed his head to the aggressors. Why did he abase himself in this unseemly way? If he backed the other states, those nearest to Ch'in would be able to face up to the bully squarely, and Ch'i itself would be better protected. If, on the contrary, Ch'in overran them, Ch'i would lie exposed to Ch'in's advancing armies.

Lastly, Su Ch'in rode to Ch'u in the south. "If even you acknowledge the superiority of Ch'in," he told the king, "all others must submit. But remember that the greatest enemy of Ch'in is Ch'u. There is no room for both of you. The only course for you is to unite with the other five states against Ch'in. Otherwise Ch'in must attack you first. And then it will be too late."

The Vertical Alliance was duly formed. Su Ch'in was appointed supreme commander and returned to Chao with a ceremonial bodyguard several miles long. Banners and standards darkened the sky, and every state sent distinguished envoys to see him on his way. Once back in Chao, where he was made chief minister, he sent Ch'in the text of the pact. The King of Ch'in was sobered, and the menace of his bid for hegemony receded. But not forever. For the other outstanding student of Master Ghost Valley was now on his side.

After Su Ch'in became chief minister of Chao, Chang I became chief minister of Ch'in, and he set out to demolish the Vertical Alliance and replace it with a Horizontal League by driving wedges between the six states, and then joining them individually to Ch'in to their west with a series of bilateral treaties. A one-man mission constantly on the move, this antique Kissinger opened the play by arranging for a Ch'in princess to marry the heir-apparent of Yen. His chances of success increased when Su Ch'in was assassinated by political enemies, but his greatest anxiety was the formidable threat that Ch'i and Ch'u could pose, and since Ch'u had a common frontier with Ch'in while Ch'i was more distant, he concentrated on pretending to befriend Ch'u in order to smash the link between the two allies.

He began the softening-up process in 313 B.C. by brazenly offering to return 600 *li* of land earlier seized from Ch'u, if Ch'u would break with Ch'i. But when Ch'u accepted, he feigned a chariot injury and stayed away from the Ch'in court for three months. This enabled the King of Ch'in to behave as if he knew no details of the bargain struck with Ch'u, and no territory was ceded.

The perplexed King of Ch'u, finally realizing that he had been cheated, turned once again toward Ch'i on his other frontier—some say to seek a new alliance, others say to threaten Ch'i and so curry favor with Ch'in. Isolated and alarmed by the supposed reconciliation between Ch'in and Ch'u, however, the King of Ch'i had hastened to make his own pact with Ch'in, leaving a highly vulnerable Ch'u sandwiched between two hostile neighbors.

Having extracted the maximum profit from this situation, Chang I later engineered a second reconciliation between Ch'in and Ch'u which was sealed by two royal marriages, and then deceitfully claimed to the King of Ch'i that all the other states except his had ceded cities to Ch'in as an earnest of their friendship, and it was now Ch'i that stood alone. "So if Ch'in were to set Han and Wei to attack you in the south and Chao to attack your capital from along the Yellow River, it might be too late for you to come to terms," he concluded slyly. "I therefore beg Your Majesty to think carefully."

The King of Ch'i saw the point, whereupon Chang I moved on to Chao, which in fact had not yet come to heel, and curtly informed the ruler that since the Vertical Alliance was a dead letter and Chao's ability to resist Ch'in had therefore disappeared, Ch'in proposed to send a punitive expedition against him. "However, before the army marches we shall first talk things over in a civilized way. If Chao sincerely wants to establish friendly relations with Ch'in, then Ch'in is willing to forgo the assault and make peace."

Chao capitulated, and after that it was easy for Chang I to browbeat Yen also into yielding territory to Ch'in, despite the marriage between their royal houses, in the overriding interest of peace and quiet.

If the wily words attributed to Su Ch'in and Chang I were the work of the more imaginative chroniclers of the *Strategies of the Warring States*, their arguments and tactics and movements were not, and while Su Ch'in cajoled his hearers into acquiescence with a mixture of cold logic and dire warnings and a mortifying disdain for their pusillanimity, Chang I tricked and bullied and lied his way to success. Like most who are too smart by half, Chang I later fell from favor and retired, but Ch'in continued to make the Horizontal League the basis of its policy, and to practice the principle of "befriending the distant while attacking the near."

Chang I had hoodwinked Ch'u into breaking with the more remote state of Ch'i, and cowed the King of Ch'i into an alliance by pointing out how vulnerable his realm had then become. With Ch'i neutralized, Ch'in invaded the four smaller kingdoms in succession, rounded off the series by defeating Ch'u, and then overran Ch'i. By 221 B.C. all six had been forged into a single empire under the dominion of Ch'in. The long agony of the "Warring States" was over.

The "vertical" and "horizontal" strategies in the distasteful combination of arts known as diplomacy and war are as complementary as *yin* and *yang*, as weakness and strength, to the Chinese, and they have a place of honor in the classical manuals of statecraft. When weak, the state must join with those who are near against the more powerful enemy farther away, and make tactical alliances even with neighbors it dislikes in order to buy time. It does not befriend the remote and untrustworthy Ch'in when it cannot even defend itself against Chao next door, for under such circumstances "distant water does not put out fire."

In modern terms, a country or a party should form a vertical "united front" with enemies who can be liquidated later, in order to be able to destroy the enemy who must be liquidated now. In 1936 Generalissimo Chiang Kai-shek was kidnapped in the famous "Sian Incident" and only given his freedom again after he had agreed in principle to a truce which united the Nationalists with the Communists against the invading Japanese. Once the Japanese were defeated, the Communists turned their full fighting strength against Chiang and swept his demoralized Nationalist armies off the mainland of China.

But as the weak becomes strong, *yin* becomes *yang*, the "vertical" strategy gives way to the "horizontal," and the principle of playing one rival off against another, of "befriending the distant while attacking the near," is put into operation. The ruler passes to the offensive, and his object now is to bracket a hostile neighboring state between his own forces confronting it and an ally he has made behind it. He can then throw his troops across the frontier under the best possible conditions, since instead of being able to hope for help from the rear, the neighbor will be looking nervously over his shoulder. Or he can bide his time, for the neighbor will not be able to anticipate invasion by attacking first, since the potential enemy at his back will be "holding him by the leg."

This instinct for making "distant allies," and for "using barbarians to pacify barbarians," twice prompted early emperors of the Han Dynasty to dispatch officers on spectacular expeditions to the far west in search of firm friends behind the Huns, who were forever worrying at China from beyond the Great Wall. One of these intrepid envoys reached the Oxus, the other the Caspian Sea.

By the 1970's the Chinese were "walking on two legs" by practicing a fine combination of horizontal and vertical diplomacy, and in circumstances changed by the passage of twenty-two hundred years and the rise of two "superpowers" as against one "Mighty Ch'in," their leaders were still echoing the catch phrases of the past. The international situation was one of "great disorder in the world" [1]—a tag used long ago to describe the era of the Warring States—and the foreign policy of Peking was summed up in the words "relations with the distant and preparedness against the near." The "near" was a superpower which by definition aimed, like Ch'in, to "lord it over all," to "commit aggression, subvert, control, and hoodwink others," as Deputy Foreign Minister Ch'iao Kuan-hua told the U.N. General Assembly on November 15, 1971.

The "preparedness" could be seen in public exhortations to store grain, in the marching militia, in the shop-floor trapdoors to the fantastic labyrinth of tunnels under Peking through which three million comrades would be dispersed in case of air attack, and in similar human honeycombs in other cities and towns. "The absence of an external enemy will lead to the ruin of the state," Mencius had said, and two millennia later Marshal Ch'en Yi, Foreign Minister of a Communist China, was to quote his words. China had her indispensable public enemy number one in "the renegade clique of Soviet revisionists, even more deceitful than the old-style imperialism"—Holy Mother Russia.

"Old-style imperialism" referred to the United States, whose President paid an unprecedented visit to Peking early in 1972. Once more the Chinese were seeking allies afar to offset enemies just across the frontier, using barbarian to neutralize barbarian, ensuring that each "held the other by the leg."

The "wandering persuader" in this drama of modern Warring States was instantly recognized and appreciated by the Chinese, although not one of them. Dr. Henry Kissinger was a dispossessed German who had been an adviser to three American Presidents. He was an academic who had an urge to turn his principles into practice and power, yet knew that power must be transitory. He traveled incessantly, he had contacts everywhere, and although he spoke loudly of the ultimate need for an open foreign policy, his was a secret, single-handed diplomacy.

Like the disciples of Ghost Valley, he decided privately what should be done and then talked men into doing it while seeming to present an objective case. He never thrust decisions on others, but listened and leaned with their arguments, steering a course through complex negotiations with the sensitivity of a helmsman feeling his way over a reef. He varied his tactics to suit his interlocutor, watchful of the other man's standpoint, learning quickly that while the Russians started bargaining by making impossible demands, the Chinese simply quoted the list price for a settlement (anyone who failed to ask for a cash discount had only himself to blame).

His high-flown references to the need for something beyond power were for the most part mere talk; he was ready to do business with anybody, more fascinated by enemies than friends, by the balance between states as Su Ch'in or Chang I might have gauged it than the modern or Moist conception of interdependence.

Chinese said that Kissinger's flair for negotiation lay in its dullness—"You sit at the table with him and for half an hour he will make irrelevant conversation non-stop without touching on the real problem," Chou En-lai is once said to have remarked. Time would drag on, and the other party become impatient, just as Kissinger hoped. Then he would put forward his ideas in sequence, mentioning a second while the others were still discussing the first to show how keen he was on a settlement. His apparent sincerity won him sympathy and popular support, and his adversaries often found themselves obliged to make concessions to preserve their own international image.

The Chinese savored the furtiveness of Kissinger's initial moves in any delicate undertaking, so refreshing after the frankness of all the Occidental loudmouths who had prated absurdly of "open agreements openly arrived at." The final, public displays of diplomacy should be like the capering of Wu Sung and the Tiger—what was important was that the two actors had struck their bargain backstage and rigged their bout before they appeared, so that it would be a finished performance with no wild, impromptu swinging that might break an arm or black an eye in front of a world audience.

The Chinese formula is simple. Only negotiate what is negotiable. Establish an understanding with the other party beforehand, and all faces will be saved. When Dr. Kissinger first stepped into a plane to fly to Peking, Chairman Mao and President Nixon already knew that his mission of reconciliation must succeed.

Kissinger was also admired for his Oriental ability to talk and fight simultaneously, to beguile and bomb the North Vietnamese into a cease-fire. Secret preliminaries and a strong army were the keys to smooth and successful negotiation, the Chinese had emphasized throughout their history, and Kissinger was comfortingly comprehensible—he also believed in bidding from strength while holding his cards close to his chest. He recommended that the United States be prepared to wage a limited nuclear war if the need arose. America must be realistic and unsentimental, ready to use her formidable powers as "incentives for conciliation" or to inflict "penalties for intransigence." This was the kind of disciplinarian jargon that had been the making of Ch'in, whose kings had learned in their time to be as mysterious and secretive as the American Secretary of State was now.

Unlike Ch'in, Kissinger did not want to hold the world in thrall, but only in balance. Yet even that was a superhuman task, for the relationship between nation and nation—and notably America, Russia, and China—was growing and changing like the Taoist cosmos. China was still comparatively weak, her nuclear power embryonic. Her "horizontal alliance" with the United States was not dictated by a desire to attack the U.S.S.R., but to limit Russian expansion in the Far East, to gain time and put on muscle, and within it America—not the People's Republic—played the stronger role of Ch'in. Chinese policy was therefore ambivalent, the horizontal line was complemented by a vertical line, and at the intersection lay Western Europe.

In Peking the Chinese gave a carefully modulated welcome to an exhausting stream of European visitors, because a united "Europe" could serve as another "distant ally" behind Moscow's back, and they pulled the linchpin out of Western political logic during 1974 and 1975 by showing favor on occasion to right-wing opposition leaders rather than "left-wing" parties in power. Chairman Mao received the defeated former British Prime Minister Edward Heath twice within two years—although Heath had meanwhile lost control of his party as well as his country. He also received Franz Josef Strauss, ultra-rightist chief of the West German opposition, three months before Chancellor Helmut Schmidt was due to take his turn on the red carpet in Peking.

But Heath was a champion of "Europe" when Harold Wilson and his ruling Labour Party were threatening to pull Britain out of the Common Market, and Strauss staunchly rejected the *Ostpolitik* of Soviet-German rapprochement, whereas Schmidt was its misguided architect. Moreover, Heath could still bounce back, and Strauss looked an up-and-coming figure at a time when harassed men in power could be broken by the formidable problems they faced.

The cultivation of deluded bourgeois-reactionary or pseudo-socialist politicians from London, Paris, and Bonn also belonged to a wider program for lining up the rest of the world against the two superpowers, as Su Ch'in had lined up the six states against Ch'in—a program which not only prompted the Chinese to champion the grievances of the Third World, but persuaded them to turn a strained smile upon their old enemy, Japan.

That did not necessarily foreshadow the last twist in the *yin-yang* spiral, however, for there is no last twist. It still remained to be seen what would happen if the day came when the internal authority of the Chinese Communist Party was absolute, the People's Republic was a major nuclear power, and modern China could be equated with ancient Ch'in—the Ch'in that had once become master of All under Heaven.

7

The Mixmasters

If the morals of Mencius the sage and the methods of Chang I the schemer seem as incompatible as silks of clashing colors, they were nonetheless to be woven into the same pattern of Chinese political thought after the great authoritarian Hsun Tzu had begun to draw them together.

Men were born good, said Mencius. "A person who lacks compassion, who has no sense of shame or hatred, of humility or courtesy, cannot be called a man." Tyrants were simply "robbers of the people," and bureaucrats were their "concubines."

No, man was born evil, said Hsun Tzu (Hsun K'uang, who was himself born in 312 B.C. when Mencius was already a crusty old septuagenarian). He had to be educated to know what was right, as tools must be ground before they could be sharp. Bent by nature, he could be straightened with the precepts of the early kings, who had known that the discipline imposed by laws and rites and the authority of the ruler was as indispensable as a plumb-line in a crooked world.

Leave men to themselves, and the strong would bully the weak, the many browbeat the few, and society soon fall into chaos. Yet the evil wanted to be good, as the poor wanted to be rich, and the ugly beautiful, and their nature could be changed by conscious cultivation, just as the farmer who plowed and sowed with care could reap a bumper crop. If

Mencius was closer to Plato in his view of humanity, Hsun Tzu was closer to Aristotle. Both were Confucians, but the clamor of their dispute was to echo down the long corridor of Chinese history, perhaps forever.

Hsun Tzu came from Chao, but like Mencius before him he lived for many years in Ch'i, whose kings tempted scholars to their court by offering them stipends and lodging and the leisure in which to study and debate. Vicious slander later forced him to move on to Ch'u, but he was nonetheless a thinker who commanded great respect, for he was the most practical of the Confucians. And this was true whether he was enlarging on the regrettable nature of man, the virtues of discipline and learning, the vagaries of the military-minded—or the merits of an expanding economy.

Shortages were solely the fault of bad government, he asserted. Controls should be imposed to stop the outrageous profiteering of salt and iron magnates and to regulate supply and demand, but instead of taxing farmers and merchants and craftsmen into their graves and wasting their hours and energy on forced labor, the ruler should provide them with incentives to grow and buy and sell more.

For it was the riches of the people that made the state strong, not the riches of the state itself. "The fuller the state granaries, the poorer will be the people, and if the people are poor, the state will become poor in its turn," he said, paraphrasing Confucius. "Any government that allows the people to profit and is not itself overanxious to be rich can unify the Middle Kingdom . . . but a government that squeezes profit from the people has taken the first step toward self-destruction." The happiness and security and prosperity of the people and state were inextricably interwoven. The wise king therefore promoted the upright and the able commoner, and demoted the base, however blue-blooded, for men frightened of their masters were as dangerous as horses frightened of the chariot.

It all has a resonant Confucian ring, but Hsun Tzu lived during the closing century of the Warring States, and he was heir to the winning and losing equations of generations of sages and persuaders consulted by the feudal lords. In consequence his teachings echo the themes of others, including some of his colleagues at Chi-hsia, the academy for scholars that the kings of Ch'i supported near the west gate of their capital. But they do not echo the exponents of the Yin-Yang school of thought.

It was at Chi-hsia that the disciples of Taoism and Moism first shrouded rational thinking in a mist of metaphysics to create this alluring "philosophy," whose founder was a man some twenty years older than Hsun Tzu named Tsou Yen. Having discovered to his chagrin that the plain Confucian principles of benevolence and righteousness and the comfortless strictures of Mo Tzu fell on deaf ears when logically propounded to arrogant aristocrats, Tsou Yen had lit upon an ingenious solution to the problem of making them listen to him. The Yin-Yang doctrine related humdrum human affairs and natural phenomena, the Way of Heaven and the virtues of frugality, to the arcane workings of the Taoist cosmos and the sibylline prophecies of the *Book of Changes,* and its success was very swift.

That in itself was predictable, for danger and uncertainty trick men into turning to mystery and magic for comfort, and it was in times of turmoil that Taoism degenerated progressively into a pop faith filled with gods and ghosts, charms and Chang Tao-ling, the first Taoist "pope" (who is said to have ascended to Heaven on a dragon in A.D. 156, aged 122). China swarmed with traveling quacks who peddled cheap spells and panaceas for all ills, and for the superstitious rulers of Hsun Tzu's day the Taoists already held an almost irresistible attraction as purveyors of occult "power," bent on the time-honored quest for the pill of immortality and the formula for transmuting base metal into gold that alchemists in the West were to pursue many centuries later.

According to Tsou Yen and his disciples of the Yin-Yang school, the five natural forces or "Virtues"—earth, wood, metal, fire, and water—brought about the interminable cosmic changes that had begun when Heaven was first separated from the world, for each enjoyed periods of growth and decay, one Virtue giving way to the next when its potency was exhausted.

The early Hsia Dynasty had the Virtue of Wood, a green dragon heralded it and its first ruler always wore green. But metal cuts wood. When the Shang Dynasty succeeded the Hsia, silver flowed down the mountains as a sign and the ruler wore silver, for its Virtue was Metal. But metal is melted by fire. When the Chou Dynasty was founded, red birds soared in the sky and the ruler wore red, for its Virtue was Fire. However, the five Virtues were linked not only with "lucky" colors and numbers and months, like the signs of the zodiac, but with planets, animals, seasons, places of sacrifice, grains, tastes, smells, human organs, and even government ministries, and during the Han Dynasty this comprehensive system held the court completely in its grip.

The residence halls of the emperor were built according to exact specifications, and he had to change them every month—as well as his clothes, his food, his music, his sacrifices, and even the ministerial business to which he attended. For eighteen days in each of the four plus one seasons (increased to match the number of Virtues), he lived in a special chamber aligned with the corresponding "lucky" point of the compass (the number of points was raised to five by including the axis), and during the Sung Dynasty nearly one thousand years later the ritual was even more complicated.

Could it survive, this mumbo-jumbo that wood occupies the east and commands the spring, metal occupies the west and commands the autumn, fire occupies the south and commands the summer? "Fire occupies the south," affirmed one of the many oracular Chinese who still believe that the authority of the ruler is divinely conferred. "Mao is a southerner. The present age has the Virtue of Fire. Therefore the red flag flies everywhere."

The Communists deride and condemn all feudal superstition, including—ostensibly—the myth of the superman, the "red dragon" whose advent was heralded by portents. But they have not hesitated to play on the Chinese sense of awe by glorifying the young Mao who defied the elements, climbing mountains in wind and rain, the old Mao who swam the Yangtse in 1966, and the "Red Sun in our Hearts" whose "Thought" could inspire the painless removal of fifty-pound tumors and the curing of deaf-mutes.

According to the official "proletarian revolutionary line," however, there are no individual geniuses—it is man in the mass that achieves all the miracles, overcoming the universe by the power of his will. Mao himself wrote the lines:

> Fight with Heaven, for limitless joy!
> Fight with Earth, for limitless joy!
> Fight with man, for limitless joy!

—and in doing so echoed Hsun Tzu, who chastised the mystics and declared that Heaven was simply the heavens and spirits were simply the forces of nature.

Heaven still has winter, even if men hate cold, he pointed out, and Heaven remains wide, even if men hate distances. Man is accident-prone, and may be stupid yet rich, wise yet needy, but good government will bring fortune, bad government disorder, and "if you till the fields and are frugal, Heaven cannot make you poor." Prayers are useless—it rains whether you pray or not. Omens are not to be feared—stars fall of themselves, the sun and moon are naturally subject to eclipse.

With human "portents" it is otherwise, however. When peasants are taken from the fields for forced labor in the sowing season, when cows and horses are left to interbreed, when men and women mingle wantonly, so that fathers are suspicious of sons and officials fall out, trouble will follow. The rites that order men's lives and impose moderation by fixing each in his allotted place are therefore vital to prosperity and peace.

For Mencius ritual was practice in propriety for men born good, but for Hsun Tzu it was a curb for the unbridled emotions of men born into evil. "Since all wish to satisfy their urges," he said, "conflict between man and man is inevitable.

The sage-kings of old therefore established standards so that in a harmonious society, human desires would be satisfied within limits, and equilibrium preserved. That is the origin of ritual." In due and proper form, a man expressed his grief through mourning, his joy through music—and his indignation "through graded penalties which ensure that no crime goes unpunished."

Hsun Tzu thus bridged the gap between *Li* and law. He was an enemy of cruelty, he denounced the iniquitous system of clan punishment whereby the kin of a criminal were killed with him. As a good Confucian he was on the side of leniency. He stressed that those who administered justice must be of the highest character, and he condemned callous and muddled moralists who confused their terms to the point of saying that "when you kill a thief, you do not kill a man."

"But if a murderer does not die, and if he who injures another is not chastised," he added, "the power of evil will increase." Civilizing exercises in rites must therefore be backed by sobering exercises in retribution when the rites fail to civilize.

In the ideal state, Confucius had said, men would not need law, but only *Li*. In an ideal world, Mencius had said, the sage-king would conquer without arms, for all men would flock to him. But Hsun Tzu moved with the times, and he discussed not only practical punishments for fallible men, but practical rules for fallible rulers, not only the virtues desirable in the lawful sage-king, but those of quite a different royal beast—the ambitious feudal lord who set out to win dominion over all the warring states.

The "good" hegemon, he suggested, opened up lands for farming as he advanced, built granaries, and saw that all people had what they needed. He was careful when appointing his subordinates and employed men of talent, encouraging them with rewards and correcting them with punishments. He restored states that had collapsed, upheld dying royal houses, protected the weak, restrained the violent. If he showed that he did not propose to annex his neighbors, the other feudal lords would warm to him, and if he treated them as equals, he would gain their favor. Then he would always be victorious.

There was little to bite on here for the aspiring overlord obsessed with dreams of bloody conquest, and Hsun Tzu was careful to predict disaster for any brutish fellow who was merely out to fill his coffers and grab the territory of others. He would alienate his peers, invite attack, and find himself with "more and more cities to defend and fewer and fewer men to defend them."

He was nonetheless giving guidance to any usurper who chose to brush aside the authority of the "nominal king"—the rightful Chou Dynasty monarch—and take effective power into his own hands. He had opened a Confucian door to dictatorship for those ready to pick what they wanted from his preachings and throw the rest away.

Directed toward the discovery of the ultimate philosophical elixir, the doctrinal alchemy practiced at Chi-hsia combined disparate elements of past Chinese thought into new, sometimes unstable potions. While Hsun Tzu postulated an ostensibly Confucian world in which men must nonetheless be disciplined with strict laws and "graded penalties," and a hegemon might nonetheless be virtuous, the Taoists postulated a pitiless cosmos in which the despot of the day was preordained, cultivated benevolence was pernicious, and the true sage treated all men like straw dogs. The two schools might be at odds with each other, but for the power-hungry eclectic their ideas were not mutually exclusive.

It was after he moved to Ch'u, however, that Hsun Tzu undertook the instruction of two students named Han Fei and Li Ssu; it was after that period of instruction that their refined if repellent "Legalist" theories won the admiration of the most ruthless tyrant in the Middle Kingdom; and it was after that again that the tyrant in question made his final bid for the hegemony of All under Heaven.

Legalism was not new to him, the "horizontal" strategy of Chang I had long since laid the groundwork for his program of total aggression, and this sequence of events therefore seems to have been almost as inevitable as the rotation of the five Virtues, ending with water. And the qualities of water were: season—winter; animal—pig; number—six; color—black; direction—north; planet—Mercury; dynasty—Ch'in.

8

Machiavellissimo

It is a measure of the subtlety with which the different elements of Chinese philosophy are blended that Legalism could claim inspiration from the man of whom the humanistic Confucius had said almost reverently: "Had it not been for Kuan Chung, we would still be wearing our hair long and folding our clothes to the left." For Kuan Chung not only strove to make Ch'i the greatest state of his time under a prince wielding absolute power, but laid stress on the immutable authority of law rather than *Li:* "Ruler and subject, superior and inferior, noble and commoner, all must obey the laws, and then the state will be governed in peace."

If Kuan Chung stressed law in the seventh century before Christ, Shen Pu-hai stressed the craft of the ruler in the fourth, for when the "technique" of the king was weak, he warned, he became the slave of his own kingdom. If, for example, his officials were ill chosen and treacherous, if they covertly exploited his royal prerogatives in order to rid themselves of rivals and protect their own henchmen, wasted public funds and victimized his subjects, a cowed people would obey the ministers rather than the monarch himself. The ruler should never let his underlings know the workings of his mind, he should never let them act outside the limited scope of their specific responsibilities, and he should never delegate his power to fix punishments and rewards.

Shen Pu-hai proved that he knew what he was talking

about, for during his fifteen years as chief minister of the state of Han, the government was reformed, the defenses were strengthened, and no enemy dared to attack. He died in 337 B.C., one year after the pitiless disciplinarian whom many regard as the first true Legalist—Shan Yang.*

To the west in Macedonia, a border state on the hem of Greek civilization, Alexander had been tutored by Aristotle, the advocate of an inflexible Logic, and was about to make himself master of his world. To the east in Ch'in, a border state on the hem of Chinese civilization, the ruler had been counseled by Shan Yang, the advocate of an inflexible Law, and Ch'in was to become master of all China.

Shan Yang's formula for success was admirably comprehensive. Under his direction, the old order of landed vassals in Ch'in was abolished, the country was divided into thirty-one counties administered by magistrates, and power was concentrated in the hands of the monarch. The people were arranged in groups of five or ten households responsible for one another's conduct, and the group was punished collectively for the crime of any individual member of it. If a man failed to denounce a miscreant, he was chopped in half, but those who faithfully reported the transgressions of their neighbors were rewarded "as if they had beheaded an enemy."

To split big families into manageable size, Shan Yang ruled that households harboring two or more grown sons should be taxed twice over. No one was allowed to leave the country, those on the move had to register wherever they stayed, and all were dragooned for periodical forced labor. The entire population was ordered to devote itself to farming, weaving, and fighting, and the families of merchants and similar parasites were enslaved. Men were ennobled only for valor on the field of battle, and nobles were stripped of their titles and privileges if they proved poor soldiers.

The rigid laws of the state were enforced by means of punctual rewards and a short list of discouraging penalties

* Wei Yang or Kung-sun Yang, Lord of Shang, normally referred to as Shang Yang or Shan Yang (c. 390–338 B.C.).

largely confined to beheading the delinquent, cutting him in two at the waist, tearing him apart with chariots, boring a hole in his skull, unceremoniously extracting his ribs, or roasting him alive on a stove.

At first everyone complained, but according to China's Grand Historian, Ssu-ma Ch'ien, "At the end of ten years, the people were content, the hills were free of brigands, men fought resolutely in war, and villages and towns were well ruled." However, when the imprudent began praising the system, Shan Yang had the "troublemakers" banished for their presumption. Kuan Chung had said that the law was above even the ruler, and Shan Yang struck at the king's son for flouting it. When the king died and his vengeful heir came to power, therefore, Shan Yang tried to flee the country unseen, but he was caught in the web of his own police system and forced to register in his real name at an inn in the mountains (he was torn apart, in due course, by chariots himself).

But Ch'in had not done with Legalism, and almost exactly one hundred years later the reigning king welcomed Han Fei to his court, just as his forebear had once welcomed Shan Yang. For Han Fei had spun into tough twine the separate strands of this stern philosophy, claiming that each by itself was too weak a thread on which to suspend the state.

For lack of a rigid, uniform law, the "technique" of Shen Pu-hai had not saved Han from the depredations of corrupt officials, he said. And for lack of "technique," of the secret art of ruling, the previous kings of Ch'in had overstressed the glory of military prowess and enfeoffed their gallant warriors so richly that if they rebelled they could not be suppressed. Both "law" and "technique" were as indispensable as clothing and food, but to these a third must be added—"power," the unquestionable authority that is born of influence, station, legal prerogative, and military might—for without this quality of the "soaring dragon," the most virtuous of men must bow to the ignorant and vile. Nor did Han Fei stop there, for his teaching is heavily weighted with the "Confucianism" of Hsun Tzu and the "Taoism" of Lao Tzu.

The enlightened ruler cultivates the art of being a terrifying, actionless, fathomless blank, notes the *Han Fei Tzu*. He is "so still that he seems to dwell nowhere, so empty that no one can seek him." He "reposes in non-action above, and his ministers tremble with fear below." He drains the wise of their wisdom, the worthy of their virtue, the brave of their valor. Their role is to work. His is to personify all their wisdom, virtue, and courage and enjoy the success of their efforts.

Han Fei Tzu agrees with Shen Pu-hai that the sage-king must never reveal his thoughts, but keep his ministers guessing. He must be like the *Tao* of the cosmos itself, showing no more preference one way or another than a balance which registers light and heavy, yet identifies itself with neither. He must be impervious to the wiles of women and sycophants, to the tug of blood relationship, to greed and luxury and extravagance, to the temptations of popularity, and to the urge to be overbearing on the one hand or to overlook faults on the other.

He must be cold-blooded in his judgments, trusting none. The carriage maker wants men rich, the coffin maker wants them dead. This is not a matter of love and hatred, but of profit and loss, and the same principle applies to those who want the ruler alive, or the ruler dead. The sovereign is therefore safest with subordinates whose loyalty has a set price which he can pay.

It follows that in choosing his advisers the enigmatic prince must suspect all who are contemptuous of honors and money. This means that he must have no favorites among the ministers he does pick, for they are mercenaries, they do not love him, and they are only interested in gain. They should never be given a chance to learn what they should do to win his royal approval. He must not praise virtue or valor or beauty, for then they will dissimulate, pretending to be virtuous, brave, or beautiful, and conceal their true nature.

Men who are already known for their good deeds and charity should be rejected, for they will only continue to curry favor with others, and this can lead to the formation of traitorous cliques that may threaten the authority and life of the overlord. For the same reason, no official should be given exceptional power, for that would be to make the shin thicker than the thigh, and those who grow too strong must be whittled down, as a man must prune his trees so that they do not block the path he walks.

The despotism of Han Fei Tzu is based on the principle of "one man, one office." No single official should hold two ministries, and a ruler should beware of the minion who exceeds his duties. What drives him? Zeal? Or ambition? "When the Marquis of Han got drunk and passed out, the royal hat keeper laid a robe over him. When the Marquis came to, he was at first pleased, but on hearing who had covered him, he punished his hat keeper for overstepping his office and his robe keeper for failing in his. The trespass of one official on the responsibilities of another was to him more dangerous than lying in the cold."

If a minister's achievement falls short of his promise, he must be punished, but if his achievement surpasses his promise, he must also be punished. A ruler must not be deceived, and his ministers must be measured not only by what they say but by what they do not say.

Technique is useless without "power," however, and Han Fei Tzu examines where that "power," the authority that keeps a king at the apex and the country at peace, resides and does not reside. It does not reside, he emphasizes, in the humanity and righteousness notionally practiced by the sages of antiquity.

For one thing, times change: "When men could not overcome beasts, a sage appeared who made nests out of wood for them, and the people were so pleased that they appointed him ruler of All under Heaven." But who lives in a wooden nest today? Humanity and righteousness may have served in another age when men were few and things many, life was easy and there was no cause for quarreling, but they are of no use in an era of dog-eat-dog war, when more men are scrambling for fewer things, and the qualities that count are cunning and courage. To practice lenient government at such a time, says Han Fei Tzu, is as disastrous as trying to control a runaway horse without touching reins or whip.

He therefore lists "five vermin" that Confucian compassion breeds, among them an exaggerated respect for filial piety. In the state of Ch'u an honest man denounced his father for stealing a sheep, he recounts, but the Confucian magistrate treated this loyal subject as a villainously unfilial son and ordered that he be put to death. On the other hand, when an officer of Lu charged with running away from the enemy excused himself on the grounds that there would be no one to take care of his old father were he killed, Confucius praised his filial conduct and had him promoted. Thereafter no one in Ch'u would denounce a thief, and few in Lu would fight on the field of battle.

Those who break the law and disrupt the state by punctiliously pursuing private vendettas are honored, he continues. Those who earn themselves riches and reputation without either plowing the land or striking a blow to defend it are admired above others. And Confucian scholars who fuddle sovereigns with their appeals for rule by love instead of rule by law are given government posts, although their tales of benevolent sage-kings who allegedly wept when erring subjects were disciplined are mischievous nonsense.

The true sage shows no clemency. He does not govern a state by depending upon people to be good, for if a fletcher "waits for arrow shafts to straighten of themselves, he will not make an arrow in a hundred generations." He simply ensures that they are not allowed to do evil, by administering a single, comprehensive system of justice under which the virtuous are rewarded handsomely, the vicious are punished horribly, and there can be no exceptions. Moreover, if there must be one code, there must also be one ruler, and as Shen Pu-hai had insisted, the "power" of the ruler rests above all in this: that he keeps to himself "the two handles of punishment and favor," the right to kill, mutilate, honor, and recompense in accordance with the uniform, inflexible laws that he alone makes. For should he delegate that prerogative to his officials, the people will fear the officials and disdain the ruler, and he may expect to be assassinated. "Punishment and reward are like the claws and teeth of the tiger that can subdue the dog. If the claws and teeth are given to the dog, it is the tiger that must submit," Han Fei Tzu warns.

In other respects also the centralized meritocracy of Han Fei Tzu closely resembles Ch'in in the days of Shan Yang. "There are no books, for the law is the sole subject of instruction, and the officials are its teachers." Ministers and generals alike rise from the ranks, and since farming and fighting are valued above all, men are eager to farm and fight. There are no private feuds, and by definition valiant deeds can only be performed in the service of the king. "Therefore in times of peace the state is prosperous, and in times of war its army is strong."

And this is the nub of the matter. Since Han Fei Tzu and all the other exponents of the "Hundred Schools" of thought whom they have consulted are answering the same questions posed by the same breed of overlords, the ultimate purpose of their guidance is also—paradoxically—the same. Whether Mencius is trying to persuade some disbelieving potentate that if he practices government by goodness all the world will rally to him and none will dare to attack him, or Han Fei Tzu is advancing his own equally drastic solutions, the object of the exercise is to give a kingdom the inner strength that will make it immune from invasion and enable it to dominate all others.

Interdependence is no substitute. "Vertical" and "horizontal" alliances are both hazardous undertakings, says the *Han Fei Tzu*, for in the first each state must trust all the others to remain loyal in an emergency, and in the second the weak state must confide its destiny to the tender care of a strong one. And when a state is strong, it does not need such devices. For "a powerful ruler can conquer his neighbors, and a well-ordered realm cannot be overrun"—provided both the power and the order have come from within.

Han Fei was not given a chance to put his intimidating theories into practice in the state of Ch'in, for his tragedy was that although he had compared treacherous officials who frightened talented men away from their royal masters to "fierce dogs" that kept good custom away from an inn, he fell victim to a "fierce dog" himself.

Shan Yang had come to Ch'in from Wei. Han Fei came to Ch'in from Han. He was afflicted with a bad stutter and had originally set down his ideas for his own ruler, but his writings had fallen into the hands of the King of Ch'in, who was deeply impressed by them and delighted when the brilliant Legalist arrived at his court.

The chief justice of Ch'in was not delighted, however. For the chief justice was Li Ssu, Han Fei's fellow student under Hsun Tzu, and he was jealous of the exceptional ability of this interloper who might now become his rival for royal favor. Li Ssu therefore insinuated to his prince that since he was a nobleman of Han, the newcomer's loyalties were suspect, that he was a dangerous, spying intruder who would later return to his own state and be a thorn in the flesh of Ch'in—"so in my opinion the best thing would be to charge him with some crime, execute him, and have done."

The ruler first agreed, then wavered. But meanwhile Li Ssu had sent poison to Han Fei, and Han Fei, isolated in prison and unable to plead his case, duly drank it. Born in about 280 B.C., Han Fei died in 233. But his Legalist teachings lived.

The King of Ch'in was a remorseless despot, a man with "a waspish nose, eyes like slits, a chicken breast, the voice of a jackal, and the heart of a tiger or wolf," who was humble when times were difficult but "swallowed men up without a scruple" when all went well. In a series of campaigns notable for cynical treachery and revolting ferocity, he conquered the other six feudal kingdoms between 229 and 222 B.C. and founded the gigantic realm that was to be called after his original fief—"China."

In the West, Alexander had united the Greek states, and in no more than fourteen years won a vast empire that fell apart soon after his death. In the East, Ch'in had welded the Chinese states into another vast empire, under a dynasty that was also to last no more than fourteen years and fall soon after the death of its founder. Unity, as the Chinese say, can lead only to disunity, and disunity to unity.

But the new "China" was not to disintegrate so easily. The "First Emperor," as the Ch'in conqueror styled himself, broke up the feudal system and divided his realm into prefectures and military districts administered by officials whom he personally appointed, and to guard further against any undesirable centrifugal tendencies on the part of the vanquished, he moved the 120,000 most important families among them to the capital.

He was the formidable tyrant who built the Great Wall, and over the huge expanse of territory "Within the Wall" imposed that cultural unity which has been the greatest strength of the Chinese ever since. He standardized the laws, the written language, weights and measures, farming implements, and even cart axles. But he did more than that after Li Ssu, by now his chief minister, had memorialized him in these immortal words: "The Empire has been pacified, and the laws of the country unified. *May it please Your Majesty to determine right from wrong,* to proscribe all unorthodox opinions, to destroy by fire all historical records but those of Ch'in, to rule that any man who possesses the writings of the Hundred Schools and the ancient literature must immediately surrender them to the magistrates to be burned, and that if any man dares to discuss these works with others, he shall be put to death and his head displayed in public; that if any man cites the old laws in order to vilify those of the present dynasty, his clan shall be exterminated, and that officers who fail to report such cases shall be similarly punished. After thirty days those who have not had their books destroyed shall be branded and condemned to forced labor on the Great Wall. As for those who wish to study the laws, let them take the officials as their masters."

To promote even greater solidarity under his central rule, therefore, the First Emperor not only decreed that anyone who quoted the Confucian Classics should be beheaded, and that all books should be burned (with a few technical exceptions), but had several hundred scholars who were caught hoarding the forbidden works buried alive. In consequence, most of the literary heritage of China went up in smoke.

When the Ch'in Dynasty was violently overthrown by its restless victims, the emperors of the great Han Dynasty who ruled China from 202 B.C. to A.D. 220 (with one short break) adopted Confucianism as the philosophy of the state. But behind the benevolent façade—the reverence for the ancients, the humanitarian magistracy, the mandarins versed in the Classics—lay the sharp half-hidden reality of Legalist practice, like a knife concealed in the robe of a priest.

The first emperor of the "Confucian" Han Dynasty confided his administration to hand-picked scholars, and the bloody suppression of provincial rebellion to able generals. But while seeming to trust his subordinates, he had them closely watched, and if he was assailed by the faintest suspicion that any man was plotting mischief, he ordered his immediate execution. The tradition did not fade. The founding emperors of the Sung and Ming dynasties that later held sway both earned unenviable reputations, the first for his suave yet ruthless assumption of absolute power, the second for his sinister "techniques" and savage punishments, so that men said "to keep company with a king is like keeping company with a tiger." Yet throughout Chinese history it has been almost axiomatic that the first ruler of a new imperial line would be the best.

Nor did the Legalist conceptions of "power" and "law" die with the empire. In the 1930's a young official was posted to a special administrative area in the south of Kiangsi Province whose corrupt and extravagant governor, behaving like an independent monarch, had silenced the criticisms of earlier intruders from the capital at pistol point. Nonetheless, the newcomer at once proscribed gaming, prostitution, opium smoking, and similar pursuits, and when the wife of the Director of the Salt Bureau ignored his orders and continued to gamble, he made her kneel before a memorial for the dead in a public park for three weeks and thereafter sweep the streets for six months.

He next had the only son of a rich and influential family

shot by firing squad for smoking opium, and within a short time gambling stopped and drug addicts fled the region. Police "technique" had enabled him to apply immutable "law," but both had been made possible by his "power"—the power of the soaring dragon—for his authority was incontestable. He was called Chiang Ching-kuo, and he was the son of Chiang Kai-shek.

Mao Tsetung has been a brilliant exponent of "technique" throughout his career. In times of trial, he makes friends with one enemy in order to destroy the other whom he cannot befriend. In times of triumph, he preserves his unique "power," and when he does delegate authority, he makes others responsible for the consequences and waits—often silently, even enigmatically—for the outcome, ready to take credit for success or sacrifice a scapegoat for failure.

Ostensibly aloof, he maintains the balance between eternally struggling factions ("One must divide into two" is the basic mechanical principle of the unending Maoist revolution), thus reducing the capacity of any group to turn against himself, while winning gratitude whenever he does give one side or the other his approval.

For in the last analysis he alone "holds the two handles of punishment and favor," since in an ideological state, the ideology is the law, and in China the ideology is the Thought of Chairman Mao, against which all words and actions are tested, and judged to be good or bad *("May it please Your Majesty to determine right from wrong . . .")*.

The pungent odor of Legalism seeps out of every seam in the Chinese Communist system. The political "law" is the main subject of instruction, and the party cadres are its teachers. All other "schools" are proscribed, and their books have been at least metaphorically burned. Old doctrines, old rites, and old humanities are anathema—as they were anathema in Ch'in.

The state is united under centralized rule. The privileged classes have been abolished, and men are promoted according to merit. The peasant, the worker, and the soldier are the darlings of the state—the merchants and other idlers have been duly dispossessed, and contentious scholars among the intellectuals are regarded with suspicion. Once again, as in Ch'in, the defense of the country against an invader largely depends on the man who can drop his plow and take up his sword when the need arises.

Frugality is urged upon all. Sons are encouraged to denounce the sins of fathers. Street committees are responsible for the conduct of the families under their surveillance. Registration of the population is rigorous. The names and the personal details of all members of each household are carefully listed. The arrival of travelers must be reported to the local police station, together with their particulars and the reason for their visit, even if they are relatives or close friends who come frequently and stay only one night. No person may move permanently to another town without permission, and none can leave the country privately. Shan Yang could no more have escaped from modern China unnoticed than he could leave ancient Ch'in unperceived.

It is not surprising that as early as 1961 Communists were favorably describing Hsun Tzu, Shan Yang, and Han Fei Tzu as "materialists" and "leftists," that by 1974 they were cursing Confucius as the champion of a slave-owning aristocracy, and praising the First Emperor of Ch'in as the "progressive" unifier of all China.

But the parallel must not be pushed too far. If the Thought of Mao has replaced the Law of Ch'in as the unique doctrine of the centralized state, it has also replaced the Confucian learning that for so many centuries was China's sole official political creed. The Communist cadre fluent in Marx, Engels, Lenin, and Mao is the heir in many ways of the Confucian mandarin steeped in the Classics.

Moreover, Chinese justice is not administered in accordance with one of those inflexible codes so beloved of the logical French. Two outstandingly ruthless Legalists, Shan Yang and Wu Ch'i, were torn apart with chariots, Han Fei notes. Why? Because "though both men spoke what was apt and true, the high ministers resented their laws, and the common people hated orderly government."

The humanistic Confucian tradition has left the Chinese with a conviction that what is just is more important than what is legal, and where the outer barbarian is concerned, this is characteristic not only of the Chinese millions but of their political masters. Communist and Nationalist leaders alike decry the "unequal treaties" under which the weak Manchu Dynasty ceded territory to the Western powers and Japan during the nineteenth century—not because they are technically invalid but because they consider them morally weightless. By the same token, they do not justify their claim to the islands in the South China Sea by waving title deeds to them, but by expostulating that they are "naturally" or "historically" part of China and "have always been" within her "time-honored frontiers." [1]

The Communists may find the thoughts of Mo Tzu, Hsun Tzu, Han Fei Tzu—even Lao Tzu—less objectionable than those of Confucius and Mencius, but while they may deplore the persistent influence of Confucian ideas that still pervade the Republic, they cannot ignore them. The people look up to their leader in Peking, as Ch'in would have wished, but they recoil from the rigid rule of law. Millions still cling instinctively to a well-worn fabric of society made up of deviationist "old beliefs" like filial piety and family loyalty. They are permeated with "feudal" allegiances to local province and patron, and even with a reverence for rites—gaudy weddings and formal burials and furtive prayers to honorable ancestors.

The essentially Chinese texture of the Maoist administration therefore has in it the feel of the earlier philosophies. For "technique" demands procrastination, if not a compromise. A regime that wants to win the enthusiasm and trust of all must be patient and flexible with the masses, must display a certain "benevolence" of its own, talking them rather than terrorizing them into conforming to the new creed.

Ironically, a soft mask of magnanimity conceals the firm bone structure of authoritarian rule in Communist China, much as it did in Imperial China. Revolution is revolution, but in a complex era that may call for a computer to work out the equation, the present is still only the sum of the past.

PART TWO
FIGHTING

9

The Gentle Art of War

The distressing frequency with which accounts of Ch'in victories end with the same throwaway line—"and a hundred thousand heads were lopped off"—sharpens the deceptively fatuous old adage that expresses the basic Chinese attitude toward the business of waging war: "Battles are dangerous affairs."

By the fourth century before Christ the warring states of the Middle Kingdom were throwing half a million men into the field at a time. Mailed veterans wearing toughened sharkskin or rhinoceros hide that "rang like metal" were armed not only with that minor miracle of its day, the trigger-operated crossbow, but with swords and spears of durable steel "sharp as the sting of a wasp" which were to become the envy of the West. Commanders disposed of shock troops, light and heavy columns, conventional armies and "special forces," and were served by staff officers trained in logistics and the use of weather, smoke, fire, and flood. They employed sophisticated tactics and launched complicated campaigns dependent on precise timing in order to vanquish the enemy.

But the more deadly the pastime became, the greater was the pragmatic prudence with which the Chinese approached it, and the more ingrained the conviction that the proper purpose of war was to defend the homeland, not to provide an occasion for brutal conquest and futile heroics.

"Weapons are tools of ill omen," Lao Tzu had said. They were not to be used in the everyday running of the state, but only when it was in peril. "Then a cool head is needed, not a bellicose, bloodthirsty mentality. A victor should not be arrogant, for then he only makes plain his delight in murder. And no murderous tyrant can win the support of the people . . . therefore men of morality are not aggressive, and men proficient in battle do not easily grow angry or lightly instigate war."

Despite his distrust of the Taoists, the Confucian Hsun Tzu echoed the Old Master: A state could not exist for a single day without an army, but it must be employed only for suppressing rebellion and resisting aggression, and the ruler must never forget that his winning weapon was the will of the people, "for if bow and arrow are not in harmony, even a famous archer cannot hit the mark."

All else was secondary. The men of Ch'i were paid eight ounces of gold for every enemy head they brought in; the men of Wei were rewarded with tax exemptions if they could march a hundred *li* in twenty-four hours, wearing heavy armor and carrying a crossbow and a sword and three days' rations; the men of Ch'in were coaxed with rewards and cowed with punishments into fighting ferociously; but before armies united by their love of a benevolent ruler, these were mere hired laborers, the stratagems and deceptions of whose masters were no more than the tricks of robber bands, and they would surely be defeated, "for it is the way of all men that if they do something only for the sake of benefit, they will abandon an undertaking as soon as it appears unprofitable or dangerous." And despite his distrust of the other Confucians, Chairman Mao has consistently echoed Hsun Tzu, emphasizing that victory depends on the spirit of men in the mass, not the mercenary with his machine gun or megaton bomb.

Hsun Tzu, however, was like a key that turns the wrong way. In theory he wanted to see law and punishments used to chasten men until they became noble enough to turn back and live by Confucian *Li.* But in practice he bridged the gap that separated *Li* from Legalism, and men moved forward to live by the dire disciplines of Ch'in. He was not at odds, therefore, with the great Chinese strategists of his century whose professional code was marked by a cold, mathematical ruthlessness.

As Han Fei Tzu pointed out, Shan Yang had shared the fate of a certain Wu Ch'i, since both were torn apart by chariots on the orders of nobles infuriated by their pitiless severity. But if Shan Yang did not spare his own prince, Wu Ch'i, who died in 381 B.C., did not even spare his wife. When the Duke of Lu shied away from appointing him commander of his armies because she came from an enemy state, Wu Ch'i murdered her to prove his loyalty, and was thus able to embark upon a brilliant military career that was to be extolled by generations of Chinese.

His teachings have a familiar ring. Success in handling troops depends on four factors, which include the "two heavies"—heavy rewards for advancing, heavy punishments for retreating—"and rewards and punishments must be reliable, otherwise troops will not halt at the sound of the gong or advance at the sound of the drum, so that even if there are a million of them, what use are they? . . . All must come to grips with the enemy, and therefore of all dangers, timidity is the greatest, and the catastrophes that overtake armies arise from hesitation."

If Wu Ch'i was ready to sacrifice his wife to win a post, Sun Wu was as quick to sacrifice the favorite concubines of a ruler in the interests of discipline, even if it meant losing one. For when the King of Wu, a state on the coastal fringe of China, tested this prestigious general by asking him to drill his palace women, Sun Wu had the two bewitching company commanders decapitated for giggling on parade and failing to obey orders after they had been repeated four times. The horrified monarch remonstrated with him ("Without them my food would lose all its flavor"), but Sun Wu replied, "A general in the field is not bound by orders from his sovereign." After witnessing a prompt double execution, the other beauties showed a marked improvement in their responses to commands.

Hsun Tzu, who called for "apt and consistent" punishments, and laid down that the commander in the field could refuse to obey his king only if he were ordered to defend the indefensible, to attack without hope of success, or to deceive the ordinary people, might have demurred. But he had himself stressed that obedience was more important even than achievement. The system of collective responsibility and the discouraging penalties so dear to Shan Yang were now the fashion in Chinese armies, and not only unit commanders but whole squads were summarily beheaded for retiring without orders (as they still could be in the Kuomintang forces of Chiang Kai-shek).

Sun Wu, it will be noted, claimed sole power over life and death for the general on the spot, much as Han Fei Tzu warned the ruler to hold fast to "the handles of punishment and favor." And where Han Fei Tzu demanded that the monarch should be a fathomless blank, "Sun Tzu" said, "The general must be inscrutable, impartial . . . he should keep his officers ignorant of his plans . . . and change his methods so that men do not know what he is doing."

Who was he? "I wish I had read *The Art of War* twenty years ago," Kaiser Wilhelm is said to have remarked ruefully after his defeat in the First World War, and he was not referring to *The Art of War* by Machiavelli, but *The Art of War* by Sun Tzu. No one knows for sure when the thirteen sections of this masterpiece were written, or when Sun Tzu lived. His mention of the crossbow and his failure to mention cavalry seem to place him squarely in the middle of the fourth century before Christ. Traditional history says that he was born in Ch'i a hundred years earlier, and that when the King of Wu employed him despite the casualties among his concubines, he made Wu powerful and feared.

This may be a legend—but then so is Sun Tzu himself. He is the unquestioned Clausewitz of China, studied by Napoleon (who warned Europe against rousing the "sleeping lion of the Orient") and revered by the militaristic Japanese. His genius is timeless, and while men may cast out the *Analects* of Confucius as a philosophical anachronism, they cannot gainsay the living precepts in *The Art of War,* with its succinct chapters on all aspects of the craft from planning to dispositions, and from the use of terrain to the use of spies.

Notwithstanding their disciplinarian outlook, both Wu Ch'i and Sun Tzu agree with the Confucian philosophers and Mao Tsetung that men come first. Do not, Wu Ch'i warns, attack a state in which the people are prosperous, the rulers are benevolent, rewards and punishments are fairly administered, and persons are promoted for their virtue. Only after these does he mention a strong enemy army as a further deterrent.

Ritual and righteousness are keys to impregnability, "for if the people are safe in their homes and friendly with the officials, the defenses are already strong; if the clans prefer their own king to all others, the battles are already won." As Mencius had said of a certain ignominious defeat: "It was not that the walls were low, or the moat shallow, or the weapons blunt, or food short, but that the *men* abandoned the city and fled." Chinese on the Great Wall and Frenchmen in the Maginot Line alike were to drive the point home across two thousand years of history.

But while Mencius saw magnanimous rule as a means of making people happy, Sun Tzu saw it as a means of making effective war—preferably without lifting a trigger finger. For since "battles are dangerous affairs" and "weapons are tools of ill omen," the true art of war is the insidious art of no war, the art of keeping the edge of your own men's loyalty keen with a nicely calculated policy of benevolence, while destroying the morale and unity of the enemy so that he cannot even take the field. He may thus be brought to his knees in an operation that combines maximum impact with minimum risk of troops and treasure. Sun Tzu was more than a tactician with a boxful of military tricks writing a handbook for heroes. He wrote for kings and commanders whose aim was not to fight, but to win, and like Machiavelli he dealt with more rewarding aspects of his highly competitive trade than improvident combat.

No country should embark upon a major campaign without carefully counting the cost, he remarks, for "there has never been a protracted war from which a state benefited." The supply problem becomes a headache, the troops impoverish the land by living off it overlong and then start to go hungry themselves. Prices rise, and the replacement of equipment takes sixty percent of all government expenditure. Plan to fight for one season only, Hsun Tzu counsels, and avoid getting bogged down in long sieges against towns. Sun Tzu concurs ("The troops will be exhausted, and your neighbors will take advantage of your situation") and so does Mao.

It is, moreover, a matter of simple common sense to be lenient with the adversary. "The army does not destroy crops. It does not punish the common people, but only those who mislead them, and men who flee from the enemy and surrender must be allowed to go free," says Hsun Tzu. Treat captives well, urges Sun Tzu. The object is to make more friends, not more foes. His chapter entitled "Waging War" cites horrible examples of what happens when victorious troops are permitted to mutilate prisoners or loot so brazenly that the enraged adversary rises again to annihilate them. Wu Ch'i gives similar advice on winning the hearts and minds of the other side, and Hsun Tzu condemns the prevalent habit of massacring the inhabitants of any town seized.

There is no greater folly than a profitless military campaign against one enemy if it lays the state open to attack from another, the Chinese believe, and will quote the flagrant case of the ruler of Wu who embarked on a series of exhausting wars with his civilized neighbors in the Middle Kingdom in the sixth century B.C., while ignoring the barbarous state of Yueh at his back. His famous chief minister, Wu Tzu-hsiu, not only expressed alarm at this folly, but sent his own son away to Ch'i for safety, whereupon the king, livid at his lack of confidence, ordered him to kill himself. The adviser did as he was bid, but cried before he expired: "Tear out my eyes and fix them on the gate of Wu, so that I may see the triumphant entry of Yueh." In time Yueh duly destroyed Wu, and the king committed suicide, "covering his face so that he would not have to meet the reproachful gaze of his minister in the next world."

Extravagance is the unforgivable sin—the extravagance of

waging unnecessary, prolonged, and bloody war in which stupidity wastes lives and money, brutality breeds enemies instead of eliminating them, and barren victories yield ungovernable territory. Wu Ch'i derides the "benevolence" of those who mourn men wantonly sacrificed on the field, for the task of the responsible commander is to do everything to make the whole process as painless as possible.

How is it done? First of all, use secret diplomacy and secret agents to "attack the strategy of the enemy," as Sun Tzu puts it. Sow dissension between king and minister, incite the people to rebellion, undermine the discipline of his army—the assassination of the ruler's best general may be enough to dislocate his plans and compel him to come to terms. Thereafter, disrupt his alliances by fostering distrust between friend and friend, wooing the first, poisoning the mind of the second, setting one enemy to restrain another. When frustrated and isolated, adversaries may well submit without losing an arrow.

Even if this does not happen, everything will have been done by way of selling lies and buying officials to establish an unfair imbalance, so that the enemy can be quickly defeated in battle without heavy loss to either side. The next move, therefore, must be to attack his army. But do not go for him blind and bald-headed. "In following the disposition and movements of the foe," says Hsun Tzu, "strive to obtain the most comprehensive reports about him and make sure that their reliability is checked." "Know your enemy and know yourself, and in a hundred battles you will not be in danger," adds Sun Tzu, and later proceeds to enlarge on the importance of spying. Do not grudge spending money on intelligence, he stresses, for foreknowledge is not to be gained from gods or spirits, but men.

Be prepared to deal with five kinds of agents, for when they all work at once, information can be drawn in by a single cord, like fish trapped in a net. First there are native agents, who are simply inhabitants of the enemy countryside. Then there are the "inside agents," enemy officials who work for you because they have been sacked from their posts or have been passed over for promotion or need money or are greedy or want to have a foot in both camps. Once you have started paying them, you have them in your hand.

Next come the double agents sent by the enemy whom you turn around and use against him, and after that the "expendable agents." Expendable agents are spies of your own to whom you leak false information and then send on missions into enemy territory. Once they are captured and tortured efficiently enough, they will pass your misleading fabrications on to your opponent with convincing reluctance (unfortunately when the enemy finds out that they are misleading, he will kill the agents, but that is the price that must be paid). Finally, there are the well-connected agents who are clever enough to appear stupid, and who can come and go between two states at war.

These are all interwoven. The commander relies upon double agents to recruit native agents, and to find out just how his antagonist can be led astray to his own destruction, so that an expendable agent may then be sent to him for the purpose of deceiving him along the right lines. It is thus important that spies discover not only the identities and strengths and weaknesses, but also the connections and foibles and loyalties of all leading enemy personalities, and even of their staff officers, chamberlains, gatekeepers, and guards in cases, as Sun Tzu says, "where you wish to strike armies, assault cities—or assassinate people."

10

The Downhill Struggle

"All war is based on deception," Sun Tzu explains succinctly, and the successful commander must therefore cheat not only with his spies but with his soldiers. When strong in the field, pretend weakness, he urges. When near, pretend to be far; when far, near. Use devious routes to take the enemy unaware. Feign confusion, and then hit him suddenly. Assume an air of inferiority and make him overconfident. Lure him on with bait and await him in ambush. Goad his generals into acting recklessly—besieged by a ruler at the head of a hundred thousand men, one canny commander sent the aggressive potentate a sealed pot of urine as a gift of "wine." This so infuriated the monarch that he threw his entire force against the town the practical joker was holding in one continuous, massive onslaught until after thirty days he had lost more than half of his army.

On the subject of first-class fraud, however, Sun Tzu is, as always, a professional, and reminds commanders that if they wish to simulate weakness, disorder, and cowardice in the face of the enemy, they must first make sure that their forces are in fact well organized, courageous, and strong. It is still characteristically Chinese for a scene of noisy, aimless, and confused activity to be the product of men who are well versed in what they are supposed to be doing and will get it done with startling speed.

The meat-grinder tactics employed in Flanders during the

First World War would have horrified and disgusted Sun Tzu—and so would many of the generals responsible for it. In the Chinese tradition, fearless blockheads and medal-seeking man-mincers are blundering amateurs engaged in a dangerous undertaking that requires skill and care. "The success of everything depends on circumspection," Hsun Tzu insists. "Be cautious and never neglectful—in your strategy, with your officers, your men, and your enemy." The good general is prudent, and leery of traps, says Sun Tzu. He knows that there are "some roads not to be taken, some armies not to be attacked, some cities not to beleaguer, some positions not to be challenged." A Chinese strategist would readily have said of the Charge of the Light Brigade, "*Ce n'est pas la guerre,*" but he would never have agreed that it was "*magnifique.*"

Two of the worst qualities in a commander are rashness and a quick temper. Impetuous officers who order forced marches in pursuit of an adversary in unknown country will end up lost and leading a straggling column ripe for ambushing by fresh troops lying in wait. Probing parties sent out to test the enemy must withdraw no matter how tempting it may be to push on. "Their sole purpose is to flee," notes Wu Ch'i. On one occasion a captain under Wu Ch'i's command, unable to curb his own zeal, charged forward before the battle had started and returned with the heads of two of the enemy. The general had him decapitated forthwith. "A talented officer," he commented sadly, "but a disobedient one." Men who advance without orders must be punished as severely as men who retreat without orders.

The tradition that professional courage and caution went hand in hand was much older. In 684 B.C. the states of Lu and Ch'i were at war, and when their armies met on the battlefield Ch'i launched a full-scale assault. The war drums were beaten in unison, murderous screams filled the air, and the massed troops surged forward like a tidal wave. The Duke of Lu was about to command his own columns to charge the oncoming adversary when an adviser * cried,

* Ts'ao Mo, the general who demanded at dagger point that the Duke of Ch'i restore territory he had taken from Lu (see page 8).

"Slowly! The enemy is now vigorous. You must not be reckless." Thereupon the men were instructed to stand firm and hold their ground. No ill-considered or hotheaded move would be tolerated.

The army of Ch'i flung itself fruitlessly against the Lu defenses three times, yelling insults at a foe so cowardly that he dared not come out and fight, before the duke's adviser finally signaled the attack. The drums rolled, the fresh Lu army delivered a ferocious onslaught, and the bone-weary troops of Ch'i were massacred in droves. But when the duke wanted his men to set off after the routed enemy, his counselor held up the advance until he had first examined the chariot tracks and hoofprints of the fleeing columns, and only then did he give orders for the Lu columns to pursue and kill for a distance of ten miles.

The duke commended his wily aide, who observed that since the outcome of a battle depended above all on the eagerness and energy of the troops, it was a sensible precaution to tip the odds by taking the wind out of the enemy in three charges while keeping one's own forces at rest, and another sensible precaution to examine his tracks when he retreated, to make sure that his chariots were in a tangle, his standards all over the place, and that he really was in headlong flight and not leading his antagonist into an ambush.

One must not be misled by the bravura of elaborate Chinese hyperbole into thinking that military theory in the Middle Kingdom mainly consisted—and still consists—of hot air. It contains much ice-cold logic. "Rise swiftly like a strong wind," intones Sun Tzu. "Attack like a raging fire. When still, be like a mountain. When you move, be like the thunder that peals too quickly for a man to cover his ears, and the lightning that flashes too quickly for a man to blink his eyes." More soaring dragons? But see how he advises a commander to achieve this mystical and terrifying effect:

"*Fight downhill*," he says curtly. The prudent general strikes only if the factors are in his favor and he is sure of winning. When he outnumbers the enemy ten to one, he surrounds him; when five to one, he launches a direct assault;

when two to one, he divides him. If the sides are equally matched, he may engage him. But if he is outnumbered he must be able to withdraw—"a small force is mere booty for a larger one."

He does not attack a powerful opponent who is advancing in good order, or who occupies the high ground, or who has the hills behind him, and if that opponent pretends to flee, he does not fall for proffered bait and chase him. He does not thwart an army that is already withdrawing to its homeland. He never presses an enemy who has his back against a wall or a river ("Wild beasts at bay struggle desperately. How much more true is this of men? If they know there is no alternative, they will fight to the death"). And when he does surround a foe, he leaves him a way of escape.

Fully prepared, flexible, fast and elusive, hitting when the blows will count, ducking when the enemy strikes back, taking nothing on the chin, the good commander keeps the initiative through sheer footwork, manipulating or "shaping" his adversary and never allowing the adversary to manipulate him. He brings the enemy to battle (and not the reverse) by tempting him with the prospect of easy gain, or by taking him by surprise, moving fast along unguarded routes and making big detours in order to appear suddenly from an unexpected quarter. By 1975 the Russians had deployed some twenty-five divisions close to the border of Manchuria, but the main Chinese armies defending the northeast were concentrated several hundred miles to the south of the frontier. The region might be a treasure chest of raw materials and giant industrial complexes, but the Chinese were not going to let the enemy take it over their dead bodies. They did not propose to fight for every inch of the ground and risk being encircled by swift-moving Soviet mechanized and armored columns. They would await them in strength, and strike back when they might catch the spent and strung-out adversary with his fuel gauges down.

A general who attacks only what his opponent does not heavily defend will win every time, for the opponent will not know what to defend. He will be compelled to disperse his troops to protect many possible targets, and "if I concentrate while he divides, I can use my entire strength to attack only a part of his at a point of my choosing . . . for when he prepares everywhere, he will be weak everywhere."

Avoiding uneconomical head-on confrontations, the commander bewilders his adversary with false reports and the fraudulent multiplication of drums and flags and cooking fires where few men are, changing his ploys, giving his force no discernible form—for "an army may be likened to water, and just as flowing water avoids heights and runs downhill, so an army avoids strength and strikes weakness."

More than a century after Sun Tzu is said to have lived, his descendant Sun Pin gave a classic demonstration of how his ancestor's precepts could be put into practice, and the very strength of an enemy used against him with almost supernatural effect. Appointed chief of staff of the armies of Ch'i when they were engaged against the formidable fighting forces of Wei, Sun Pin advised his commander: "The soldiers of Wei are fierce and bold, and despise the men of Ch'i as cowards. A skillful strategist should make use of this and lure them on with a promise of advantage. According to *The Art of War,* an army that rushes a hundred *li* after profit loses its general, and if it rushes only fifty *li,* no more than half of it will arrive." Therefore to draw the confident enemy on, Sun Pin suggested, "let us light a hundred thousand fires when our army enters Wei, fifty thousand on the next day, and only thirty thousand on the third."

This plan was put into operation, and P'ang Chuan, the commander of the Wei armies sent against the column from Ch'i, exclaimed with delight: "I knew the men of Ch'i were cowards, and after only three days more than half of them have deserted!" So leaving his heavy infantry behind, he hastened after his apparently depleted adversary with lightly armed crack troops, moving twice as fast as before.

Sun Pin estimated that by dusk his pursuers would reach the narrow defile into which he was leading them. Accordingly, he stripped the bark from a big tree, painted on the trunk: "P'ang Chuan dies beneath this tree," and deployed ten thousand archers in an ambush. P'ang Chuan arrived at dusk and kindled a torch to see what was written on the peeled trunk. The ambush was sprung, the doomed troops of Wei were thrown into confusion, and the chagrined General P'ang cut his throat. Sun Pin, who was for long believed to have edited *The Art of War* himself, had "shaped" his powerful enemy to a nicety.[1]

Balancing the wiles of Sun Tzu, the military genius, are the Confucian ethics of Hsun Tzu, the military philosopher, who holds that deception is unworthy of the army of the benevolent ruler. Risky sleight of hand based on no greater security than the hope that the enemy will be fooled cannot be tolerated in the field. All legitimate stratagems must be properly backed by adequate strength and sound logistical support.

Commanders, says Hsun Tzu, must be cautious, thoughtful men who keep their word, are never in a hurry for glory, never seize upon apparent advantage without calmly weighing disadvantage, never forget in the joy of victory to ask themselves why the other side lost. They must above all be able to gain the confidence of their men and respect for their authority. They must painstakingly study the enemy and his dispositions, and whether they are garrisoning the frontier or on the march, they must ensure that the defenses of their camps, their stores, and their stocks of food and arms are impregnable. If Sun Tzu suggests Rommel, Hsun Tzu suggests Montgomery, and throughout Chinese history generals have been heavily influenced by their two schools of thought—and often identified with one or the other.

The semi-legendary Chuko Liang, regarded by many as the greatest Chinese strategist of the Christian era, is said to have played his most sublime trick when his army was far away and a force of 150,000 enemy was seen approaching the isolated city in which he had remained with only a small garrison. To meet this disconcerting situation, he ordered his few troops to take down all flags in sight and to hide themselves. He then had the city gates thrown open, sat on the wall dressed in a Taoist robe, lit some incense, and began strumming a lute. The enemy host approached in a cloud of dust, but when its experienced commander saw his renowned opponent perched unarmed on the wall of an undefended town, he at once suspected a hideous trap, and withdrew.

This tale is usually cited as a splendid example of how a vulnerable Chuko Liang disposed of a mighty adversary simply on the strength of his reputation as a military wizard. But there is subtlety within subtlety. For Chuko Liang was a "Hsun Tzu" man who would never normally have tried to bluff without having concealed high cards, the enemy commander knew he was a disciple of Hsun Tzu, and Chuko Liang knew he knew. Caught defenseless, this was the only occasion on which he was obliged to take such a chance, and as he acted out of character, he successfully deluded his opponent.

As Hsun Tzu had laid down nearly five hundred years before, Chuko Liang built all his granaries and garrison camps exceptionally strong, and his wells, cooking pits, and latrines were of a high standard. He was solicitous of the population around him, and "when he led an army out, it was like a foreign guest traveling abroad, for there was no rape or plundering; or like a woodsman bent solely on cutting down trees, who does not disturb the wild animals in the mountains."

His integrity won him the unquestioning faith of his men, with whom he was strict but merciful, and his officers were wholeheartedly devoted to him. When the enemy attacked, and his subordinates suggested that soldiers who were about to go on leave should be kept back to strengthen the defenses, Chuko Liang replied: "I command a great army. It is founded on trust. The minds of those who have been given permission to depart are already set on home like arrows. Their wives and children are counting the hours that they must wait for them. Although the battle before us may be fraught with danger, that trust cannot be broken." He then personally urged the men to go, but they insisted on remaining behind to fight, and the enemy was decisively defeated.

Wu Ch'i also had a reputation for treating his troops like

brothers, wearing their clothes and eating their food. When the army was on the move he did not ride, but marched with the men, carrying his rations on his back and sharing all their hardships. When one of them developed a boil, Wu Ch'i sucked the pus from it. Soldiers were ready to lay down their lives for him, as they were for Chuko Liang, and his fighting record was unblemished.

Chinese military instructors quote examples not only from the history of China, but from accounts of past Western generalship to prove somewhat chauvinistically that when the principles of Sun Tzu and Hsun Tzu were respected, all went well—and when they were not, disaster followed. In the freezing northern Italian winter of 1796, students are told, the still young Napoleon commanded a half-starved army of between 30,000 and 40,000 troops, short of supplies, poor in equipment, and disposing of no more than twenty-four mountain guns and four thousand scrawny horses. Yet if he did not attack Austria, the Austrians might invade France at any time.

"Soldiers," he therefore told his men, "you are famished and nearly naked. The government owes you much, but can do nothing for you. Your patience, your courage, do you honor but give you no glory or gain. Today, however, I shall lead you into the most fertile plain in the world. There you will find great towns, rich provinces. There you will find honor, glory, and riches. Soldiers of the Army of Italy, will you be wanting in courage?" The troops responded with a will, for while his discipline was strict, Napoleon had the reputation for being a just and courageous general who at the most critical moment in a battle might suddenly appear beside his beleaguered men. He was energetic, an outstanding strategist who never spared himself, and he had earned the affection of all his subordinates.

He now laid plans for crossing the southern Alps before the snow melted, in order to take the enemy by surprise. Sending two hundred men ahead to reconnoiter a route over the passes, he led the main French army up the freezing heights until it was able to strike down upon the Austrians on the other side as if from Heaven, and so win a brilliant victory. One hundred and sixty-six years later the Chinese Communist general Ting Sheng was to outflank the strategic Sela Ridge during the Sino-Indian war by putting an entire division over a snow-covered mountain 13,000 feet high, from which his troops fell upon the unsuspecting Indians in the rear and inflicted on them a humiliating defeat.

Solicitous of his men, but moving with speed along an unguarded route to take his enemy by surprise from an unexpected quarter, Napoleon had behaved like a model disciple of Sun Tzu, and by 1812 his name resounded throughout the world. But goaded by anger and ambition, he then launched 450,000 troops on a punitive adventure into the bleak immensities of the Russian Empire which could only have a melancholy ending. As the Chinese see it, he had flouted Sun Tzu. He had lost his temper. He had led a weary army against an enemy who awaited him on his home ground and who could choose his own battlefield and effectively deploy both "normal" and "extraordinary" forces. The Russians eluded Napoleon and scorched the earth; the French froze and starved.

The "normal" and "extraordinary" forces that harried the Napoleonic armies in Russia and Spain were, respectively, the regular troops pitted against them and the local partisans. But these are terms of Sun Tzu, and they have a wider meaning. The two work together—"who can say where one begins and the other ends?" In the field the "normal" may be the main army that pins the enemy down, and the "extraordinary" the outflanking task force of anything from guerrillas to tanks that annihilates him. In the course of the war as a whole, the "normal" may be the military, the "extraordinary" the fifth column, the specialists in economic warfare, political disruption, espionage, and assassination. It is the interaction of these elements that obliges the enemy to split his own forces, and so permits the more astute commander to concentrate his whole strength against one tenth of his opponent's.

Faced with a modern Japanese army in the Second World War, the Chinese opted for a protracted resistance, frequently avoiding battle and letting their adversary overstretch as he occupied more and more cities which had to be fed from a guerrilla-ridden countryside. When the Japanese set out to suppress the guerrillas, the Chinese used "magnet tactics," luring the enemy into the hills by making and breaking contact and then fleeing back through prepared ambush positions.

Hsueh Yueh, the Chinese Nationalist general commanding the "normal" and "extraordinary" forces defending Ch'angsha, the provincial capital of Hunan which the Japanese failed three times to take, explained his success to us in the following words: "These are border regions of mountains and lakes, the roads are rough and steep and we can quickly destroy them. The enemy has to penetrate deeply in order to get at us, but the mountains fit together like dog teeth, and it is easy for a waiting army to conceal itself anywhere in the broken terrain. Our troops are in ambush on every side, making pincer attacks on the Japanese, and he is trapped as in a net. The transportation of rations and ammunition depends on pack animals, and mechanized troops are useless. Therefore the enemy is routed." It was the type of country of "precipitous cliffs, deep caverns, tangled thickets, and treacherous quagmires" from which, as Sun Tzu put it, the prudent commander "must depart as fast as possible without entering."

The general had concocted a typical Chinese mix of "normal" and "extraordinary" forces. The "normal" Nationalist army confronted the enemy north of Ch'angsha, while "extraordinary" guerrillas operated behind the Japanese lines. But other "extraordinary" guerrilla units were simultaneously active in the immediate vicinity of the city itself, assisting the "normal" army, and within these guerrilla contingents there were in turn "normal" troops. "Their combinations are endless," Sun Tzu had remarked. "No one can comprehend them."

Mao Tsetung, who once said, "The operations of the people's guerrillas and of the main forces of the Red Army complement each other like a man's right and left arms," was the most subtle exponent of the use of the "normal" and the "extraordinary." The stages whereby the handful of irregulars he first commanded on the heights of Chingkangshan in 1927 grew into an irresistible steamroller of five field armies twenty-two years later constituted an exercise in combining the two forces within the framework of a "people's war" that was almost as intricate as the workings of *yang* and *yin* themselves.

But it will already be obvious that Mao provides the most convincing proof that the theories of Sun Tzu still live—and work. Mao's flexible guerrilla strategy differs from the teachings of the Master in only one important respect: Sun Tzu opposed protracted war, while Mao was obliged to wage one against both the Chinese Nationalists and the Japanese, for most of the time he was heavily outnumbered. Yet it was precisely this weakness that persuaded him to be faithful to all else Sun Tzu had taught. "My strategy is one against ten," he said, "my tactic ten against one," echoing Sun Tzu's advice to disperse the enemy and then concentrate all available forces against a fraction of his army. The most famous of Mao's military jingles neatly summarizes Sun Tzu's advice to avoid strength, hit weakness, tire the adversary, and engage only when victory is certain:

> The enemy advances, we retreat;
> The enemy camps, we harass;
> The enemy tires, we attack;
> The enemy retreats, we pursue.[2]

"If you can win, fight; if you cannot win, flee!" advises Mao in effect, and his military writings paraphrase Sun Tzu time and time again, whether he is talking about the overriding need to "know your enemy," the uses of deception, the dangers of rashness (but the advantages of speed and decision), the desirability of feeding off the other side, the logic of treating prisoners leniently and winning over the civilian population, the folly of fighting an opponent who is stronger or who holds a fortified position, or the cardinal error of attacking cities first.

The modern Chinese responds to the pragmatic callousness of the ancient strategists (Sun Tzu: "There are five ways of attacking with fire: the first is to burn personnel"), to their pragmatic caution (Lin Piao: "In making war there must be three parts risk and seven parts security, in addition to one's own subjective effort"), and to their pragmatic concern above all for the spirit of the men involved.

"What is the true bastion of iron?" asks Mao. "It is the masses, the millions upon millions of people who genuinely and sincerely support the revolution. That is the bastion which it is impossible for any force on earth to smash. Rallying millions upon millions of people around our revolutionary government and expanding our revolutionary war, we shall wipe out all counterrevolution and take over the whole of China." [3]

And he did.

11

The Knight and the Nobody

Rebuffing those who pretended that rule by fear made for greater stability than rule by love, Hsun Tzu pointed ironically to the miserable fate of one tyrant who "murdered and massacred in all seasons, so that his ministers and people were filled with dread, yet when the enemy swept down on him, none of his commands were obeyed." Monarchs should let their authority inspire awe, but seldom wield it. "Ch'in has been victorious for four generations, yet has lived in constant terror and apprehension of destruction."

The First Emperor of Ch'in, the mightiest man in the world of his day, went in such fear of his fellow men that the two hundred and seventy pavilions of his fantastic palace at Hsienyang were all connected by covered passages so that he could hurry between them in secret. He slept in a different apartment every night, and anyone foolish enough to reveal his movements in advance was beheaded at once. When he himself died during an imperial progress in the provinces, only his Legalist minister Li Ssu and a handful of eunuchs knew, and they concealed their dangerous knowledge by filling a cart behind the emperor's carriage with salt fish to mask the smell of the decomposing corpse.

For the heir-apparent had opposed the burning of the books, and both Li Ssu and his close confederate, the chief eunuch Chao Kao, were frightened that he might now order their immediate execution. They therefore forged an imperial decree commanding him to commit suicide. The prince, thinking his father still alive, obeyed the edict, and his younger brother became the "Second Emperor."

Chao Kao then bullied this twenty-one-year-old weakling into delegating all authority to him, whereupon he sacked the closest advisers of the First Emperor, had Li Ssu tortured to death, tightened the already painfully constricting laws, imposed exorbitant taxes, and seemingly set about ruining the country in the shortest possible time. Before the Second Emperor had been on the throne for twelve months, in consequence, the first rebel raised his voice, the empire "answered like an echo," and in 207 B.C. the Ch'in Dynasty fell.

The cliché-ridden scenario is repeated with variations throughout Chinese history. The day arrives when the eunuchs find themselves the closest attendants upon a young, impressionable emperor isolated from the millions he rules within a vast, walled-off palace, and embark upon the impossible task of satisfying their own insatiable appetites for power, luxury, and wealth. That marks, quite literally, the end of the line. A hero arises to overthrow the old, corrupt regime and to inaugurate in its place a new, vigorous dynasty which will not grow old and corrupt in its turn for another two or three centuries.

Before this man of destiny appears, however, there are sometimes a few false starts. Yuan Shih-k'ai, the first "president" of republican China to assume the mantle of the Manchu Dynasty in 1912, committed the fatal error of privately planning to supplant one imperial tyranny with another, and more than two thousand years before him, Ch'en She made the same mistake.

A farmhand conscripted for garrison service who was afraid of being decapitated for reporting late for duty, Ch'en She chose the alternative of mounting an insurrection in 209 B.C., proclaimed himself king of the old feudal state of Ch'u in defiance of the Ch'in emperor, and ruled ruthlessly for six months before he was killed. Rebel generals arose to follow his example in other states, but as the eliminating rounds between rival contenders for supremacy plunged the empire into ever greater disorder, the field was cleared for the final, dramatic duel in which the teachings of the great Chinese strategists were to be put strikingly to the test—or disastrously ignored.

It is said that Hsiang Yu had double pupils to his eyes, one inside the other, but it is more certain that he had a single purpose, and when as a young man he saw the Ch'in emperor passing in a procession one day, he remarked contemptuously, "This fellow could easily be deposed and replaced." He was himself the scion of a long line of enfeoffed generals of the state of Ch'u, a huge, high-tempered aristocrat who could lift a bronze cauldron unaided. Orphaned as a small child, he lived with his uncle, Hsiang Liang, whom he exasperated by showing scorn for such gentlemanly pursuits as studying calligraphy and practicing swordplay. "Writing is only good for keeping records of names, and a swordsman can only fight one foe," he objected. "I want to learn how to fight ten thousand."

To his great satisfaction, therefore, his uncle agreed to instruct him in military strategy, but he was too impatient to continue with it once he thought he had grasped the bones of the matter. He was essentially a man of simple action and simple virtues—gallant, loyal, full of lofty aspirations, stubborn and unyielding and impetuous, six feet three inches of easily angered hero and formidable fighting soldier. His career began when the tide of revolt surged around the region of Wu Chung,* in which he lived, and his uncle decided to mount his own insurrection. Hsiang Yu opened the play by slicing off the head of a local governor, and then butchered a few dozen of his staff in order to chasten the rest.

Hot and cold murder was natural to the make-up of this daring, damn-your-eyes bravo who balked at nothing and was never to know why he won the battles but lost the empire. The defenders of the first city that resisted him were massacred to the last man, he was to slaughter 200,000 Ch'in soldiers who surrendered to him, to raze the Ch'in capital and to

* Now Wu County, Kiangsu Province.

slay all in it, and he was only talked out of killing everyone over fifteen in another stubbornly held city by a boy of twelve who appealed not to his compassion but to his common sense: "How can you win the hearts of the people like this?" the child protested. "There are still more than a dozen towns east of here, and now they will all be too afraid to submit to you."

Hsiang Yu was to have an unwise joker boiled for calling him a "monkey with a hat on" when he expressed a provincial nostalgia for his home village, to burn one enemy general and boil another after hearing that their cornered king had eluded him by a stratagem, and to threaten to do the same to a venerable hostage if his son did not yield. Yet if he was disdainful of the lives of others, he was equally disdainful of his own. His wholesale savagery was matched by his uncaring personal courage—he once stopped a champion archer from shooting him at close range merely by shouting furiously at the man—and it was employed solely in the service of his own armies and ambitions, for business and not for pleasure. In his private dealings he was cruel or kind according to impulse, and his leniency rather than his callousness was to prove his undoing.

This was not immediately apparent. Once he held the seals of authority of the dead governor, Hsiang Liang roused the region against the tyranny of Ch'in. The flower of Ch'u rallied to him, and he sensibly established the legitimacy of his rebellion in their eyes by seeking out the grandson of their last lawful ruler, whom Ch'in had deposed, and installing him as King Huai of Ch'u with great pomp and ceremony.[1] His army was soon one hundred thousand strong, and at twenty-four his nephew Hsiang Yu was already a respected and feared general. But he was to go further.

Hsiang Liang became overconfident, and was routed and killed in battle. The Ch'in army then turned north to attack the state of Chao, which was also in revolt, and the King of Chao asked Ch'u for help. Sung Yi, the Ch'u commander in chief, set out for Chao at the head of a relief force with

Hsiang Yu as his deputy, and that gave the swashbuckler his big chance.

When only halfway to Chao, Sung Yi encamped for forty-six days. Rain and snow fell, food was in short supply, the men were soon shivering and hungry, and Hsiang Yu fumed with impatience. "I hear that the Ch'in army is already besieging the King of Chao," he protested. "If we cross the Yellow River now and attack from without while Chao attacks from within, we are sure to prevail."

But Sung Yi shook his head. "If the attack on Chao is successful, the Ch'in army will nonetheless have been weakened and we can destroy it all the more easily. If the Ch'in army is defeated, we can chase it all the way to Hsienyang. 'When the snipe and the mussel struggle, the fisherman gets the benefit.' Why should our army not be the fisherman? For desperate fighting, I may be no match for you. But for strategy and tactics, you are no match for me," he concluded, smiling superciliously.

Sun Tzu might have savored the old Warring States military fable of the snipe that seizes the mussel, only to have the mussel clamp down on its beak, so that the fisherman can take both at leisure. It is a basic principle of Chinese strategy to encourage rival states to wear each other down until both may be dominated—to "use the barbarian to pacify the barbarian." But Hsiang Yu was not amused, and Sung Yi found it necessary to issue an order stating, "Officers who do not recognize the binding nature of commands, be they as fierce as tigers and as greedy as wolves, shall be beheaded according to army law."

The order was clearly aimed at Hsiang Yu, who burst into his commander's tent on the following day wearing a sword and shouted hotly: "Although we joined forces with Chao to attack Ch'in, and the King of Chao has been surrounded, the Ch'u army does not advance. The year is lean, the soldiers eat roots, yet you will not lead them across the river so that we may both obtain food and combine with Chao to strike Ch'in. Meanwhile, if a strong Ch'in attacks a feeble Chao deprived of reinforcements, Chao is sure to be defeated. And if the forces of Ch'in destroy Chao, they will be stronger, not weaker. Our king has committed all our troops to the fight against Ch'in under your command, and the very security of our state now depends on one move, yet you attend only to personal affairs. You are therefore betraying the men of Ch'u."

This said, Hsiang Yu drew his sword and hacked off his commander in chief's head, and having coolly told his alarmed subordinates that he had acted on the orders of the king because Sung Yi was a traitor, he assumed command himself. He then ferried his entire force across the Yellow River and hurled it against the Ch'in army, after scuttling all his own boats, smashing all cooking pots, and burning down all the shelter available to his troops along the far bank.

He was practicing Sun Tzu's principle of "death ground"—do not press the enemy at bay or when he has his back to a river, for if he has no alternative, he will fight like a tiger to the end. And what is true of the adversary is true of a commander's own troops. There was no going back. Hsiang Yu had committed his whole army to death or glory. His men fell upon the Ch'in with irresistible ferocity, bringing them to battle nine times and burying the field in enemy corpses, while hesitant reinforcements from the other rebel states of Ch'i and Yen looked on in amazement. Hsiang Yu had staked all on a single risky throw, and he had won.

When it was over he sat in his tent like a conqueror, acknowledged as the supreme commander of the combined armies of the feudal lords, whose shamefaced generals came to kneel before him in obeisance. The three senior generals of the defeated Ch'in also submitted to him with 200,000 troops. Doubtful of their loyalty, however, and conscious that they might still prove a powerful hostile force within his own camp, he changed his mind about accepting their surrender and had them massacred to a man instead, sparing only their commanders.

It was Hsiang Yu's moment of triumph. He now marched his mighty army toward Ch'in, the "Land between the

Passes," the heart of the crumbling empire with its jewel of a capital at Hsienyang, which the King of Ch'u had promised to the man who reached it first—only to find that Liu Pang had got there before him.

Hsiang Yu had come far, but Liu Pang—his sworn brother and comrade-in-arms and fellow general in the service of the King of Ch'u—had come further. For while Hsiang Yu was the heir of a noble family, Liu Pang was a peasant, a former village headman responsible for arresting local robbers and running a staging post for official couriers in the district town of P'ei.* But if Hsiang Yu was tall and muscular, Liu Pang was also striking—a barrel-chested fellow with a straight, prominent nose, a high forehead, alert, deep-set eyes, and splendid whiskers. And if Hsiang Yu had double pupils to his eyes, Liu Pang had seventy-two black moles on his left leg and the "air of a dragon."

Whereas Hsiang Yu was forthright, obstinate and overbearing, loyal to his own peculiar sense of honor, a capable commander determined to cut his way to the top, Liu Pang was a mediocre general but always listened to advice. A rough-tongued, openhanded rascal who quickly attracted affection, he concealed his cold appraisal and crafty manipulation of his fellow men behind a mixture of coarse good humor, warm fallible humanity, and bold presumption, according to mood. When still a headman he carried a three-foot sword and frequently flaunted a high helmet of bamboo skin to show that he was above the common herd. But he spent much of his time lolling about in wineshops and running up bills, and most of the rest in womanizing.

The humility that this highly complex man could display when advantage lay in humility was matched only by his sheer effrontery when effrontery showed a profit. He contracted a genteel marriage after calling on his future father-in-law (whom he had never met) with a card that purported to convey with it a congratulatory gift of ten thousand cash (which he did not possess), and calmly taking the seat of

* P'ei County, Kiangsu Province.

honor above all the other guests in his house. But it was not his abundant cheek or his nonexistent wealth that won him his bride—her superstitious father had seen in his physiognomy the signs of future eminence.

Eminence may have strange origins. The First Emperor having died, forced labor was raised to excavate his tomb, and Liu Pang received orders to escort a gang of convicts from P'ei to the site. This chore was to be the making of him. So many of his charges slipped off on the way that he had every reason to fear he would be beheaded when he reached his destination. He stopped to think things out over a flask of wine, therefore, and like Ch'en She concluded that it would be safer to take to the mountains. Some of his prisoners went with him, but while Mao Tsetung started out with four hundred fugitive peasants, Liu Pang started out with only ten.

Not long afterward the insurrection of Ch'en She threw the officials of P'ei into an agony of uncertainty, for who could say which was safer—to remain loyal to Ch'in or to go over to the rebels? Either course might mean death. However, after some discussion they decided to support the rebellion, arguing that they could call back Liu Pang and similar ruffians in the hills who, as outlaws from the justice of Ch'in, must support the uprising and could intimidate all others in P'ei into doing the same.

But once Liu Pang approached the town with a hundred men, the dithering local magistrate changed his mind and closed the gates. This provoked the infuriated ex-headman into firing an arrow over the wall with a message urging the inhabitants to kill the poltroon and open them up again at once if they did not want to be slaughtered. The people promptly did as they were told, and Liu Pang, having become their protector, was soon able to set out with three thousand men and the title of Lord of P'ei to play his part in one of history's most untidy revolutions.

Finding that the powerful armies of Hsiang Liang were close by, the Lord of P'ei judged it prudent to put himself under the leadership of the as yet undefeated general, who gave him command of five thousand troops. It was thus not long before Hsiang Yu and Liu Pang met for the first time—both bold and open in manner, but one secretly secretive—and embarked on a joint operation against the forces of Ch'in during which they enthusiastically massacred the inhabitants of a large town. Liu Pang nevertheless earned a name for clemency—not because he was softhearted, or had the military wit himself to follow the advice of Sun Tzu and make friends rather than enemies, but because he had an outstanding adviser in a certain Chang Liang.

Descendant of a family of distinguished administrators from the state of Han, this gentleman had tried to right the wrongs of his time economically by hiring an assassin to kill the First Emperor with an iron hammer. The attempt had failed, and Chang Liang had then settled down to the long-term alternative, which involved spending ten years studying the ancient strategists. And it was he who advocated pity where pity paid.

In consequence, the King of Ch'u chose Liu Pang as the right man to move directly against Ch'in when Hsiang Yu accompanied Sung Yi north to go to the rescue of Chao, for it was argued by his advisers that the very ferocity of the arrogant Hsiang Yu might stiffen Ch'in resistance to a point where, in those wild hills between the passes, it could prove unbreakable. Liu Pang, on the other hand, could display a wonderful adaptability—with or without his tongue in his cheek—and he once obtained valuable information during this campaign by bowing deeply and begging forgiveness from a village gatekeeper who had upbraided him for failing to show him proper respect as a man older than himself.

However, it was Chang Liang who was responsible for the stratagems that won Liu Pang his victories on the battlefield—the use of unexpected routes, the changing of flags to deceive the enemy, the duplication of pennants to make him think that the Lord of P'ei disposed of twice as many men as he had under command. And it was also Chang Liang who was responsible for the stratagems that gave Liu Pang his bloodless triumphs. Most important of all were his systematic purchases of city governors with promised fiefs and Ch'in commanders with gold ("You will have plenty of time to die later," one desperate worthy was assured), the clemency that he showed to the ordinary people, and the stringent injunctions that stopped his men from pillaging homes and seizing civilian prisoners. The discouraged Ch'in armies were whittled down and broken, and in December of the year 207 B.C., Liu Pang entered Hsienyang.

As the empire collapsed, the six other states rose against the tyranny of Ch'in, and Nemesis approached in the shape of the burly Liu Pang, the chief eunuch Chao Kao compelled the Second Emperor to commit suicide in order to save his own skin, and the Lord of P'ei was met outside the city by his young successor, who had been on the throne for only forty-six days. The last of the Ch'in rulers arrived in an unpainted cart drawn by a single white horse, with a rope around his neck and the imperial seal in his hands. He and his retinue then knelt in the dust before Liu Pang, to whom he offered the seal in submission. It was a delicious moment for the village headman who had been treated with contempt and showered with insults by haughty officials on his previous visits to the capital.

When some advised him to behead the young monarch groveling before him, he nevertheless demurred. The King of Ch'u expected him to be merciful, and to kill a man who had already given himself up would bring bad luck. Liu Pang issued strict orders that all ranks should behave with restraint in the city. There was to be no rape, looting, or murder. However, once he saw the fabulous array of riches in the great palace of the Ch'in emperors, the storehouses piled high with gold and silver, the precious hangings, the treasuries filled with pearls and jewels and jade ornaments, the splendid horses and hounds and hundreds of women as beautiful as clouds, he was intoxicated by the heady affluence of it all, forgot his responsibilities, and made plans to live there in luxury while he gently plundered the place at leisure.

Chang Liang dissuaded him. "The Ch'in emperor lost his throne through indulging his greed for wine, women, and opulence," he remarked tartly, "and if you follow the same path, you will simply be outdoing the despot." This sobered Liu Pang, who sealed up the treasures of the palace and camped outside the city.

Solemnly playing the role of noble conqueror, he summoned the local dignitaries and promulgated a new code of laws consisting of only three articles: those who murdered would forfeit their lives; those who injured or robbed others would be punished according to the gravity of the offense; and the laws of Ch'in were abolished. He retained all officials at their previous salaries, telling them, "I have come only to save you from further harm, not to exploit or tyrannize." Everyone was happy and the people hastened to bring wine, cattle, sheep, and other food to the Ch'u camp. But fairy-like as this tale may seem, they were not to live happily ever afterward. In fact, they were not to live for long at all.

12

Armies for Two

It was not more than one month later that Hsiang Yu arrived at the eastern pass into Ch'in at the head of an army of 400,000 men, to find his way blocked and to learn that Liu Pang had already taken the coveted capital at Hsienyang. In a towering fury, he at once prepared to fling this huge force at the defenders in what threatened to prove a bloodbath, for he was twice the general that Liu Pang was, he had four times as many men, and it was he and not the Lord of P'ei who had decisively defeated the main Ch'in armies on the Yellow River.

His fury was fed by reports that, having reached the pass first, that bucolic upstart nonetheless planned to make himself King of Ch'in, and he was further incited to annihilate his rival by his seventy-year-old counselor Fan Tseng, who believed—as the ancient Chinese strategists had also believed and Machiavelli was one day to stress—that a task must be executed with absolute ruthlessness where necessary, or not undertaken at all. "This village headman was greedy only for riches and women, but since entering the Pass he has not been led astray by wealth, wine, or sex," Fan Tseng remarked. "That shows he is aiming high. The signs in the firmament are those of a Son of Heaven. You must lose no time in settling with him."

It seemed that Liu Pang was to be destroyed by his own absurd attempt to hold the pass against all comers, but Chang

Liang urged him to assure Hsiang Yu that he had had no intention of opposing him, and introduced into the camp an intermediary who was ready to take that message back to the enraged commander. "Since I entered the Pass," Liu Pang told this man (who was Hsiang Yu's uncle), "I have not touched so much as a hair of the head. I have sealed up the gold and silver in the treasuries and made an official register of the population against the day when the commander would arrive. I sent officers to guard the Pass to stop bandits from entering, not to stop his army. Night and day I have been awaiting him, ready to hand everything over in good order. How could I dare to rebel against him and set myself up as king?" Liu Pang's voice was trembling with sincerity, but Hsiang Yu's uncle advised him to seek an audience with his nephew and present his apologies personally.

Well knowing that this was a moment that demanded, very literally, a low posture, Liu Pang accordingly rode at the head of a hundred men to the camp of Hsiang Yu, who was now only thirteen miles away and therefore uncomfortably close, and addressed him in the humblest and most flattering terms. "I have striven body and soul in union with you, O Chief Commander, to obey the orders of the King of Ch'u to attack Ch'in," he began. "The road that you took led north, the road that I took led south.* I did not suppose that I would enter the Pass first, for it was you who enabled the armies of Ch'u to smash the forces of Ch'in as swiftly as splitting bamboo. Now we meet again here, and evil men have sown doubts in your mind, but you are certainly too astute to be deceived by them."

This nimble argument was typical of the sly, hardheaded peasant, and the response was typical of the straightforward, hotheaded prince. Obliged to recognize that by forcing the pass in the first place Liu Pang had made his own task easier, and mollified by his pleasing words, Hsiang Yu softened and invited the Lord of P'ei to stay in his camp for a banquet. Fan Tseng was incensed by what he considered his commander's

* Liu Pang attacked Ch'in from south of the Yellow River, advancing from modern Honan into Shensi.

absurd scruples, and begged him to give a signal for troops concealed behind a screen to rush out and cut the shifty fellow down. But even when they were seated at a low table, drinking and talking, Hsiang Yu made no move.

Finally the exasperated Fan Tseng sought out a cousin of his and said: "Our Lord is too kind. Go in, perform a sword dance, and strike Liu Pang where he sits. Otherwise we shall become *his* captives in the end." The cousin started to do as he was bid, and Chinese today use the expression "Hsiang Chuang's sword dance" to mean to divert with harmless passes when you intend to kill, to assail a man with light banter when you propose to assassinate his character.

However, as he whirled his flashing blade within inches of the discountenanced guest, Hsiang Yu's uncle, who did not wish to see murder done under the guise of hospitality, jumped up and began dancing also, interposing his body between the killer and his intended victim. Meanwhile, Chang Liang hurried out of the camp to warn the escort, and when the onetime dog butcher from Liu Pang's home district who was now his trusted bodyguard heard what was happening, he broke through the sentries at the gate like a maddened tiger and burst into the banqueting tent, sword and shield in hand.

Faced with this glaring apparition, Hsiang Yu slowly rose and reached for his own weapon as he asked who the intruder was, but when told he commented approvingly, "Fine fellow! Give him a jar of wine and a leg of pork. Can you drink more?" he inquired, as the man settled down to carving his raw pig with his sword.

"I'm not afraid of death," the bodyguard growled. "Why should I shrink from wine? All men rebelled against the tyranny of Ch'in, and the King of Ch'u promised that whoever reached Hsienyang first would rule this state. Now the Lord of P'ei entered the Pass before all others, yet he has not touched the treasures of the capital, but has waited for the chief commander to come and receive them. Nevertheless, although he has labored hard and his merit is great, you do not reward the hero with noble rank, but listen to slander and plan to kill him. Is this behavior any different from that which led to the downfall of the First Emperor?"

While Hsiang Yu sat speechless in the face of this tirade, Liu Pang swiftly took advantage of the distraction to go to the privy, and presumably it was his long purse (which had already proved a better weapon than his long sword on previous occasions) that enabled Chang Liang and even the bodyguard to slip out and join him. The Lord of P'ei then galloped back to his own camp with a small escort, taking a shortcut over the mountains and leaving Chang Liang to face Hsiang Yu with a gift of jade disks and whatever excuse he could find to make for his master's abrupt disappearance. "For," as his bodyguard had trenchantly reminded him when he spoke diffidently of taking formal leave, "in big matters you cannot observe small courtesies. They are the chopper and block, and we are the meat and fish."

With great aplomb Chang Liang told his host that Liu Pang had drunk too much and was unable to reappear, and presented the disks on his behalf. Where was he then? "Knowing that Your Lordship intended to censure him, he left alone. He will be in his camp by now." Hsiang Yu accepted the disks graciously enough, but Fan Tseng dashed the jade cups that he had been given to the floor and vindictively hacked them to pieces with his sword. "Bah!" he cried disgustedly. "One cannot plan with a simpleton. Liu Pang will steal your empire yet and make us all his prisoners."

Rage is catching, and finally abandoning his laudable hesitation to condemn the Lord of P'ei (which he would live just long enough to regret), the chief commander thereupon bent his energies to the most senseless act of savagery in his bloodthirsty career. He marched on Hsienyang, killed the young Ch'in ruler out of hand, massacred the inhabitants, looted all the palaces, seized all the womenfolk, and then burned the whole place down in a fire which was still smoldering three months later.

Now all-powerful, he conferred on the King of Ch'u the title of "Righteous Emperor" and treated him with specious deference, for this elevation in the rank of the nominal ruler left the way open for him to promote himself and his most trusted generals to be kings. "When the rebellion against Ch'in broke out, we put the descendants of the old royal houses on the thrones of their respective states purely as a temporary measure," he said in effect. "But we are the men who risked their lives to overthrow the dynasty. The Righteous Emperor did nothing. Let us therefore share out the land and make ourselves monarchs."

He then set himself up as the Hegemon of Western Ch'u, usurping the capital at P'engch'eng and the effective authority of the Righteous Emperor and creating eighteen kings from among his commanders. He deprived Liu Pang of Ch'in itself, however, by dividing it among the three enemy generals who had earlier surrendered, and gave him the former Ch'in dependency of Hanchung [1] in the far west instead. This was the best and the worst he could do without blatantly reopening their quarrel and thereby alienating some of the other commanders. For in the remote, mountainous region of Hanchung, to which convicts were traditionally exiled, Liu Pang would be virtually banished beyond the barrier of Ch'in. Having settled these geopolitical matters to his satisfaction, Hsiang Yu next matured plans for murdering the Righteous Emperor and commanded all his kings to disperse to their kingdoms.

Liu Pang set off with the 30,000 homesick men who remained to him to penetrate the forbidding fastnesses of his new realm, taking the difficult and dangerous route westward, where crags and peaks crowded the sky and the ancient trees pierced the clouds. In the intimidating Li Gorge the road deteriorated into a string of precarious wooden trestles that wound around the precipitous cliffs, supported by stakes driven into the rock and held up by chains. On the advice of Chang Liang, Liu ordered these flimsy shelves to be burned after the troops had passed over them, not only to prevent possible pursuit by Hsiang Yu, but to prove to the hegemon and the neighboring Ch'in generals that he did not intend to move his army eastward again, and that they need fear no attack from Hanchung.

As might have been foreseen, the pent-up wrath of frustrated rulers of the former royal houses, who had been edged out of their best domains when Hsiang Yu created eighteen extra kings, soon began to explode into local rebellion. By the time Liu Pang and his sad company had been in Hanchung for only a few months, the moment had arrived to make the next move. In accordance with plans worked out by Chang Liang and another able commander called Han Hsin, therefore, troops were dispatched to rebuild the wooden trestleways.

The news was deliberately leaked to the commanders in Ch'in, who heard it with equanimity, even amusement. For while it might have taken no more than a few hours to burn the ledges, they knew that it would take at least eighteen months to replace them. With the stage set for a masterly act of military legerdemain, Liu Pang then marched his army secretly along an antique and forgotten path over the mountains [2] and fell upon the three unsuspecting kingdoms into which Ch'in had been carved, rolling them up like a mat. It was a copybook Sun Tzu operation—total deceit as to intention, timing, and route, capped by a sudden onslaught from an unexpected quarter after a march over an unguarded road. "Feint in the east and attack in the west," as Mao Tsetung was to say more than two millennia later (for this was the winter of 206–205 B.C.).

By the following spring Liu Pang had reached Loyang on the Yellow River after his generals had won an almost unbroken series of victories. And it was at Loyang that a Confucian scholar gave him the bad news that the Righteous Emperor had been assassinated, and the good news that he could turn the bad news to account. He must, said this venerable elder, have a valid and dignified reason for campaigning against Hsiang Yu. And here it was. The hegemon had killed the lawful ruler, and now Liu Pang would not be "attacking" him, but "punishing" him. Always quick to take sage advice, Liu Pang ostentatiously put his whole army into mourning and, calling on all men to rally to him, sent envoys to the other rulers asking them to join him in punishing the murderer of their chosen emperor for his "most treasonable and heinous offense."

Within a year he was marching east with 560,000 men and five feudal lords as allies. They sacked Hsiang Yu's riverine capital at P'engch'eng and captured all the ladies of the court. But since Liu Pang personally set the pace for the uninhibited feasting that followed, Hsiang Yu was able to surprise his army with 30,000 picked men and to inflict such slaughter on the forces of moral retribution pitted against him that his inebriated adversary lost 100,000 killed in action and another 100,000 drowned. The corpses were piled so high and packed so tight that the river Ssu ceased to flow, and Liu Pang himself only escaped thanks to a providential wind that blew up a sandstorm and "turned day into night."

The fickle nobles went over to Hsiang Yu, and the fortunes of war changed. Liu Pang was cornered in a beleaguered city unnervingly short of food, and in some alarm sued for peace. Hsiang Yu was ready to discuss terms and lift the siege, and once again Fan Tseng was the fierce advocate of ruthless, decisive action. "Crush him now," he counseled tersely. "If you let him go, you will be sorry later." But he was only digging his own grave.

Liu Pang employed a talented deserter from Ch'u named Ch'en P'ing to "control battles" for him in the best traditions of Sun Tzu by operating a spy network that could draw on the army's coffers for up to half a million ounces of gold. This worthy now dispatched agents into the Ch'u camp to spread rumors that Fan Tseng had made a secret pact with Liu Pang, and Liu Pang added force to his simulated displeasure on discovering that it was Hsiang Yu and not Fan Tseng who had sent an envoy he was feasting by having the succulent dishes he had ordered removed, and plainer fare served in their place. The envoy reported the revealing incident to a distrustful Hsiang Yu, who stripped Fan Tseng of all office, and shortly afterward the invaluable old warrior died.

Liu Pang was still trapped, but he escaped from the surrounded city as he had escaped from the sword dance—by putting a trusted general at risk. First he dispatched two thousand women dressed in armor through the east gate, and when the besieging troops closed in to attack them, a senior commander followed them out, riding in the royal chariot with its distinctive yellow canopy and feather pennant flying on the left. "There is no more food in the town," this officer announced, impersonating his lord. "We therefore submit." And as the soldiers of Hsiang Yu cheered and broke ranks to stream over and see the famous "King of Hanchung," Liu Pang escaped through the unguarded west gate with a score of horsemen. When Hsiang Yu discovered how he had been tricked, he burned the general alive.

In the course of the next year Liu Pang won new allies and raised another army, only to find himself fleeing almost alone through the north gate of another beleaguered city, and not long after that he was confronted by Hsiang Yu yet again across a ravine. But now it was Hsiang Yu who was running perilously short of food, and the hegemon therefore tried to end the duel between them on the spot by playing his one high card. During the fighting he had captured Liu Pang's father, and he now stood the old man on a high scaffold, shouting, "Surrender immediately, or I shall boil your father alive!"

"But we are sworn brothers," Liu Pang called back derisively. "So my father is your father also. If you insist on boiling your own father, send me a bowl of the soup!"

The infuriated Hsiang Yu wanted to carry out his culinary threat forthwith, but was dissuaded by an adviser who said, "A man who aspires to be emperor will not trouble about his family. Killing the father would achieve nothing."

Hsiang Yu's next move was to challenge Liu Pang to single combat, the winner to take the empire, "instead of involving all these other men."

"I will meet you in a battle of wits," retorted Liu Pang, "not in a trial of strength," and in an insufferably self-righteous manner proceeded to enumerate all the crimes that Hsiang Yu had committed. The outraged hegemon snatched up a crossbow and shot him in the chest, but the cunning peasant covered up quickly and, seizing his own foot, yelled, "The rascal has hit me in the toe!"

Compelled to suppress the rebels further east who had cut his supply lines, Hsiang Yu finally withdrew and left the defense of his nearby headquarters at Chengkao on the river Ssu in the hands of his senior marshal. "Keep it secure," he ordered. "If challenged, do not give battle. I shall be back in fifteen days." But after the army of Liu Pang had challenged the defenders of Chengkao several times without being able to draw them out, soldiers were dispatched day after day to hurl vile insults at Hsiang Yu's generals until the marshal, losing his temper completely, launched a full-scale assault across the river. "Wait until half of his army is over, then hit him," Wu Ch'i had prescribed for such occasions. Liu Pang's men annihilated the enemy, and on taking Chengkao found that they had captured the entire treasure of the kingdom of Ch'u. The three commanders of the hegemon responsible for breaking the cardinal rule never to attack in anger killed themselves on the riverbank.

The tables were turned again. Liu Pang disposed of a strong, well-fed force while Hsiang Yu commanded only an exhausted and hungry remnant of his once great army, and this time it was Hsiang Yu who proposed peace. He sent Liu Pang's father back to him, and the two heroes agreed to divide the empire, Hsiang Yu taking the east, Liu Pang the west. But as Fan Tseng had once urged Hsiang Yu to show no mercy to the stricken enemy, so Chang Liang now urged Liu Pang to destroy him: "To let him go would be like rearing a tiger that would later devour you." Unhampered by the scruples of his rival, Liu Pang coolly repudiated their treaty, and two months later Hsiang Yu's adversaries had surrounded his army and were ready to move in for the kill.

Hsiang Yu broke out of the cordon with eight hundred men, was deliberately misdirected by a traitor, found himself in a swamp, lost all but twenty-eight of his followers, and was finally brought to bay by a pursuing force of five thousand cavalry. He charged this legion twice, slaughtering a score of enemy, cutting down one general and frightening the mount of another so much by glaring and bellowing at its rider that it bolted several miles.

He then gave his own horse to a boatman who had offered to help him escape across the river Wu * ("I cannot bear to kill him") and went for the cavalry on foot. Coming up against an old friend in the press of battle, however, he shouted, "I hear Liu Pang has offered a thousand pieces of gold and a fief of ten thousand families for my head. Let me do you a favor"—and slit his own throat. "I have fought more than seventy battles and was never defeated," he had said earlier. "Yet now I am hemmed in here. It was Heaven that destroyed me, not my generalship that was at fault."

"What a fool!" comments the Grand Historian Ssu-ma Ch'ien. "He banished the Righteous Emperor so that the lords turned against him. He trusted only his personal judgment and did not follow ancient precedents. Considering himself an overlord, he tried to win an empire by military conquest. Yet he never realized his mistakes or blamed himself for his folly."

* Ho County, modern Anhui Province.

13

Empire for One

"Can your courage and presence be compared with those of Hsiang Yu?" Han Hsin once asked Liu Pang.

"I'm afraid not."

"Yet while Hsiang Yu's air of authority may awe a thousand men, he is incapable of employing good generals because he is envious of the able. He does not reward merit or share spoils, and he is not farsighted. He can be affable, and sympathetic toward the sick. But that kind of petty benevolence is not required of those who do great things. On the other hand, wherever he goes he leaves a trail of death and destruction and the people hate him.

"Now you employ the most sagacious officials and valiant generals in your service. The cities that you have taken have all been conferred on meritorious men. Who would not gladly trust you? You have abolished the cruel laws of the Ch'in Dynasty, and won the love and respect of the people. You can advance and take the empire."

Han Hsin's analysis appeared to be justified. All the kingdoms of China now submitted to Liu Pang except that of Lu, but he magnanimously refrained from massacring its inhabitants in the usual way. Instead, he displayed the head of Hsiang Yu to them in order to persuade them to capitulate, and then gave his old enemy a state funeral as "Duke of Lu." He refused the imperial title three times before accepting it and reigning as Han Kao-tsu, the founding emperor of the great Han Dynasty. He rewarded his generals, disbanded the feudal armies, and proclaimed a general amnesty.

He never lost the common touch, and after he had been emperor for eight years he visited his native P'ei, invited all his old acquaintances to dinner, danced and drank and cried and sang a song he had composed, and exempted the citizens from taxes forever. He remained for ten days of merrymaking, only left because he felt that the needs of his huge retinue were too heavy a burden for the small community to bear, and even then, unable to tear himself away, set up tents outside the town and stayed for another three days.

At court the tried and trusted friends around him were men of the same humble origins as himself—dog butchers, drapers, grooms, runners, robbers and jailers, and the low musicians who blew trumpets at funerals. There was much horseplay and badinage, drinking and yelling and quarreling and hacking at the woodwork with swords, and the palace was constantly in an uproar. He cursed the architects of the imperial pavilions in his new capital at Ch'ang An, finding them too luxurious and fancy for his taste, and when a dignitary quoted from the *Book of Odes* one day, he exclaimed with irritation. "I won the empire on horseback," he boasted. Why should he bother with the Classics? "Yes, but can you rule it from horseback," came the bold retort.

The village headman had become valiant emperor of all China by weighing the words of others, and although he was contemptuous of scholars at the outset, his canny instinct was already prompting him to coat all this raw rusticity with a thin Confucian gloss calculated to please men who had rebelled against the Legalist tyrannies of Ch'in. He displayed a filial piety that earned him murmurs of approval. He visited his father every five days, carefully conforming to the *Li* demanded of a respectful son, and when a steward advised the old man to treat him not as his son but as his sovereign, Han Kao-tsu accepted the new relationship but conferred on his parent the title of "Grand Emperor" (while privately bestowing half a hundredweight of gold on the perspicacious steward).

He also bowed to the argument that he must dwell in magnificence if he wished to preserve his authority as the Son of Heaven and pass it on to his heirs, and commanded that a solemn court ritual be drawn up so that *Li* might replace license in his palace. At dawn the high officials entered the gates according to their rank, chariots in line and banners flying. The ruler sat on his throne with hundreds of attendants on either side of him, the Master of Ceremonies intoned the word "Advance!" and the ministers and nobles and generals came forward one by one to tender their congratulations in soft voices and a reverent manner, withdrawing thereafter in correct and seemly order. "Now I know what it is like to be an emperor," Han Kao-tsu sighed.

But could he rule the empire from horseback? The very price of the animal was relevant to the question, for the country had fallen into ruin during the rebellion, and a single horse had cost three hundred pounds of gold. In 196 B.C. he issued a decree calling upon all men of merit and distinction to come forward, and from among these he chose his advisers and administrators.

He judged them by the impression they made upon him in audience, and candidates for office would not be required to take written examinations in the Classics until nearly a hundred years later. Nonetheless, most of the men he appointed were scholars, and they were the forerunners of the great Chinese civil service of educated Confucian "mandarins" that would still be running the empire at the turn of the twentieth century. The very title of "gentleman" which had belonged to men ennobled by their birth was in the future to belong to men ennobled by their moral studies, so that by 120 B.C. it was possible for a pigherd to become chief minister.*

If splendid palaces provided the indispensable setting for the *Li* surrounding the Son of Heaven, however, they also provided an indispensable setting for the expression of his mystical "power." And if the hierarchy of imperial mandarins

* Kung-sun Hung, under Han Wu-ti.

promised a benevolent Confucian meritocracy based on the precepts in the ancient books, it also presaged the end of the feudal system that Confucius himself had upheld, and the revival of the omnipotent central government first conceived by the Legalists of Ch'in.

Han Kao-tsu may have made a pilgrimage to the temple of Confucius and sacrificed innumerable oxen, sheep, and pigs to the frugal sage, but he deprived the vassal kings of their right to confer high office, and sent to every corner of his realm the new officials whom he had selected personally, who represented his overriding imperial authority, and who were his private agents, reporting back solely to him. And not even the First Emperor of Ch'in was a better judge of a cat's-paw.

"How was it that I won the whole world?" he once asked his lords and generals, and like Han Hsin they told him that although he was brusque with others, he had never failed to reward virtue and share the spoils of victory with his loyal followers.

"That is one reason, but there is another," rejoined the emperor. "In devising stratagems I am no match for Chang Liang, in organizing supplies for the army I am no match for Hsiao Ho, and in winning battles I am no match for Han Hsin. These are men of extraordinary capabilities, but it was I who gained possession of the world, for I used them and took their advice. Hsiang Yu did not even listen to Fan Tseng."

The deserter from Ch'u whom the emperor had employed as a master spy to drive a wedge between Hsiang Yu and his unhappy counselor was a perfect example of Han Kao-tsu's almost soulless selection of men as tools. The fellow was a glib and personable turncoat who was habitually lazy and would devote much of the day to drinking and wenching and pocketing bribes. But his new master made him provost marshal of the army (to the disgust of his own generals), for the sound reason that he had a genius for duplicity. There was no sly trick or foul deceit that his devious and conniving mind failed to engender, and he saved Han Kao-tsu six times by means of subtle artifices the details of which have never been revealed.

He himself once had the grace to say, "All my crafty ruses are not in harmony with the *Tao,* and once the fortunes of my heirs decline, they will never rise again because of the evil I have done." But Han Kao-tsu was not concerned with such niceties. As the worthy who had first recommended the man had pointed out, what was required was not a virtuous gentleman but a brilliant strategist in his own field. He was the right rascal for the job. What had his private life got to do with it? Who cared if he was dissolute and corrupt and slept with his sister-in-law?

For all his brutality, Chinese say, Hsiang Yu was not relentless enough. The free lance who wants to be king must be ready to spend money like water and cut people down like hemp. For all his calculated clemency, on the other hand, Han Kao-tsu killed when it counted without compunction, and he continued killing after he mounted the throne. On the way up the hero should at times be lenient, and loud in his advocacy of honorable conduct so that he may attract support, but once at the top he must be ruthless if he wishes to stay there, liquidating all challengers and thus "demolishing the bridge after crossing the river himself."

This often means that he must also "forget the good that men have done him." Liu Pang—ex-headman, Lord of P'ei, King of Hanchung—might bind much-needed followers to him by "rewarding merit and sharing spoils," but the all-powerful Emperor Han Kao-tsu soon stripped his commanders of the kingdoms earlier conferred upon them. Even Han Hsin was degraded and murdered, and only Chang Liang survived by abandoning the court to become a Taoist mystic in the mountains. For popular and successful generals can be even more dangerous than those who merely lose battles.

The death and disgrace of Lin Piao in 1971 underlined the rule. Chairman Mao remained Chairman Mao because he consistently called to account any rival who threatened his supremacy. And although in the early 1960's his policies were being eroded and his hold on China appeared to be slipping, he made a sudden and spectacular comeback against his opponents in Peking when, from his political base in Shanghai, he launched the Great Cultural Revolution that swept them out of office. This tactic of feigned withdrawal and sudden attack is still known among Chinese as "burning the trestles, to return by the secret path." But then, as the soothsayers have pointed out, Mao was also a burly, canny, chili-chewing peasant from Ch'u, with a bluff, earthy manner, fond of a cup of wine and destined to have four wives, a flexible and formidable general—who had the same long arms as Han Kao-tsu.

The Chinese claim that Mao has been the outstanding figure of his day, and there is little doubt that Han Kao-tsu was the outstanding figure of his. Remorseless where remorse was out of place, he rarely displayed arrogance or savagery or anger, he overthrew a greater tyranny to give the people a lesser, and he founded a dynasty that was to endure for four hundred years—even if it was also to be the prologue to further chaos.

14

Prologue to Chaos

For sixteen years after the death of Han Kao-tsu his widow, the Dowager Empress Lu, dominated the palace by the simple expedient of replacing her illustrious husband's relatives with members of her own family in all positions of power. But when she in turn died, the wily deserter from Ch'u who had been the emperor's most trusted hatchetman was able to encompass the slaughter of her clan, and the son of an imperial concubine ascended the throne as the Emperor Wen. His was a reign of rare tranquillity, during which schools in the Confucian Classics were founded, the court observed commendable thrift, and the ancient sacrifices were reintroduced. Imperial control over vast regions of China appeared to be loose, yet there was prosperity and peace.

But while honest scholars were painstakingly putting together the antique books burned by the Ch'in, there was much deceitful re-editing by academic cheats, and Legalist tags sanctioning arbitrary imperial decisions crept into humanistic Confucian doctrine. When Han Wu-ti ascended the throne in 141 B.C., he was able to set an example for future emperors by seizing upon the convenient formula these insertions offered for practicing autocratic Legalist rule behind a formal mask of Confucian benevolence. In the palace at Ch'ang An a watchdog secretariat supervised and censured the mandarins on behalf of the ruler, and the law was progressively codified (by the end of the dynasty it ran into nearly 18,000,000 characters).

In the West, Carthage had just been destroyed by Scipio Africanus, and Rome was shortly to succumb to the depredations of Marius and Sulla, but for China this was to be a period of military expansion. Han Kao-tsu, still saddled with the task of taming an empire, had signed a treaty with the powerful Hun state that menaced him from the north and had coaxed the ruler of the extensive kingdom of Yueh to his southeast into recognizing him as suzerain. Under Han Wu-ti, however, Chinese armies overran and colonized Korea as far as modern Seoul, made the mountainous southwestern territory of Yunnan a tributary, and subdued Nan Yueh (or "Nam Viet"), whose new masters in the region of Canton held sway as far south as Tongking.

But the emperor's perennial problem was how to neutralize the obstreperous Huns who continued to harass the northern frontiers of his realm. In 138 B.C., accordingly, he sent an officer named Chang Ch'ien off into the wild west with only one hundred men and orders to enlist the aid of "distant allies" in the shape of a people living on the far side of the hostile Central Asian wastes beyond the Great Wall.[1]

Chang was captured by the Huns and held prisoner for ten years, but when he finally escaped he steadfastly resumed his mission. He caught up with his quarry beyond the Oxus, only to be told that they were no longer interested in fighting Huns. He then made his hazardous way back to China, twelve years after he had set out. He brought with him alfalfa, which the Chinese did not know, and also an unimpressive little plant on which grew a strange, sweet fruit—the grape. He had been to the Hellenized kingdoms of Sogdiana and Bactria, the heritage of Alexander's conquests. The civilization of China had met the civilization of Greece.

Of Sogdiana he wrote, "The people have many superb horses, which sweat blood when they perspire." His appetite whetted, Han Wu-ti dispatched an embassy and then an army to obtain some of these fabulous brutes, but the embassy was killed off and the army defeated. In 102 B.C. (the year Julius

Caesar was born), the emperor therefore sent a vast punitive expedition across the desert to teach Sogdiana who was master, and of this 30,000 parched and hungry men reached their destination and made sure that he got his horses.

Half a century later it was the Chinese, intervening again, who installed Hermaeus, the last Greek king to rule in northwestern India. West and East were moving closer together. The first images of Buddha were to be executed by craftsmen who took Apollo the sun god as their model, the Chinese began to sell gold and silk and fine-cast iron to the Occident, they bought pearls and glass (which they considered as valuable as jade), and they acquired the ass and the pancontinental camel. They were overlords of Mongolia and Eastern Turkestan, their arts were developing rapidly and gracefully, as their wall paintings and glazed pottery attest. Moreover, in Ssu-ma Ch'ien, whom Han Wu-ti had castrated for defending a disgraced general, China produced one of the greatest historians the world has known.

The relationship between Rome and China, separated throughout the Han Dynasty by the power of Parthia, tantalizes because they never quite touched. In A.D. 73, twelve years after Boadicea had massacred the Roman garrison in Britain, another officer named Pan Ch'ao trekked westward through the poorly charted wilds beyond the Wall to find "distant allies" and to prevent the Huns themselves from uniting against China. In the course of a model exercise in pitting "barbarian against barbarian," this resourceful commander subjected more than fifty petty kings of Turkestan and marched unopposed to the shores of the Caspian Sea with a vassal army 60,000 strong. "Ta Ts'in"—the Rome of the Emperor Nerva—lay just across the water and the mountains of Armenia. But when Pan Ch'ao sent an envoy to make contact with the Romans, the man was so daunted by the tales of the Parthians (who feared a Sino-Roman alliance and lied to him about the dangers of the journey) that he turned back.

It would be absurd to pretend that the Chinese had never been greedy for ground—they started life in the valley of the

Yellow River and ended by possessing a gigantic empire. But their instinct when they absorbed territory was nonetheless defensive—the acquisition of more fat against the cold threat of Barbaria without—and their expansionism cultural. The emperor was not so much the conqueror of most of the states that bowed to China, as their suzerain, and he often exacted from their rulers little more than homage and tribute.

While Chinese accounts of Rome were flattering, painting it as a just if luxury-loving state, there could be no doubt which of the two empires was in better trim. The Romans were deplorably extravagant and the cultural solidarity represented by the word "Rome" progressively melted as the frivolous citizenry became increasingly dependent on slaves, and the state on barbarian mercenaries. In China not more than one man in a hundred was a slave, and all Chinese knew that theirs was the "Middle Kingdom" of the world, knit together by one written language, one true philosophy, one true civilization.

In Han Wu-ti's day China was further stabilized by the economic measures of a shopkeeper's son named Sang Hung-yang, who became the emperor's most trusted adviser. By 120 B.C., one year after Gaius Gracchus had been murdered in the streets of Rome for his tax reforms and commercial legislation, the Chinese ruler had decreed that iron and salt should be state monopolies and had imposed taxes on carriages and boats and accumulated capital to pay for his campaigns. Sang then ended much misery and hardship (and filled the empire's granaries and treasury in the process) by creating a government department to "level" trade. Officials were authorized to buy up goods in times of glut and sell stocks cheap when they were scarce, and each province was allowed to pay its imperial tribute in the commodity of which it had most. This would be transported to regions which lacked it, instead of to the capital as before, so that speculating, hoarding, and manipulating prices were reduced to a minimum.

What is the quality of life in Han China after the birth of Christ? There are water clocks of an accuracy that Europe will have to wait another twelve hundred years to achieve, and a lunar calendar has been established that will still be consulted in 1927. Sunspots have been observed (Galileo will be the first European to write about them, but not until 1613), 11,520 stars have been charted, and the elliptical orbit of the moon measured. The silk loom and the seed-sowing machine have long since been invented, and now farmers have foot-treadle trip hammers for dehusking grain, wellhead pulleys, and water pumps.

The population of China is already about 60,000,000, and although the empire still includes twenty petty kingdoms nominally ruled by royal kinsmen, it is otherwise divided into more than eighty prefectures effectively administered by Confucian mandarins. Life in the countryside is nonetheless harsh. The peasant must do one month of forced labor every year, and if harvests are bad he may have to sell children or turn bandit. Comparatively few men may be slaves, but punishments are barbarous. Wrongdoers are still beheaded, cut in two at the waist, castrated or otherwise mutilated—and they may transgress the law merely by using the central part of a highway reserved for the emperor.

A careful register of households is kept, for all males must serve their time in the army—fed, clad, but unpaid. Once conscripted, they are posted as infantry to a city garrison or to the Great Wall or to pioneer farming settlements. Military administration is sophisticated. On the Wall units keep nominal rolls with complete personal details of all effectives, firing (archery) test results, document registers, stores lists and meticulous accounts. In any one of the watchtowers there are heavy crossbows fitted with sights as well as triggers, grease and glue to maintain them, suits of armor and helmets, codes for pulley-operated signal flags, medicines and tools.

The men are jacks-of-all-trades. They not only cook and mend and carpenter for themselves; they may raise cattle, grow vegetables and grain, construct irrigation works, make bricks, and erect granaries for their own crops. Chinese units have always been labor organizations, ready to build and till when there is no fighting to be done. The thirty-odd static armies in the provinces of Communist China run their own workshops and farms, breed pigs, build roads and dams, manufacture their own pills and boots.

For the casting of swords and plowshares alike, forty-eight iron agencies operate throughout the Han empire, with towers, pits, foundries, furnaces, and cooling tanks. In the marshes, other government agencies mine salt, employing bamboo pipelines and winding gear, raising brine that has been tapped by drills up to two thousand feet below the surface of the earth.

The Chinese have elegant light carriages with dish-shaped wheels of bronze and wood, and the wheelbarrow that Europe will not see for centuries. Their books are written on silk or inscribed on long bamboo wafers strung together and rolled into neat bundles, but after A.D. 100 paper begins to replace these, and the first dictionary, containing 9,000 characters, is presented to the emperor.

In tile-roofed, multi-storied houses the staircases are painted, the rafters carved, the floors strewn with skins and rugs and embroidered cushions. Men sit on mats, or kneel at low tables to eat. There are no chairs, but the hard beds are covered with fine-worked cloth and discreetly screened. The wealthy can wear fox fur, and shoes and slippers of silk or inlaid leather. Women adorn themselves with delicately worked jade, pearls, and tortoiseshell, and rich families keep their own orchestras—bells, drums, zither and syrinx, flute and lyre.

Silk is a lucrative export. Craved by the Huns as early as 200 B.C., it now goes far beyond them to eager buyers in the Roman Empire. The long, dangerous caravan routes lead, with variations, through Kashgar, Samarkand, and Antioch. In Christ's time ships also carried silk from what is now Haiphong, through the Straits of Malacca and around India to the Red Sea, from where it was transported to Alexandria. The traders were mainly Indians and Arabs, but in A.D. 166 Roman "envoys" from Marcus Aurelius arrived in Tongking "offering ivory, rhinoceros horn, and tortoiseshell" which they had purchased en route.

The silk was unraveled and respun into finer cloth in Syria so that, as Pliny commented, "the Roman matron may appear in public in transparent garments." The Romans had no idea how silk was made—Pliny wrote of the Chinese removing "down from leaves"—but they tried hard to find out, spurred on by the unscrupulous profiteering of successive middlemen which became almost intolerable once the Persians had cornered the trade. The Chinese manufacturing monopoly was finally broken in A.D. 552, when monks from the East smuggled silk-moth eggs hidden in sections of bamboo to the court of the Byzantine emperor Justinian—an early case of industrial espionage.

Both the Roman and Chinese empires were later to fall to the barbarian, but although in theory each sank into its own "dark ages" thereafter, Roman civilization was submerged, whereas China's muscular culture survived. It also survived the cyclical disasters brought about not only by palace eunuchs, but by palace women like the Dowager Empress Lu. For even if she were not ambitious, an imperial consort and her family had to fight for the upper hand at court, since they were automatically the focus for the often murderous jealousy of the emperor's own clan, and if the emperor died, their only salvation might lie in usurping the Mandate of Heaven themselves.

When Christ was perhaps five years old,* therefore, a certain Wang Mang, nephew of another dowager empress who had been carefully placing her relations in key posts since the death of her husband, seized the throne and held it for fourteen years before he was cut down by a common soldier.

Living a century after Sang Hung-yang had died, the new emperor was another innovator who jolted the Chinese economy. He stabilized prices again by storing commodities in short supply, demanded a voluntary cut in salary from mandarins, broke up big landholdings, prohibited the ownership of private slaves, and started a credit system to enable landless peasants to buy and till the soil. But the sanctimonious

* A.D. 9, accepting the modern calculation that Christ was born in A.D. 4.

upstart introduced these ostensibly "socialist" measures solely in order to strip possible rivals of their wealth and fill his own coffers, and he justified them by quoting from fraudulent classical writings "found" hidden in the wall of the house of Confucius which most conveniently proved that he was merely emulating the ancient sages.

His most sensational act was to corner gold. He laid his hands on five million ounces of the metal, and even the Emperor Tiberius nine thousand miles to the west was obliged to prohibit patricians from wearing Chinese silk for a time because Rome was suffering from a gold drain. However, neither his family nor his policies were appreciated, and his one-man dynasty (the Hsin) is no more than a thin wedge between the Early (Western) and Late (Eastern) Han, to whom the throne was finally restored in A.D. 25 after much bloodshed.

China recovered. The Chinese reconquered a recalcitrant Yunnan, subjugated Tongking and Annam and held them for nearly a thousand years thereafter, and tightened their grip on much of Korea and Manchuria. In Central Asia they pushed back the Huns and consolidated their own hold by unrolling a creeping carpet of agricultural colonies stiffened by the army—much as today the Communist leadership stiffens the settlements along the Sino-Soviet frontier in Sinkiang with armed, trained, and uniformed pioneers of the so-called "Production and Construction Corps." But all this imperial muscle flexing concealed a cancerous growth of palace intrigue within, and when a Chinese emperor died in A.D. 189 leaving no direct heir, the country dissolved into rebellion and anarchy.

China's political history is not one of constant minor carping and change, but of superficially calm periods of suppressed exasperation punctuated by sudden explosions of pious popular rage. It was accordingly a peasant insurrection, led by a mystical society called the Red Eyebrows, that first challenged the rule of Wang Mang and precipitated the turmoil that led to his murder. In A.D. 184 the Yellow Turbans rose in their turn, and although their revolt was shattered, they brought down the Han Dynasty with them. Later the White Lotus sect was to mount successive rebellions against the Mongol dominion of Kublai Khan, the native Chinese Ming Dynasty that replaced it, and the Ch'ing Dynasty of alien Manchus that supplanted the Ming.

Since the violent overthrow of a degenerate dynasty is evidence in itself that the Mandate of Heaven—that Chinese Heaven whose ire the misdeeds of monarchs can so quickly kindle—has been withdrawn, it follows that any successful revolt must be righteous. The fall of the Eastern Han (so called because the capital was moved to Loyang) did not immediately bring a new emperor to the throne armed with a new "Mandate," however. Instead, another of China's disruptive agents appeared—the warlord—for the mere size of the country encouraged military chiefs to make a bid for power in the provinces when the court was corrupt and the ruler weak. Ambitious soldiers were to found a succession of ephemeral dynasties between the fourth and sixth centuries, to destroy the T'ang Dynasty early in the tenth century, to install the Sung Dynasty toward the close of it, and to carve most of the empire up between them when the Ch'ing Dynasty relinquished effective power in 1912.

At the end of the period of confusion that marked the collapse of the Han in A.D. 220, therefore, China was not reunited under one emperor but divided into three kingdoms, and the bloody acts of betrayal and callous brutality that characterized the subsequent struggle for supremacy among them have been immortalized in wonderfully embellished fable. The fable is nonetheless as important as the facts, for both have had an all-pervasive influence on Chinese military and political traditions.

The biased, factual history contained in *The Annals of the Three Kingdoms* is matched by a balanced, fictional epic called *The Romance of the Three Kingdoms*—China's first full-length novel, published in the fourteenth century. The inspiration of a hundred popular operas, this great saga has been an almost inexhaustible well from which millions of ordinary Chinese have drawn their knowledge of history, of policy, of generalship and skulduggery, even of logic and argument and morals. Its heroes are household names, and it has been carefully studied by modern military leaders from Chiang Kai-shek to Chairman Mao, for it is full of practical illustrations of the doctrines of the earlier strategists.

Its lessons converted a "Christian" rabble into an army during the Taiping Rebellion of the last century, say the Communists; and they converted a Communist rabble into a military power in this century, say the Nationalists. The period threw up men of outstanding talent, as only convulsive situations can, and to say that its larger-than-life figures have been immortalized is not always mere metaphor, for one of them has long since been deified and is today the Chinese god of war. But the first to take the stage was a man more equivocally described in his day as "a capable minister in an age of tranquillity, a treacherous hero in an age of chaos"—Ts'ao Ts'ao.

15

Talk of Ts'ao Ts'ao

He is a very Chinese hero—beloved and execrated and admired and abhorred for the knave he is—and it is significant that his compatriots, who do not believe in a Christian Devil, should instead use the expression "Talk of Ts'ao Ts'ao . . ." even today. "I would rather betray the whole world than let the world betray me," he retorts in *The Romance of the Three Kingdoms* when someone remonstrates with him for slaughtering the family of a man he quite wrongly suspects of treachery. The story may be apocryphal, but the philosophy is that of a very real person, famous for his commentaries on Sun Tzu's *Art of War*. Mao Tsetung may have said, "Revolution is not a dinner party," but seventeen centuries before, Ts'ao Ts'ao had written just as sardonically, "An army cannot be run according to the rules of etiquette."

The Chinese applaud a many-sided rogue who can wield both pen and sword, and Ts'ao Ts'ao was a man of parts. When young he led the life of a sprig of the nobility, breeding falcons, hounds, and horses and displaying great prowess in the chase. Yet he was also a studious and cultivated classicist, and as he grew older composed elegant verse of a sparkling rhythm that could be set to music. But he passed his days in scheming and fighting, and his nights in reading and writing more than just poetry. "Bypass what the enemy defends, hit him where he does not expect you," he advised students of Sun Tzu, and, perhaps somewhat ruefully in view of his own fate, "To use fire, rely on traitors." He, too, reiterated, "The general need not be bound by the commands of the ruler"—and not surprisingly, for he was to hold the emperor himself in his hand and treat him as a mere pawn in the power game.

Ts'ao Ts'ao was a short man of enormous spirit with a sharp eye and a long flowing beard. He was careless in his dress and deportment, his speech was expressive and rich, his laugh loud and unrestrained, and when excited he would say the first outrageous thing that came into his head. Yet he was very thrifty. His cushions were plain, and his curtains and screens were patched when old, for he could not bear to put new ones in their place. He did not allow his wives, his concubines, or daughters-in-law to wear embroidered finery, and as a soldier to whom the frugal way of the scholar had become a habit, he hated show of any kind.

He did not need it. Waiting to receive an envoy from the Huns one day, he was suddenly seized with misgiving, fearing that his appearance would fail to awe the barbarian. So he ordered an imposing official of dignified mien to impersonate him and receive the fellow on his behalf, while he stood beside the make-believe Ts'ao Ts'ao, pretending to be a bodyguard. Afterward he learned that the envoy had nonetheless taken the bodyguard with the big sword to be the true hero all along.

Ts'ao Ts'ao did not rise from obscurity. His grandfather had been tutor to the heir-apparent, and when the heir-apparent became emperor, was made an imperial adviser. His father had paid ten million cash for the office of military counselor to the ruler. The family was extremely rich, its wealth and power a springboard for this ambitious and gifted young blade for whom "only those who have exalted aims in their breasts and fine stratagems in their bellies" could be considered men of destiny.

But as was common practice in China until the present century, his grandfather had had himself castrated in order to be eligible for a post in the palace, and his father had been adopted. In consequence, when the storm that was to wash away the Han Dynasty first broke over Loyang, Ts'ao Ts'ao discovered to his disgust that instead of counting him among the disaffected soldiers and scholars in the capital, men assumed that he was on the side of the unsavory court eunuchs who surrounded the isolated emperor.

The clouds had been gathering since A.D. 159 when a dowager empress died and the eunuchs arranged for her entire clan to be exterminated for the greater comfort of the new emperor. This foolish young man then found himself utterly dependent on the creatures, and delegated such powers to them that they were able to squeeze the realm like a ripe orange. They filled the administration with their own kinsmen, and every official or general who required a service or sought preferment was obliged to pay them in gold. When the emperor died, his heir was only twelve years old, the extortions of the eunuchs multiplied, and the impoverished military commanders and mandarins were forced to meet their irresponsible demands by exacting more and more from the peasantry. The pitiable condition of the peasants was then aggravated by a plague of locusts which destroyed the crops, leaving millions starving, desperate, and looking for a focus for their fury.

Their messiah was already moving among them, an itinerant quack called Chang Chueh who treated all ailments with a magic potion consisting of plain water over which he had pronounced a few well-chosen words. Renowned for his sensational cures, this Taoist faith healer exploited the awe he evoked among simple men in A.D. 184 by calling on the wretched and hungry to rebel, and within a few months hundreds of thousands of his ragged and roughly armed followers were robbing and killing and making for Loyang from all corners of the empire. These were the Yellow Turbans, whose leader set an example in peasant revolution that was to be emulated by a long line of Chinese rebels, down to another ideological faith healer named Mao Tsetung.

To suppress the insurrection a vast new imperial army was mobilized in which Ts'ao Ts'ao, now thirty-four years old, served as a subordinate general. But the emperor had given supreme command of the force to a eunuch, while appointing as his deputy a powerful and competent minister named Yuan Shao. In consequence the army was split into two, one subservient to the eunuch influence, the other outraged by it, for operations were hampered by the inefficiency and corruption and treachery of meddlesome geldings who even took bribes from the rebels.

All this aroused the undisguised fury of the mandarins and the nobles, some of whom, having long since learned that the eunuchs would never allow them to win leverage at court by gaining the ear of the emperor, had left the capital and set themselves up as semi-autonomous masters of the provincial *chou,* the big administrative regions into which China was then divided. It was when resentment reached flash point in the palace, and these warlords already dominated much of the realm outside it, that the emperor died in the year 189 without male issue.

A decisive confrontation between soldiers and eunuchs was inevitable, for the leading scholars who might have acted as a buffer between them had by then been beheaded for conspiracy, after they had protested against the abuses of the emperor's doctored confidants. The champions for the military were the imperial commander in chief, his sister the empress, and the deputy commander of the anti-rebel army, Yuan Shao. And in order to strip the eunuchs of their infamous prerogatives, the commander in chief secretly called upon the most intimidating of the new warlords to bring an army into the capital to help him.

The warlord was a sly and cruel general of almost superhuman strength from northwestern China named Tung Cho, many of whose soldiers were Huns. Hearing that he was coming, the eunuchs tried to overawe the military by murdering the commander in chief himself, whereupon an enraged and frightened Yuan Shao mustered his own troops, and without further ado they butchered two thousand of the *castrati,* decapitating some unfortunates simply because they had no beards.

Tung Cho had meanwhile reached Loyang with his army

of ruffians from the Great Wall, and as the government collapsed beneath a confused emperor drawn from a collateral line of the imperial family, he snatched power from under the noses of other, bewildered contenders, and made himself master of the palace. Assuming the role of chief minister, he treated the Son of Heaven as a trifling appendage only useful for the authority of his imperial seal, swaggered about in court wearing a sword, and generally behaved in a debauched and bestial fashion while his troops pillaged and murdered wherever they pleased. Finally deciding that Loyang was not safe from the Yellow Turbans and his own military rivals, he unceremoniously packed the emperor off to Ch'ang An, looted and burned the capital, and rode west again himself, dragging along with him more than a million hapless citizens, most of whom died of exhaustion and starvation en route.

Tung Cho was murdered in 192, whereupon one of his barbarous generals "inherited" the woebegone emperor. But this roughneck became so embroiled in a bloody struggle with his rapacious brothers-in-arms that he left his charge to languish in the ruined palace at Loyang again while he went off to do battle. And it was there that yet another general found the imperial puppet and carried him away to his own stronghold—Ts'ao Ts'ao.

The clear-sighted Ts'ao Ts'ao had long since realized that the leprous clique of eunuchs at court had no future and that he must cut his compromising links with them: on one occasion he had ostentatiously advertised his hostility toward them by charging into the reception hall of the chief eunuch when that mutilated monster was at the height of his insidious power, and flashing his sword around to the terror of all. Once under Yuan Shao's command, he cultivated the minister so that they might plot to exterminate the parasites, and when the eunuchs were dispatched and Yuan Shao slipped out of Loyang to raise an army against Tung Cho, Ts'ao Ts'ao joined him, spending his fortune on arming and mounting a contingent of 5,000 men.

There was a severe limit to his loyalty to Yuan Shao, however, and having heard that the Yellow Turbans had attacked Yen Chou in northeastern China and killed the warlord of the region in battle, he offered to annihilate the marauders if the local officials would then make him their "protector" in place of the dead man. The officials agreed with alacrity, Ts'ao Ts'ao swept away the Yellow Turbans, and having taken the surrender of 300,000 officers and men, organized the best of them into a disciplined force.

He now had a big army and a base of his own, he no longer needed Yuan Shao as a patron, and he was ready to fight his former commander and all other contenders for the domination of the strategic Central Plain for which men had been dying for a thousand years. But he was to acquire even more than an army and a base. For when he heard that the emperor had been left unguarded in Loyang, he hastened to seek him out, persuaded him that he could not stay in that wrecked and starving city, and inveigled him into accompanying him to Yen Chou.

Once more the authority of the Han Dynasty had changed hands. Ts'ao Ts'ao was quick to make himself an imperial minister in his turn, and to chasten other warlords and draft more men into his own army by invoking the name of the legitimate ruler. In the years that followed, he galloped his proud and beautiful horse through fields of blood, his dripping sword raised high, his immoderate, triumphant laugh ringing out over the stricken dead. Tung Cho was only a memory, and now Yuan Shao was decisively defeated.

But although Ts'ao Ts'ao dominated the north, the rest of China was still divided between the single sprawling domain of Wu in the southeast, and a patchwork of smaller *chou* elsewhere, each under its own local governor or condottiere. These remained at least nominally loyal to the Han ruler, however, and so, armed with his power over the imperial seal, Ts'ao Ts'ao turned south to impose his personal will on the entire empire—only to be stopped by a man of modest demeanor and kindly disposition called Liu Pei.

16

The Keys of the Kingdoms

In 1973 visitors to the Royal Academy in London were able to contemplate a stiff, sinister shroud fashioned from 2,160 tiles of jade which had been threaded with gold wire into a gleaming carapace of silicate to encase a princess who had died two millennia before. The lady's husband had been unearthed in China, similarly packaged, but this elaborate and futile attempt to fight decay was to be among the last extravagances the family could afford.

For it is said that Prince Liu Sheng, the man crumbling to dust within that second suit of jade, had a son who failed to make a sacrificial offering and was therefore deprived by the emperor of his noble status. His clan was reduced to honest poverty, and his descendants worked as petty officials in North China * until Liu Pei was born as the latest of the line.

Liu Pei's father had died young, and he kept his mother by selling hempen sandals and making straw mats. He was a big, grave fellow with long ears, fine features, and lips as red as rouge. Believing him to be a man of destiny, older members of his clan later helped him to make a living and encouraged him to study, but as soon as times became easier he idled over his books and preferred to spend his hours with dogs and horses, wearing handsome clothes and making new friends. That image of him is only a deceptive half-truth,

* Cho County, modern Hopei Province.

however, for he was not only a warm and generous person, but a humble one. If he did not care for learning, he did not care for wealth either. He was a man of moral conviction who had suffered with the poor and understood their needs and longings.

And that is another half-truth, yet the whole truth is still not there. Liu Pei nursed a dream. He had taken an oath of brotherhood in a peach garden with two boon companions.[1] They had sworn to save the empire and restore peace. And to this improbable end he cultivated without undue difficulty sympathetic scholars and landlords and rich merchants, two of whom provided the money, the weapons, and the horses that were to enable him to keep his appointment with fate. For the man sewn up in the suit of jade had been of royal blood. In Chinese eyes, Liu Pei was an uncle of the Han emperor now languishing in the unscrupulous hands of Ts'ao Ts'ao.

With five hundred men behind him, Liu Pei set out to rid his own region of the terror of the Yellow Turbans and earn himself a reputation for military prowess that would attract others to him. He succeeded. For although he had nothing of the cunning and ability of Ts'ao Ts'ao, his energy and his pity for the people and his constant care for his followers won him love and trust wherever he went. He could touch the common humanity and decency in men, because he never betrayed the moral qualities which he believed should be those of a prince.

Even when his enemies pursued him, thousands of ordinary people would flee with his army at the risk of their lives, and on one day of ignominious defeat his officers begged him to shed this encumbering mob so that they could make their escape quickly. But they were wasting their breath, for although his consideration for these useless supernumeraries exasperated more practical soldiers, his strong point was that he remained true to it. "All great matters are founded on men," he said. "If the masses follow me today, how can I lightly discard them?" Mao was to take the same view.

If Liu Pei appears to have been an enthusiastic amateur,

Ts'ao Ts'ao was a cold-blooded professional, and where Liu Pei dealt in compassion, Ts'ao Ts'ao dealt in competence. "Even if they bear shameful reputations," he once ordered, "even if they are mean and despicable in their conduct, or inhuman and unfilial, men who know the art of ruling the state or of commanding troops must all be employed and promoted by local authorities."

It was one of Ts'ao Ts'ao's qualities that although he was treacherous and cruel and suspicious as his destiny demanded, he would rarely listen to those who blackened the names of the able. A clever commander, like a mettlesome charger, was by nature not easy to tame, he said, and only a talented man who could handle other talented men could survive in times of ferment. Moreover, promotion of the accomplished, however deplorable their habits, opened the ranks of service to all and removed the threat posed by privileged families for whom preferment was a right and whose power was therefore cumulative.

Ts'ao Ts'ao would certainly have employed the scheming deserter from Ch'u who had been the master spy of Han Kaotsu, for he could coolly turn a blind eye even to disloyalty in his own ranks if the situation so demanded. After he had overrun the positions of Yuan Shao in a major battle, his advisers discovered documents proving that some of his own generals and high officials had been in secret communication with the enemy, and urged him to have them all arrested and killed. But he ordered that the documents be burned, and did not inquire further into the matter. No cold rage or hot lust for vengeance could obscure that fact that of those who had contemplated treachery, the generals were fighting at his side and the high officials were back in his own base. The consequences of opening an immediate investigation, and then slaughtering all the guilty while Yuan Shao was still in the field with several hundred thousand troops, were unthinkable. Retribution could wait.

In similar circumstances Han Kao-tsu had ennobled a general who had plotted rebellion against him, so that he himself would then have no cause to fear assassination by brother officers who might otherwise have been tempted to eliminate him before he could eliminate them. With the advent of peace, all Chinese leaders faced a new hazard, for their commanders well knew that when war ended they were expendable, that "generals who defeat the adversary are nothing more than meritorious dogs," as Han Kao-tsu had once said. And dogs can have their day in more senses than one—unless they move fast and first.

A disarming "liberality in great measure," therefore, is the best defensive weapon of the ruler who must play for time, say the Chinese. After the Great Cultural Revolution, cadres humiliated and dismissed from their posts by left-wing "rebels" urged on by Mao Tsetung were restored to office—including Vice-Premier Teng Hsiao-p'ing, who by 1974 was being photographed sitting at the right hand of the Chairman himself. Whether the Chairman was feeling that destiny had been fulfilled—or the moment for the next twist of the wheel had not yet arrived—is another matter. But the tradition of caution that tells Chinese to fight only when they can win also tells them to destroy only when they can do so without loss.

Conversely, Ts'ao Ts'ao would kill a loyal lieutenant in order to forward his affairs with no more concern than if he were killing a fly—and at the same time demonstrate his regard for the man. While laying siege to a city in the Central Plain and waiting for supplies of grain to arrive, he was compelled to order his chief of commissariat to reduce rations, as food was running short. Soon informers reported that the troops were grumbling and accusing him of deceiving them. So he summoned the chief of commissariat and said, "I want to ask you to lend me something, and you must not refuse."

"What do you wish?"

"I want the loan of your head to expose to the troops."

"But I've done nothing wrong!"

"I know, but if I do not put you to death, there will be a mutiny. After you are gone, your family shall be my care, so do not grieve." The man was beheaded, and the soldiers accepted the obvious scapegoat.

Not long afterward the army was on the march again, and in order to encourage the peasants to harvest their wheat, Ts'ao Ts'ao ruled that anyone trampling the crop would be put to death. The soldiers were then scrupulously careful, but his own horse shied into the standing corn one day, flattening a big patch of it. Ts'ao Ts'ao at once called upon his provost marshal to punish him for the crime, but the general objected that he could not decapitate him, because the army needed the services of its supreme commander. Moreover, the Classics exempted the most honorable from the rigors of the law. Ts'ao Ts'ao thereupon seized his sword, cut off his own hair "as an attack on the head," and ordered a subordinate to display it to all units.

The gesture was typical of the man in more than one way. In his commentary on Sun Tzu he estimated that if one hundred thousand conscripts were called up for military service, the farm work of seven times as many families was affected. He was no mere glory hunter, but an efficient soldier and imperial administrator keenly aware that food and a firm social fabric could be winning weapons. Within the regions of China that he controlled he built a school for every community of five hundred families, and to make life secure for the peasants, he either kept the more pugnacious barbarians firmly on the far side of the frontier or employed them to fight in his own armies.

He constantly appealed to the country people not to neglect their work in the fields, whatever was happening around them; he redistributed the land, and he detailed troops to help with the sowing and harvesting. Farmers could borrow oxen for plowing from the local government and still keep forty percent of their crop for themselves, while those who already owned oxen could keep half of it, the other half going to the state. The peasants, who had been fleeing hopelessly from one place to another as war ebbed and flowed, gradually settled down to the soil again, deserted and ruined villages were restored, and Ts'ao Ts'ao accumulated a great hoard of grain while repeatedly attacking the food supply of the enemy of the moment. It was to be the secret of his success—after he was dead.

Nevertheless, Ts'ao Ts'ao was to be labeled a "treacherous hero" and Liu Pei the "benevolent master," and although the benevolent master knew that he did not have the qualities of the treacherous hero, he also knew where his power lay. For a time the fortunes of war threw them together, but once they were irrevocably drawn against each other, Liu Pei laid down his policy in simple terms. "Today Ts'ao Ts'ao and I are as irreconcilable as fire and water," he said. "Ts'ao Ts'ao deals with men hastily, violently, and deceitfully, while I am lenient and humane and loyal. To be successful I must be the opposite of Ts'ao Ts'ao in everything I do, and I shall certainly not sacrifice the faith the people have in me for the sake of petty gain." "What the enemy opposes," Mao was to pronounce intransigently, "we support. What the enemy supports, we oppose."

Mao embodied in himself something of both men, hero and villain. Immediately after the Wuchang Uprising against the Manchus in 1911 he rushed to join the rebels, and his capacity for passion and naïve heroism, his massive countenance and frame, his vigorous speech, and his determination to conquer the world with his bare hands had in them something of Liu Pei. Behind these warm and attractive characteristics lay a brain of ice, however, and had he not possessed Ts'ao Ts'ao's aptitude for ruthless intrigue he would never have risen above his opponents. But if for Mao the issues and allegiances were not always clear-cut, in the turbulent closing years of the Han Dynasty and the heyday of Liu Pei and Ts'ao Ts'ao loyalty and treachery became inextricably confused.

The two antagonists—the *yin* and *yang* of Mao in terms of man's basic, unchanging characteristics—first encountered each other in the year 194 when Liu Pei, who was still a minor condottiere protecting no more than a single county, successfully beat back an assault by troops of Ts'ao Ts'ao on the walls of the regional capital of Hsu Chou.[2] But Liu Pei's small force was no match for the main army of the "imperial minister," and he was soon compelled to submit to him. Ts'ao Ts'ao rejected all advice to take the sensible precaution of killing this "cockerel" to prevent him from making a nuisance of himself in the future, and characteristically raised him to the rank of a subordinate general.

However, the emperor secretly issued an edict commanding Liu Pei to kill Ts'ao Ts'ao and so restore full authority to the Han Dynasty. Liu Pei therefore rebelled against the imperial minister, and from that moment there were two challengers for China, both of whom could claim legitimacy—for while one was the custodian of the emperor's person, the other was the guardian of his will.

They were nonetheless absurdly ill matched. At first Liu Pei joined Yuan Shao against Ts'ao Ts'ao, but when Yuan Shao was vanquished he was forced to withdraw into North Ching Chou. The local governor welcomed him as a protector, but was not interested in mounting provocative military adventures, and since the frustrated Liu Pei lacked money, men, horses, and food and could not levy a large army on the spot, he was obliged to settle down in the regional capital and kick his heels.

It was not until 207, nearly eight years later, that he seems to have woken up to the fact that he was leading an unhealthy, sedentary existence, had gained a paunch but lost his military momentum, and had done nothing to honor the command of his nephew the emperor that he overthrow his redoubtable adversary. He was forty-seven years old and a failure, and it was time to stir. He began to recruit again, to seek out men of ability to be his lieutenants, and it was then that he first heard of the "Sleeping Dragon."

The Sleeping Dragon was a recluse venerated by the people of Ching, and Liu Pei did not summon him to his own headquarters, but humbly presented himself at his thatched hut three times before he was able to meet the elusive mystic and ask for his advice. Not that Chuko Liang, whose name was to ring across the centuries like a great bell, cut a particularly terrifying figure. He was tall, thin, and only twenty-six

THE THREE KINGDOMS
A.D. 220 – 265

years old, a solemn northerner from Shantung with a craggy face and a dry complexion, who walked with a measured stride, dressed simply, and despised frivolity. He had been raised by an uncle on a secluded farm at the foot of a mountain, but the uncle had been murdered by wandering soldiers, and thereafter he had tilled the land himself and spent his leisure hours in study, somehow earning a reputation as a political thinker although he had no experience of affairs of state or any other obvious qualifications.

This was the unlikely fellow to whom Liu Pei explained his problem. The house of Han was in ruins. The emperor had lost his throne and become the puppet of a ruthless and powerful general. Despite all his dreams, he himself had achieved little. What should he do?

Chuko Liang was young and spirited, keen to create, touched by the appeal, and drawn to the distressed general whose honorable aims and responsibilities he would gladly share. But he was, as always, coldly analytical.

"Ts'ao Ts'ao has an army of a million men. Therefore you cannot for the moment challenge him militarily. The Han emperor is in his hands. Therefore you cannot for the moment challenge him politically," he began (and what followed calls for a glance at the map).

There was nonetheless no cause for despair, the Sleeping Dragon went on. Liu Pei was the military commander of Ching Chou. North Ching was easy to defend, South Ching was being opened up, the resources of the region were inexhaustible, and it was the key to the great granary of Shu to the west. "Ching Chou is an ideal base," said Chuko Liang, "the political capital that Heaven has bestowed on you."

The terrain of Shu was very difficult, it was a natural bastion, yet the land was wonderfully fertile. At the same time the region was politically weak. It had been threatened several times from the north, and further shaken by an internal crisis that could lead to the overthrow of its present lord. In such circumstances, the valiant and the good men in Shu would certainly be willing to rally to Liu Pei, for he was a descendant of the imperial house and known for his humanity and loyalty.

"Now if you can possess yourself of the two *chou* of Ching and Shu," concluded the Sleeping Dragon, "and if you can pacify the barbarian tribes and act with political wisdom in these territories, the day will come when the situation will change, when you can order a trusted commander to lead your army in Ching against Nanyang and Loyang, while you yourself lead your army in Shu against Hanchung. The people will rise to welcome you. Thus the house of Han may be restored."

To hear his lucid appreciation, Liu Pei remarked later, was to be "like a fish in the mud getting water." But the sternest advice of Chuko Liang concerned the vast domain to the east of Ching Chou whose masters were the powerful Sun clan. "Sun Ch'uan dominates all the lower reaches of the Yangtse, as his family has done for three generations," he said. "His defenses are solid, and he has many talented and loyal subordinates. You must win the Sun over, so that they give you outside support. On no account should you make them an object of attack."

Liu Pei had just been dealt his hand in a three-cornered game of cutthroat which was to last for seventy years.

17

Chinese Cutthroat

These Suns of Wu, who held sway over the great belly of southeast China, were the redoubtable descendants of none other than Sun Tzu, the author of *The Art of War.* The father had distinguished himself in battle against the Yellow Turbans, but the elder brother had proved even more capable, and when he served under Yuan Shao in the long campaigns against Ts'ao Ts'ao, he expanded his hold on the lower Yangtse so fast that by the time the imperial minister had eliminated Yuan Shao and could turn his main weight against him, it was too late. He was already a fully fledged eagle in his own aerie, and there was no economical way of dislodging him, except assassination.

He therefore died suddenly at the early age of twenty-six, after bequeathing his heritage to his younger brother, Sun Ch'uan, and counseling him to employ as his right-hand man a nimble-minded and loyal tactician known as Chou Yu—"Lustrous Jade"—who was also related to the clan. Throughout history writers have extolled the bearing and beauty of this general, his elegance, his learning and intelligence, and his indomitable spirit. And with Lustrous Jade as their adviser, the powerful Sun family in the east were to defend the third corner in a triangular struggle with Ts'ao Ts'ao in the north and Liu Pei in the west.

It was a struggle in which no holds, blows, kicks, or falls were barred. "Do what your enemy would be ashamed to do," Shan Yang had recommended, and the contenders for empire used weapons, water, fire, and the assassin with total ruthlessness to gain their ends, murdering men simply as a precaution, luring armies on to annihilation with tempting displays of unguarded plunder, and offering to defend neutral cities against a notional enemy in order to be able to pass through the gates and seize them from within themselves.

But their bloody massacres were interspersed with much bloodless sparring, for the Chinese general was taught to run in the morning so that he might stay alive to ambush in the evening, and two opposing armies meeting face to face might both retire if neither commander felt he had the edge over the other. Lose now, win later, was the slogan of the times, and only the foolish wasted men to save face. "Swallow the teeth and the blood," the wise said. Do not risk all to redress a brutal blow in the face today when the stake is an empire tomorrow: "if small things are not suffered, great matters are imperiled."

By the same token, it was also a struggle in which few loyalties were fixed, for the same flexibility dictated that at a time when the imperial claim to fealty had been palmed by the fraudulent Ts'ao Ts'ao, even champions could change chiefs if the exigencies of the moment called for them to move sideways instead of forward. Liu Pei once served Ts'ao Ts'ao, and after he had crossed the lines in order to fight for Yuan Shao, one of his two "brothers" who had sworn the solemn oath in the peach garden with him still remained with the enemy.

Why? Because Ts'ao Ts'ao had captured the man, treated him well, and made him a marquis. He was honor-bound to repay the debt. He did so by cutting off the heads of two of Yuan Shao's generals in battle, after which he felt free to desert Ts'ao Ts'ao and rejoin Liu Pei on the other side. In this manner he was able to appear neither ungrateful to his generous enemy, nor disloyal to his frugal friend, according to the arithmetic of the Chinese moral abacus.

Throughout history the Chinese have displayed the greatest reverence for *chung*—loyalty—but also the greatest reverence for the double standards of appearance and reality by which they have lived. Blood brothers would swear not to harm each other, yet fight to the death on the battlefield if they found themselves in opposite camps, for their fealty to their current leader was overriding, even if they planned to assassinate him once honor was satisfied and they need no longer be loyal to him. Allegiance was no light matter. It must be accurately defined and carefully measured, and leniency shown to those who remained steadfastly true to the foe. One general rewarded the wife of an enemy commander because she cut off her nose when her husband perished, and another ordered an honorable burial for the wife of a cowardly adversary because she had hanged herself when her husband had surrendered the city to him.

Traitors were not always welcomed as friends, but often treated as mere "tools of ill omen," and a commander might execute a turncoat just to please the opposing general the man had betrayed, and so soften him up. The wise have always been ready to sacrifice a pawn to gain a knight, or a scapegoat to win a compromise. The heads of Chairman Mao's foes rolled during the Cultural Revolution, but so did the heads of some of his henchmen. Their fall from grace often sealed a bargain between the extremist and moderate factions within the Chinese Communist Party which was satisfactory to both sides, and among them was Ch'en Po-ta, Mao's personal secretary and a high-ranking member of the Politburo in Peking.

Inspired by Sun Tzu, the Chinese brought a matchless subtlety to the use and counter-use of the disloyal and deceitful, and Chuko Liang (who had willingly agreed to become the principal counselor of Liu Pei) was a master of the art, as the episode of a deserter named Cheng proved.

When this Cheng came over from the enemy, he explained that he had been most unjustly passed over for advancement to the rank of senior general in favor of his closest friend and "thrown out like a weed," and that he therefore wanted to join the ranks of Liu Pei. But while he was speaking, news arrived that the officer who had been promoted in his place was outside the camp bawling that Cheng was a traitor and a horse thief who had stolen his mount when he deserted, and demanding that he come out and fight him.

"If you go out and kill him," said the Sleeping Dragon, "that would remove my doubts about you." So Cheng left the tent, engaged his challenger, and cut him down in the first encounter, whereupon Chuko Liang at once shouted, "Decapitate this man! That was not the general who was given the post you coveted. How dare you deceive me?"

Cheng confessed that his challenger had been another man altogether, and when Chuko Liang accused him of being a false deserter sent by the enemy commander to practice some ruse, he admitted it. "How did I know?" echoed the Sleeping Dragon, when asked later. "If the other had really been made a senior general he would certainly not have been so lacking in skill as to be overcome by this fellow Cheng in the first bout."

The Sleeping Dragon then said that he would countermand his order of execution if the spy would write to his commander, telling him that Chuko Liang had accepted his story and that he should lead an attack against the camp on the following night. Cheng would show a light as a signal, and cause confusion within to synchronize with the onslaught. "I will spare you on condition that you compose this letter," declared Chuko Liang, "and I shall give you all the credit and repay you handsomely."

The letter was dispatched by hand of a persuasive officer who pretended to be a malcontent stranded in Liu Pei's territory, and who misleadingly confided to the enemy general that Chuko Liang had already rewarded Cheng for coming over to him by giving him command of the van. After some hesitation, the general swallowed the bait and mounted the assault, and his whole army, ambushed from four sides, suffered a grievous defeat. "The victory was complete," concluded the account, "and the first order that Chuko Liang issued on returning to camp was that Cheng should be put to death."

The Sleeping Dragon was not to be beguiled by the paltry

promises of a man who offered to kill his closest friend to prove his loyalty to his new commander, for the *Spring and Autumn Annals* narrated the story of an officer who had cut off his own arm as a pledge that he would assassinate an enemy, yet had done nothing of the sort. Besides, Lustrous Jade had employed a similar device to gain a victory that had already given a sudden new twist to the macaronic conflict for the mastery of China—a victory that was to deny Ts'ao Ts'ao the hegemony and split the empire into three realms.

Such a development would still have seemed inconceivable in 208. Ts'ao Ts'ao had eliminated Yuan Shao and pacified the north. His armies were rolling down on Ching Chou, whose governor had hastily offered his submission. Liu Pei had been compelled to withdraw to the south bank of the Yangtse, and the Sun family had been peremptorily warned to offer no challenge to the oncoming troops of the imperial minister.

The reaction of the Suns, however, was to send an envoy to Liu Pei to propose that between them they open up a corridor along the Yangtse and hold as much of Ching Chou as they could. The Suns were solely bent on enhancing the security of their domain of Wu, while Chuko Liang had plans of his own, but since these included a decisive confrontation between north and south, the parties had no difficulty in coming to an agreement to join forces.

Meanwhile Ts'ao Ts'ao had acquired a river fleet of several thousand vessels from the governor of Ching Chou, and had begun moving his mighty army of 800,000 men eastward along the Yangtse. Now as Liu Pei's positions constituted the first obstacle to his advance downriver, the Sleeping Dragon asked Sun Ch'uan for help. This split the Sun camp into fiercely wrangling factions, the peace party arguing that Ts'ao Ts'ao was irresistible, that his expedition had been launched in the name of the emperor and must not be defied, and that it was ridiculous to enter into an alliance with Liu Pei, for the man could not even defend himself.

The chief commander, Lustrous Jade, was at first among those who were all for submission, but the Sleeping Dragon taunted him by suggesting obliquely that he could best save his skin by yielding his wife to Ts'ao Ts'ao, who had conceived an inordinate lust for her, whereupon the affronted general swung around like some "persuader" of old who could present both sides of a case equally convincingly, and begged Sun Ch'uan to protect his hard-won inheritance and drive off the concupiscent bandit.

Ts'ao Ts'ao was in no position to attack anyway, he argued coolly. His army consisted of northerners who knew nothing of river warfare, and of local troops from Ching Chou who had no feeling of loyalty toward him. The weather was bitterly cold, the men were exhausted after their long march south and in no fit state to fight. Furthermore, his supply lines were overstretched, there were rebels loose in the north who were only waiting for a chance to move against him, and he could not risk committing the bulk of his forces to a long campaign on the Yangtse. Liu Pei still had ten thousand men, and if they pooled their resources, they could win.

Sun Ch'uan, unwilling from the first to surrender without a struggle, found in favor of Lustrous Jade. Driven on by the habitual mania for heroics of the Sun family, he drew his sword, struck off a corner of the table in front of him, and announced, "If any officer dares to mention capitulation, I shall treat him as I have treated this table."

At Ch'ih-pi * on the Yangtse, the van of Ts'ao Ts'ao's army met Lustrous Jade at the head of a combined force of 40,000 men—and was defeated on contact. For the river was a mile wide at this point, the waves rose and fell steeply and ceaselessly, and the troops from the north were so sick that they were for the most part unable to give battle.

With an initial success under his belt, Lustrous Jade withdrew to his camp, rewarded his men, and in the evening climbed a hill to observe the enemy. The fires and lights of Ts'ao Ts'ao's main army seemed to fill the west, so that it was almost as bright as day, and he realized that he would be hard put to it to fight for long with his few troops against this

* Near modern Hankow (Wuhan).

multitude. Victory must be snatched in one quick, decisive battle.

The plan for that battle first began to take vague shape when Ts'ao Ts'ao started to infiltrate spies into the Sun lines as ostensible deserters. Although Lustrous Jade saw through these frauds, he said nothing, allowing them to lull themselves into a comfortable state of false security. But when he discovered that to stop his men from spending so much of their time vomiting, Ts'ao Ts'ao had arranged for the boats in his massive floating camp at Ch'ih-pi to be bound together with iron hoops into stable groups of thirty and even fifty vessels, he decided to put the intruders to good use.

First he called a meeting of his generals and ordered them to ferry their units to the north bank of the Yangtse with three months' rations. At this, one commander, having been suitably rehearsed, protested vigorously, insisting that if they fought against Ts'ao Ts'ao they must surely be defeated and proposing that they surrender at once to save their lives. Lustrous Jade angrily accused the coward of striking at the morale of the army and bellowed out a command that he should be decapitated at once. Other officers begged him to relent, but by the time he had reluctantly agreed to do so, the man had been beaten unmercifully until he bled and had fainted several times. Ts'ao Ts'ao's spies reported what had happened to their master, and on his orders secretly approached the disgruntled general, who agreed to desert upriver, bringing with him a squadron of ships filled with military supplies. He would fly a green dragon flag on the leading vessel as a signal.

In the dead of night, when the wind was just rising in the southeast, ten large craft were quietly maneuvered into the middle of the river, where they hoisted all sail and sped under a steady breeze toward Ts'ao Ts'ao's water camp. The vessels were loaded with kindling and reeds soaked in oil and concealed under canvas covers, and each towed a small cutter astern in which the sailors manning these fire hazards would make off and save their lives if they could. When

Ts'ao Ts'ao saw them coming, he was still uneasy about the well-lacerated traitor who was bringing them, and as he watched he noticed that instead of being low in the water as they would have been had they been heavy-laden with rations and supplies, they were riding high and moving lightly and fast.

Suddenly he was convinced it was a trick, that the enemy was going to use the southeasterly wind to launch an attack with fire ships. He at once dispatched ten of his own vessels to meet the advancing squadron in mid-river and make sure that it anchored well away from his army. But he was too late. The squadron veered abruptly toward the shore, the boats were set alight, and as sharp rams fixed to their prows struck into the nearest of Ts'ao Ts'ao's transports so that they could not be dislodged, the fires roared skyward in the wind and flickered across his inflammable floating camp in long tongues and fingers of flame.

The combined legions of Sun Ch'uan and Liu Pei then attacked from the land and took terrible toll of tired troops wedged between the charging enemy coming out of the night in front of them, the holocaust behind them, and the dark, turbulent waters of the Yangtse beyond. Men and horses were burned to death, slaughtered, or drowned, the grand army was smashed, and Ts'ao Ts'ao was sobered and stripped of his former ebullient confidence.

His driving ambition and the callous, violent haste that it provoked in him had betrayed him. In his impatience he had pushed his men too far. They had fought a wearisome war against Yuan Shao and his brothers for fifteen long years, only to be reorganized to overrun Ching Chou immediately the last campaign was over, and from Ching Chou to be pitched, exhausted, into their rout at Ch'ih-pi—a battle fought in the dark under strange, incapacitating conditions against an enemy who held the initiative and all the surprises in his own hands.

The cruelty of Ts'ao Ts'ao was a byword. "Cities that are surrounded and do not surrender at once shall be put to the sword without mercy," he decreed. And they were, down to the last dog and chicken. Discipline in the army was savage. Officers and men who failed to obey orders were immediately beheaded, and if a soldier deserted, his whole family, male and female, would be killed.

This was not unusual, however. When Chuko Liang saved a city by pretending it was open and empty and therefore an enticing trap, he threatened to punish with instant death any of his concealed soldiers who made a sound. He beheaded a young general whose negligence had been responsible for a defeat (while promising that his bereaved family would be given a monthly allowance after his execution). Another senior general was summarily decapitated when a hole in a bridge that he had passed as safe to advance over nearly brought down the horse of his commander in chief. Death for disobeying an order was the rule, not the exception, and any beaten general might well be made to pay for his failure with his life. Ambassadors were not sacrosanct: "Messengers are slain to emphasize one's own dignity and independence," as Lustrous Jade once put it disdainfully when dispatching an envoy sent by Ts'ao Ts'ao.

None of these men was a merciless blockhead, all were leaders of commendable duplicity and guile. But the guile of only one of them was infinite, and if the Sleeping Dragon was to reduce Ts'ao Ts'ao to fury, he was also to reduce Lustrous Jade to crying on his deathbed, "Since Heaven gave birth to Lustrous Jade, why did it have to give birth also to Chuko Liang?" For Chuko Liang was a military miser in the best Chinese tradition, a something-for-nothing strategist par excellence who would leave others to play snipe and mussel and himself play the waiting fisherman who caught both locked in each other's grip.

He had goaded and cajoled Lustrous Jade into fighting Ts'ao Ts'ao and shaping the complex battle for Ch'ih-pi, generously yielding to him all the honors of the victory—while conserving most of his own troops and energies on behalf of Liu Pei. But getting someone else to break the armies of the emperor's minister was one thing. Gaining dominion over Ching and Shu as bases for the conquest of all China was another. There were therefore more chestnuts for Lustrous Jade to pull out of the fire.

18

Third-Party Risk

The key that would open the first lock to the empire was the city of Nanchun. It had been the imperial capital of Ch'u during the Warring States era, and fought over for century after century, for it dominated a strategic pass on the Yangtse River, it was the gateway to Shu in the west and to the main cities of Ching to the north. Once Ts'ao Ts'ao was pushed onto the defensive, the immediate object of Lustrous Jade was to take this prize away from him, and he was much put out to find that Liu Pei had also moved troops into the surrounding country. Smoothly assured, however, that they were only there to help him if the need arose, he swore on the spur of the moment that if he could not seize the town himself, they were welcome to it. It was a cheap promise because, as he told a confidant afterward, "I can take it with a flick of my finger anyway."

He then closed in on the city and quickly routed the defending army of Ts'ao Ts'ao that came out to do battle with him. But instead of drawing back through the gates after this reverse, the discomfited enemy fled in disorder, leaving banners flying on the walls but no man in sight. Lustrous Jade therefore abandoned all pursuit and thrust his way into Nanchun itself, only to run into a large-scale ambush, and as the crossbow bolts rained down he took one in the side.

By way of revenge, he now pretended that he had died of the wound, sent glib "deserters" to carry the sad news to the enemy, and so tempted Ts'ao Ts'ao's commanders to attack his demoralized and mourning army. The defenders of Nanchun accordingly sallied out in strength to launch a night assault on his encampment, only to be ambushed in their turn, thrown into disarray, and scattered.

But when the triumphant Lustrous Jade made for the exposed city, he was startled to see fresh flags on the walls, and to find that while his own troops had been battling fiercely with its powerful garrison outside, one of Liu Pei's junior generals had taken Nanchun with no more than "a flick of the finger." Cheated of his objective, the wrathful general at once stormed the ramparts, only to be met with a convincingly sharp shower of arrows that persuaded him to retire and take counsel.

He was still taking counsel when the news arrived that Chuko Liang, using a military seal of Ts'ao Ts'ao captured in the much-contested city, had forged orders which had induced the subordinate enemy garrisons holding the other vital centers of Hsiangyang and Nanyang in North Ching Chou to move out and hasten hotfoot to the relief of their comrades-in-arms at Nanchun. Liu Pei's commanders, waiting in the wings, had then occupied these defenseless towns without undue trouble.

With one masterstroke the Sleeping Dragon had gained at no cost three cities that gave him control of Ching Chou and access to Shu, having left Lustrous Jade to do all the fighting while he took all the fruits. Ts'ao Ts'ao had been cut to size. Liu Pei had his military base. From that moment on, China was effectively divided into three rival states—Wei in the north under Ts'ao Ts'ao, Wu in the east under Sun Ch'uan, and Shu-Han in the west under Liu Pei.

By now Lustrous Jade was raging to get at the throat of his tormentor, but cooler counselors quickly pointed out that if pressed too hard, Liu Pei might return the three cities to Ts'ao Ts'ao and join him against Wu. Meanwhile, for similar reasons, Liu Pei soothed the ruffled Sun Ch'uan by emphasizing that his need of the towns was only temporary, and promising that he would later cede them to him.

Furthermore, when the frustrated Lustrous Jade died at the early age of thirty-six, having failed to best the Sleeping Dragon, Chuko Liang offered sacrifices before his coffin, and spoke with great emotion of the dead hero and his victories. Mourning profoundly, falling into a deep melancholy in the sight of the assembled notables of Wu, he had them making excuses for all that he had done to them before the obsequies of the man he had so impishly used for his own ends were decently over.

In most circumstances, the Sleeping Dragon was the last man to make an ally out of a weak state if it meant arousing the fury of a strong one, but that principle could not apply when Ts'ao Ts'ao had from the outset been the declared, implacable foe. His aims now were to keep the friendship of the lesser rival in order to defeat the greater, to use Wu to counterbalance Wei, and to dissuade both from either uniting against him or fighting each other prematurely, for if the weaker was then eliminated the stronger could turn on Shu.

If Sun Ch'uan was anxious not to push Liu Pei into the arms of Ts'ao Ts'ao by threatening him with war over the cities Chuko Liang had filched in Ching Chou, Chuko Liang was equally anxious not to push Sun Ch'uan into the arms of the enemy by arousing his ire unnecessarily. For when any two of the parties joined forces, the third was bound to be thrashed.

But not all had the perspicacity of the Sleeping Dragon, who was no soldier but a cryptic strategist, a mystic who went into action in a small carriage, wearing a cloth turban and a cotton gown and languidly waving a white feather fan. Ironically, his calculations were to be upset by the warrior of warriors, the immaculate and magnificent general who had taken the solemn oath in the peach garden, and who had paid his debt of honor to his generous adversary Ts'ao Ts'ao yet proved his unwavering loyalty to his sworn brother Liu Pei—Kuan Yu.

Kuan Yu has been eulogized as the redoubtable "enemy of ten thousand" who once left a cup of warm wine in camp, mounted a charger and smashed his way into the grim northwestern army of Tung Cho single-handed, cut off the head of a senior general, and returned to fling it onto the ground in front of his own chief before the wine grew cold. He, was a giant of a man with a red face, the long, curling eyes of a phoenix, eyebrows like sleeping silkworms, a strange, handsome beard, the voice of a bronze bell, and the flourish of born authority.

Famed above all for his martial courage and resolution, his dexterous work with his "Green Dragon" halberd, he was not without cunning or perception. But while he saw clearly that Sun Ch'uan only cared about the defense of his own lands, sacrificed long-term loyalties for short-term gains, and was a dubious partner for Liu Pei, he failed to realize that for want of a better he was nonetheless indispensable to their plans.

In consequence he treated the Lord of Wu with contempt, and referred to him as "that fox"—a term Chinese still use to portray a base man paradoxically born to riches and power as a sharp-nosed creature in an opulent fur coat. And when Sun Ch'uan's son sent an envoy to ask for the hand of his daughter in marriage, Kuan Yu dismissed the fellow with the words "How can the daughter of a tiger marry the son of a dog?"

Sun Ch'uan was livid. The offer of marriage dovetailed with the Sleeping Dragon's declared desire to "resist Wei in the north and keep peace with Wu in the east." It was to have been the first move toward a new alliance, and it had been rebuffed with an intolerable insult that prompted "the Fox" to turn his head questingly away from his natural allies and toward Ts'ao Ts'ao. Kuan Yu was to pay for his arrogance.

By the year 220 Liu Pei's commanders had some excuse for arrogance, perhaps. Under the guidance of the Sleeping Dragon they had marched west into Shu and captured the strategic city of Hanchung in the north, and in the autumn of that year Kuan Yu inflicted a calamitous defeat on a vast army of Ts'ao Ts'ao's outside the key town of Fanch'eng in North Ching Chou. Taking advantage of the rainy season, he dammed the Han River and later released the floodwaters into the valley in which the adversary was unwisely camped.

The enemy commander was captured and decapitated, all but a fleeing remnant of his troops were drowned, and Kuan Yu then mustered river transports in order to lay siege to the city itself, the walls of which were already beginning to crumble under the insidious pressure of the surrounding water.

Other insidious pressures were at work, however. Ts'ao Ts'ao could not fail to note that Liu Pei's lieutenants had provoked much useful resentment among the Sun clan by finessing three cities in North Ching Chou for which their own armies had campaigned, by holding on to the region of South Ching Chou which Sun Ch'uan had only "lent" to Liu Pei as a base when he had nothing, and finally by insulting Sun Ch'uan himself. He therefore sent an ambassador to the Fox to persuade him to attack Kuan Yu in the rear while his own troops moved to the relief of the waterlogged city of Fanch'eng.

The Fox agreed, and plans were laid to seize the regional capital at Nanchun from its depleted garrison once Kuan Yu had concentrated the bulk of his army outside Fanch'eng. It was soon discovered, however, that the garrison in the capital was still strong, its defenses were in good order, and a string of beacon towers had been built along the riverbank to give warning of any attack. Kuan Yu had not underestimated Lu Meng, the resourceful Wu commander, and was not to be caught napping. What was to be done?

"Pretend inferiority and encourage his arrogance," the Fox's prestigious ancestor had written. An arrow carrying a message that help was at hand was shot into beleaguered Fanch'eng in order to stiffen the morale of the defending troops, so that Kuan Yu could not easily take the city. Meanwhile, Lu Meng feigned illness, and was replaced as army commander by an obscure young general of no particular repute, who sent an envoy with gifts of fine horses and beautiful silks to Kuan Yu and proposed that they form a new alliance.

When the messenger had gone, Kuan Yu shouted with laughter, dismissed the new commander as a "mere scholar," and since the man was obviously no match for him, he now gave orders that half of the troops left in Nanchun should march out and join the army already besieging Fanch'eng in a major assault on the walls. At this Ts'ao Ts'ao dispatched a column to keep Kuan Yu occupied outside Fanch'eng, while Lu Meng secretly assumed control of the operation to take the regional capital itself away from its pretentious protector in his absence.

The sly Wu commander packed his soldiers into the holds of big, shallow-draft transports and dressed the few sailors who would remain visible on deck as river traders. Moving slowly upstream, his vessels anchored inshore and close to the beacon towers, their inoffensive crews complaining of contrary winds when challenged. But once night had fallen, the troops emerged from their holds, captured the unsuspecting detachments guarding the signal fires, and made sure that none was lit and no alarm was given.

Lu Meng then won the prisoners over with suitable gifts and a show of clemency, and they were persuaded to accompany the main force to the capital and call on the watch to open the gates for them. The watch, recognizing their own comrades, did as they were bid, and Lu Meng's veterans stormed into Nanchun. The surprise was complete.

The Wu commander now demonstrated his sagacity by confirming all the officials in the city in their posts, setting a special guard to protect the family of Kuan Yu, and issuing orders that any man who plundered or killed should be executed. When a subordinate took a broad bamboo hat away from a peasant during a tour of the walls on a wet day in order to keep his armor dry, Lu Meng had him decapitated and his head exposed as an example to all, although they had been friends from the same village.

With the fall of the *chou* capital, two more cities dependent on it for supplies surrendered, and the relief force from Ts'ao Ts'ao raised the siege at Fanch'eng, obliging Kuan Yu to withdraw. The desperate general gathered his strength for a bid to retake Nanchun, but his men, having heard how humanely Lu Meng had treated their families, deserted him to slip into the city they had been commanded to assault, and his army dwindled away. Trapped in the nearby hills, he was caught like a wild beast in a net of ropes and hooks, and the Fox reluctantly ordered his execution after an adviser had reminded him of the eternal Chinese truism: "Destroy him now, or you will be sorry. Only evil will come of it if you spare him."

The masterly deception and tactical sense of mercy of Lu Meng had won the day, while the obdurate Kuan Yu had broken almost every rule in Sun Tzu's book. Yet it is Kuan Yu who is China's god of war, and his fierce red face and massive middle-aged figure—he was fifty-eight when he struck his last blow—that grace Chinese temples and the shrines of soldiers, policemen, and secret-society gangsters alike. For as much as they admire the fly, the Chinese love the fearless.

Kuan Yu had cost Liu Pei the mastery of Ching Chou, but he was still a sworn brother, and Liu Pei now made the worst mistake of all. Distraught with grief, he raised a great armada to punish the Fox of Wu, thrusting aside all reason and launching a classical "profitless war" in his determination to revenge the death of his friend. Chuko Liang might have been tempted to echo reproachfully, "Tear out my eyes and fix them on the gate." The policy of the Sleeping Dragon soon lay in ruins. The army of Shu was routed and slaughtered, the power of Liu Pei shattered, the alliance against Ts'ao Ts'ao turned into a feud, and it was left to Wei, as the sole winner, to set about taking all.

But not Ts'ao Ts'ao himself. He had fallen ill with a "malignant humor" in the brain. His physician offered to remove it after anesthetizing him with hashish, but was flung into jail for plotting his murder. The oversuspicious Ts'ao Ts'ao died, aged sixty-six—after ordering seventy-two different grave sites to be marked as his, so that none would know where his corpse lay and be able to dig it up.

Ts'ao Ts'ao had never usurped the throne. He had contented himself with the real power and the title of Prince of Wei. But his son Ts'ao P'ei displayed no such becoming modesty, and invented a simple and tasteful ceremony for the legitimate deposition of the rightful ruler. Stripped of frills, the process required that the court repeatedly petition Ts'ao P'ei to become the Son of Heaven and he repeatedly refuse until the Han emperor, seeing what was in the wind, personally offered in writing to abdicate in his favor and sent him the imperial seal. He rejected this offer three times, but accepted it on the fourth occasion, formally taking possession of the seal in a public ceremony at which he sacrificed to Heaven and received the celestial mandate for the new house he proposed to found.

In this fashion Ts'ao P'ei made himself first emperor of the Wei Dynasty in 220. He was in effect only King of Wei, however, and Liu Pei and Sun Ch'uan were not slow to follow his example and designate themselves "emperors" in Shu and Wu respectively. The three warring states that had existed independently since the defeat of Ts'ao Ts'ao at Ch'ih-pi were now three kingdoms that could not possibly find peace, since the first ruler in Wei claimed title to all China as reigning emperor of a new dynasty, the second ruler in Shu claimed title to all China as the champion of the deposed house of Han against this usurper ("Han and bandit cannot coexist"), and the third ruler in Wu had no claim at all but wanted neither of the others as overlord.

Just as the Warring States had been harried by the peoples on their fringes who took advantage of their disunity, so the rival contenders of the Three Kingdoms era were bedeviled by the importunities of outer barbarians. The Fox of Wu wasted an endless stream of men and cash on campaigns to cow those in the southeast, without noticeable success. Ts'ao Ts'ao, on the other hand, had solved the problem in the north very largely by recruiting these fierce aliens into his own armies, and then marching them well into the interior to fight in his own wars against his fellow Chinese.

Chuko Liang pursued a policy of "using barbarians to control barbarians," and pacified rebellious border tribes by first defeating them in battle and then restoring their chastened chiefs to their own domains, leaving their lands intact but demanding their allegiance to his king. As he pointed out, that relieved him of the trouble and expense of either garrisoning inaccessible frontier regions with Chinese troops or posting Chinese officials to them who would inevitably be at each other's throats when the natives were not at theirs. It also bought him useful allies among benighted hill peoples grateful for his clemency. His methods belong to the tradition whereby the Chinese do not attempt to occupy territory just for the sake of occupying it, no matter what the cost (which accounts in part for their readiness to withdraw their victorious troops from India in 1962), and it is accepted that he shored up the defenses of the kingdom with barbarians out of sheer necessity, for Shu was sadly lacking in manpower.

It was both rugged country and rich in grain, however, and while he lived and acted as its chief minister it enjoyed a certain prosperity behind an effective screen. For the Sleeping Dragon was a man of many talents and much inventiveness. He constructed multiple bows which could fire whole flights of arrows in quick succession, and he used the pulley and lever principles to build supply carts which the troops themselves could manhandle with ease over rough mountainous terrain without needing oxen or horses. He had a genius for converting all natural phenomena from mist to fire into weapons of war, and is famous for his battle formations.

The Chinese were always adept at marshaling their armies to good effect in the field and picking out the weakness in the pattern of the enemy. Their "fish couple" was led by a wall of chariots with a file of soldiers strung out behind each car, so that there always seemed to be another man to take the place of the one who had fallen. The "goose" was a flying wedge, the "three-covered" a treble ambush, and there were the "fives," the "three gates," the "six flowers"—three hundred and sixty-five dispositions in all, of which Chuko Liang's "eight trigrams" was the most renowned.

This involved eight standards representing Heaven, Earth, Wind, Cloud, Dragon, Tiger, Bird, and Snake, and the deployment of small fast-moving units with special roles within the more conventional framework of the larger formations, giving the whole an infinitely fluid quality. Responding to any penetration by the enemy, the troops would disperse and converge, turn and retreat, only to let others advance in their place, the van becoming the rear guard, the rear guard the van, in a series of complex evolutions, so that what appeared to be headlong flight might mask a sudden concentration of overwhelming force.

Chuko Liang never lost his touch, and he even selected his own successor from among the hostile generals of Wei by tricking the enemy into believing the man a traitor, so that he was obliged to rally to the Sleeping Dragon. But in Ssu-ma Yi, who for long commanded the armies of Wei in their bid to overthrow Shu, he had a worthy opponent.

After suffering a stinging reverse and finding himself at a dangerous disadvantage, this subtle general warned his subordinates that if any of them allowed themselves to be drawn into making an imprudent and premature attack on the Shu army, he would be executed. Chuko Liang therefore tried to goad him into seeking battle by accusing him of being a coward, and underlined the insult by sending him as a "suitable gift" a woman's dress (not, this time, a pot of urine labeled "wine"). The provocation put Ssu-ma Yi in a quandary, as Chuko Liang knew it would. He could not at that moment make a sortie without risking another defeat and he was prepared to swallow the affront, but his outraged officers somewhat obstreperously demanded the right to redress the dishonor.

His solution was to memorialize the distant King of Wei, warning him that he would one day have to do battle to wipe out this shame. The royal advisers of Wei at once realized that he really did not want to engage the enemy, and an edict forbidding him to do so was duly dispatched so that he could display it to his troops.

Chuko Liang knew how the advisers knew that Ssu-ma Yi was inviting a royal veto. "He never had any intention of fighting," he remarked wryly when he heard the news. "For as is well known, a general in the field does not have to accept the command of his ruler anyway." He had not been obliged to consult his king. He had played for time, saved face, placated his men, and no taunt could now tempt him into the open.

Sun Tzu's advice on the use of "death ground," which compels men to fight to the bitter end, also inspired two ferocious actions during the campaign of Wei against Shu—one when a powerful force defending Shu was deliberately deployed with a river behind it, and another when a Wei general had his army lowered over a precipice so that his troops could then only go forward. In each case, the unhappy adversary had no way of observing the principle that he should "always leave the enemy a way out"—and paid accordingly.

The Romance of the Three Kingdoms is coated fiction that never conceals the bitter core of history. Ts'ao Ts'ao died a sick sexagenarian in his bed, Kuan Yu and Liu Pei muffed an empire between them, and the day came when Chuko Liang and his humane but only too human master expired without having defeated Wei. The Wei commanders nevertheless remained wary of the possibility of a conspiracy between the other two kingdoms, and when planning what was to prove a decisive campaign against Shu, the last of these generals gave it out that he was going to invade Wu and gathered a great fleet on the Yangtse to lend the lie body. "For if Shu hears we are going to attack, they will ask help from Wu. But if I pretend I am going to attack Wu, its leaders will not dare to divert forces to Shu for at least a year. Then when Shu is beaten, the ships will be ready for an expedition against Wu."

Both the ruse and the campaign were successful, and in 263 Shu surrendered. The ruling descendant of Liu Pei went out of the north gate of his capital with his courtiers and his coffin to kneel in submission to Chung Hui, one of the two commanding generals of Wei who arrived to take over the city. But the general raised him up and had the coffin burned (his colleague had also advanced through Shu with a white flag inscribed with four characters reading, "Secure the state, comfort the people").

The "Conqueror of the West," as he was to be styled, then memorialized his own monarch, suggesting that it might be possible to occupy Wu "without fighting at all," for an envoy could be sent in advance to point out how isolated and vulnerable the domain of the Sun family now was. With this in view, it would be well to treat the King of Shu generously and make him a prince in his own territory for the present. That would set the minds of the men of Wu at rest, and dissuade them from offering any useless resistance. He "*could be taken away to the capital next winter,*" once Wu had been vanquished.

Wu was duly overrun, although not without a fight, and the profligate member of the Sun clan who sat on its throne was deposed, removed to the imperial court, and made a marquis.

In the meanwhile, however, one final act in this tale of irony had been staged to ensure that all the heroes and villains were to be losers—except the last. In 265 the descendant of Ts'ao Ts'ao who was sitting on the throne of Wei found himself going through the solemn mockery of abdicating it—the repeated court petitions, the four offers of the imperial seal, the concluding public ceremony—that his own forebear had invented in order to be able to seize it. The Mandate of Heaven had passed to a scion of the all-powerful family of Ssu-ma Yi. The sum of all the struggles for a century of unremitting bloodshed and intrigue was the foundation of a new dynasty—the Tsin—which was to stagger uncertainly down the years until its collapse in 420.

But the "Three Kingdoms" were to live forever, and Mao Tsetung himself was to be accused by certain pro-Soviet critics in Peking of paying too much attention to their legends and lessons. For in many Chinese minds their counterparts are still fighting it out today under other names—"China," "Russia," "America"—or "Japan."

19

The Drama in Modern Dress

The first instinct of the skeptical barbarian may be to list the differences that divide a triangular struggle for supremacy in the underpopulated past from the tensions of an overcrowded present shared by Russia, America, China, Japan, "Europe," and the Third World. But the historical instinct of the Chinese is much keener, the sense of analogy far sharper (if less discriminating) in a tidy-minded people who will add a fifth season and a fifth point of the compass to the original four in order that they may be precisely equated with the five elements, the five colors, the five senses, and the "five planets."

Educated men from Peking to Hong Kong will still typecast their contemporaries according to their physical, mental, and moral likeness to ancient heroes, even breaking them down into fractions on occasion—"He's two thirds Ts'ao Ts'ao, one third Han Kao-tsu." And since for better or worse this Chinese quirk is a fact of life, the intellectual scorn that any Westerner may pour upon it is totally irrelevant.

What many Anglo-Saxons see as a novel problem in the balance of power whose solution may lie in interdependence, Chinese tend to see as a more specific reflection of their own past. In their eyes, political tactics must be based today as they were seventeen centuries ago on a careful calculation of profit and loss, the "profit" to be measured in terms of protective alliances and advantages gained at the expense of the main enemy, whose "loss" may be measured in terms of his *ultimate* isolation.

Friends and foes may meanwhile be interchangeable, and what passes for loyalty among nations may be as plastic as the allegiances of generals like Kuan Yu, who could serve Ts'ao Ts'ao one year and Yuan Shao the next. Kuan Yu scrupulously paid his accumulated debt to Ts'ao Ts'ao and then crossed the lines to join his adversary. In the 1960's China scrupulously paid her accumulated debt to the Russians, and in the 1970's turned to smile upon their American rivals.

But this reconciliation between the Communist leaders in Peking and the arch-imperialists in Washington was above all reminiscent of Chuko Liang's policy of befriending Wu in order to counterbalance Wei, and of stopping Wu and Wei from ganging up on Shu. The danger of war between Russia and China receded, for the Muscovites were now obliged to look over their shoulder to the west before contemplating aggression in the east.

America was the lesser foe with whom, as the ancient strategists had laid down, the wise commander must sometimes ally himself against the greater. The Americans had tried to contain China, had supported Nationalist Taiwan, had fought the Chinese Communists in Korea and the Vietnamese Communists in Vietnam, and they and their capitalist system were ideological anathema. The mutual antagonism that had crystallized between Peking and Washington was nonetheless still soluble, given the application of a little warmth.

As Soviet nuclear power waxed and the Soviet navy filtered into the Pacific, the Indian Ocean, and the Mediterranean, a United States sapped by an unequal war of moral attrition in Indochina which it could not possibly win was compelled to realize that the tilting balance could best be redressed by a shift of diplomatic weight toward Peking. The Chinese therefore regarded the visit of President Richard Nixon to the People's Republic in 1972 and all that followed it as natural consequences of what had gone before, and—as individuals—approved or disapproved according to the degree to which they mistrusted or missed the friendship of Russia.

China and America disputed no borders, laid no claim to each other's sovereign territory. But Chinese maps still mutely protested that under "unequal treaties" signed during past centuries, Russia had fleeced the Celestial Empire of more than half a million square miles of territory. Chinese and Russian troops clashed intermittently along the uneasy fringes of Sinkiang and Manchuria—the Chinese more than once taunting Soviet troops in the best traditions of the past in order to goad them into opening fire, so that they would put themselves in the wrong in the eyes of the world.

President Nixon—and his Republican Party as a whole—enjoyed the backhanded respect that the Chinese have always accorded to opponents loyal to their own cause, and to censorious critics who stick to their opinions. Their private contempt they kept for naïve armchair revolutionaries from Western seats of higher learning who slavishly licked up their propaganda. Their real wrath they reserved for the bourgeois-reactionary turncoats in the Kremlin who they felt had betrayed the cause of Communist revolution, and whom they would happily have treated as Chuko Liang treated the doubly deceitful Cheng. And since their quarrel was with the "revisionist socio-imperialist clique" in power, and not with the Russian millions (with Ts'ao Ts'ao and not with the men of Wei), they naturally devoted their energies to trying to split the Soviet party and alienate the Soviet people from it, with the object of supplanting the usurpers of the moment in Moscow with the "legitimate line"—a Marxist-Leninist leadership that would be in harmony with their own.

The Chinese could afford to provoke the Soviet Union along their mutual frontier in the early 1970's, for Russian lines of communication were still tenuous, and Russian troops on the Manchurian border too far from the main industrial centers of the U.S.S.R. to be able to sustain without difficulty a long conventional assault against their vexatious neighbors. Conversely, however, Chinese resources and industry in the north of the People's Republic became increasingly vulnerable as the Russians opened up and populated Siberia. It was this factor that sounded alarm bells in Peking when Moscow and Tokyo began to discuss joint exploitation of the region, including the laying of railways and oil pipelines which might innocently profit their economies but could also serve Russian armies deployed along the Sino-Soviet frontier.

As the Chinese saw it, the Russians wanted to keep China and Japan divided, to seduce the Japanese with the dangled promise of oil when the Middle East proved an unreliable source of supply, to improve logistical support for their army in the Soviet Far East, and to counterbalance the influence of the Americans in Tokyo. The Russians were also in a position to return or withhold the Kurile Islands seized from Japan at the end of the Second World War, according to how amenable the Japanese themselves decided to be.

The Soviet Union pulled both stick and carrot out of the bag when in 1972 the Chinese, fearing that they would be isolated by a Russo-Japanese agreement, much as Shu had been isolated by the alliance between Wei and Wu, made plans to establish diplomatic relations with Tokyo. The immediate reaction of the Russians was to propose to the Japanese that they both start talking about the future of the Kurile Islands.

But Premier Chou En-lai knew what he was doing. The Japanese Prime Minister was given a warm welcome in Peking. The Chinese waived their claim to war reparations, and in the course of a six-day visit the two parties agreed to conclude a treaty of peace and friendship as well as accords covering trade, navigation, and fisheries—all of which contrasted so blindingly with China's previous hostility toward Japan that, like a great sheet of lightning, it made men blink.

Once again, however, China's masters could be confident that the ex-enemy was ready to meet them halfway. The Japanese depended upon the Americans for their defense, yet the Americans had already paid court to Peking without even telling them of their intention. Tokyo was uneasy. Japan was wealthy but weak, China poor but potentially strong. In this context Japan was very much the Wu of the three-kingdom drama now being played in modern dress, the least of the rivals, and so to be sought by all as the one that could change the balance of power among them without proving a menace to her own ally.

Tokyo was nonetheless troubled by the Sino-Soviet quarrel, which made it almost impossible for the Japanese to cultivate Moscow and Peking simultaneously. As a counterweight, Japan might be the key to the power game, but she did not possess the initiative. And if by befriending Russia she made it difficult for China to check the expansion of Soviet influence in the Far East, she herself might fall victim to that expansion in turn, as Wu was to fall after Wei had defeated Shu. In this situation all concerned "held each other by the leg." The Chinese therefore knew that both the Americans and the Japanese must agree to bury—or half bury—the hatchet with them, and that the Russians could be contained.

But the game was not played out.

Chuko Liang fostered trade between Shu and Wu to the benefit of both territories, and of the flickering friendship between them that slowly grew under his hand from the acrid embers of the past.[1] He opened up virgin land, built irrigation works, improved bridges and roads, and reformed the amenities for public health. He suppressed the hereditary aristocracy, ennobled men only according to merit, and enforced the laws without fear or favor. The public granaries were kept full, the army was well equipped, and the frail were protected against the powerful.

He died, and nearly thirty years later Shu fell. But he had been preparing the kingdom for the moment when it would be close enough to Wu and strong enough in itself to put an end once and for all to the danger of domination by any self-styled overlords in the north. And all the striving of the Communists to build China into a just, modern, nuclear state, friendly with all the right allies and enemies, indicated that the leaders in Peking were now doing the same. By 1974 the Chinese had developed multi-stage ballistic missiles with a range of some 3,500 miles capable of hitting Moscow. Premier Chou En-lai had sworn several times that they would never be the first to use nuclear weapons, but could the unimaginable day come when Peking would nonetheless launch an offensive against the U.S.S.R.?

Futurologists are frauds whose escape clause is that they will die before the doomsday they predict. Whatever might lie ahead was unforeseeable, but it could be said that the traditions of Imperial China and Communist China alike dictated a policy of defense. Only fight if you know you can win, the ancients had warned, and China was still weak. From the days when Han Wu-ti first "pacified" what are now North Korea and North Vietnam and sent armies through the Great Wall to chastise the Hun, the Chinese had normally dispatched military expeditions abroad for one of three reasons: to "punish" (not "attack"), to keep aggressive nomads at a comfortable distance, or to coerce their more sedentary neighbors into accepting Chinese suzerainty and acting as buffers against barbarians further afield.

The sages of old had condemned the conquests of the would-be overlord as evil, and in the mid-1970's Chinese Communist leaders were reiterating that they sought hegemony over none. Their armies had fought in Korea to keep the capitalists out of China, and they had crossed into India to teach the Indians humility. But they claimed no physical empire beyond what they conceived to be their territorial limits, and the ideological realm of Maoism would have to be won by native Communist guerrillas fighting their own "people's wars" in their own countries, just as Chinese guerrilla armies fought their "people's war" against Chiang Kai-shek under the command of Mao Tsetung.

The experience of those armies also engendered in Mao a taste for all-engulfing defense founded on the principles first voiced by Sun Tzu and Hsun Tzu and Wu Ch'i, and echoed through century after century of imperial history.

Mao took the first step toward winning the Mandate of Heaven and founding a new Chinese state in 1927, when as a young revolutionary leader he regrouped his defeated followers on the heights of Chingkangshan, and began to imbue them with a sense of loyalty toward his substitute for an imperial seal—the authority of the Chinese Communist Party. The Party would command the army, and its cadres must develop the "party nature," so that the one overriding ambition to win a decisive victory for Communism would wipe out all other allegiances, and like Han Kao-tsu they would be willing to drink the soup of their own boiled father rather than submit. "Cultivate a firm and correct political orientation, an industrious and simple style of work, and flexible strategy and tactics," Mao instructed them. "Be united, alert, earnest, and lively."

A rustic army whose main task was to rouse the millions of oppressed peasants among whom it must swim "like a fish in water," this force ate as frugally as Mo Tzu's fighters and its officers shared the privations of the soldiers as Wu Ch'i had always done. It was plain-living and hard-working, it came from the poor villages of China and could melt back into them. And it was a human object lesson in the wisdom of learning from the wisdom of Sun Tzu. It had been formed out of the defeated remnants of revolutionary "regiments" that had ill-advisedly tried to take cities by direct assault, but now Mao was to become as practiced a something-for-nothing strategist as Chuko Liang. Outnumbered and outgunned from the start, his men were organized as hit-and-run guerrillas who had to win the confidence of the peasants and to offset the strength of the Kuomintang enemy by deceiving him with ruses, tracking his every move through spies, ambushing his small parties, and avoiding his big battalions.

Under Mao's guidance the Communists husbanded their own forces while whittling down their adversary's, taking what he did not defend and skirting what he did, until they dominated the countryside and encircled the towns that were to be their last targets, not their first. In an article published in September 1965, moreover, Lin Piao later expanded this principle into a formula for world revolution, whereby the have-not "country" nations whose raw materials and labor the imperialists exploited would eventually isolate and overcome the "city" nations of the industrialized capitalist West that were, in the last analysis, dependent on them.

During the Sino-Japanese War, Mao's army continued to "conserve its own strength while destroying the enemy," fighting few pitched battles, operating behind the lines, only attacking secondary targets, and leaving the Japanese and the Nationalist Kuomintang to devour each other if they were foolish enough to do so. When it was over and the Japanese had surrendered, the Communists pushed Chiang Kai-shek back into the "death ground" of Formosa—and left him there to rot.

By the mid-1970's the People's Liberation Army disposed of armored and airborne divisions, jet bombers and fighters, and its first nuclear-powered attack submarine. It was rich in generals who had studied in Russia or faced the fearsome firepower of a modern Western army in Korea, and it was permeated with officers who wanted it to be a professional force fit for the laser age. In 1975 it began to look as if they were at last beginning to get their way. The PLA was—to quote one American expert—in "poor shape" for ambitious operations against a powerful enemy like the Soviet Union. Its equipment was obsolescent, its soldiers were suffering from a surfeit of indoctrination, and its morale had been roughly shaken by the campaign of hatred directed against the late Lin Piao and commanders loyal to him. But there were now signs that Chinese scientists were trying to produce miniaturized warheads and so put tactical nuclear weapons in the hands of the troops. The army was getting less political talk and more military training, and it was to receive more trucks and tracked vehicles, better guns and better tanks.

In essence, however, it was still being shaped for a "people's war" based on the concepts of the dim past that Mao had put into such effective practice against the Kuomintang. Its troops were instructed above all in close-quarter combat and night fighting, the ambush in the mountains, guerrilla action in intense heat and cold, fast get-in-get-out surprise attack, rapid concentration and dispersal.

The role of the regular infantryman was to fight an in-depth war of resistance against all comers in conjunction with the militia, who were to provide the bulk of the defense while he provided the bone. The militia were drawn from among party cadres, peasants, and workers, and it was estimated in 1974 that at least five million of them—and perhaps far more—had been adequately trained and armed as local auxiliaries.

Their organization had been founded on the principle that "all citizens must be soldiers," and with the intention that it would become a huge, fine-meshed "net of Heaven and Earth" in which any intruding enemy would be trapped, or "a hostile sea" in which he would be drowned. For he must be absorbed and stifled without any need for extravagant or profitless confrontations, exterminated by men who knew the ground, were skilled in the art of deception, and whose peasant eyes and ears would be everywhere.

The cadres of the militia, it was laid down, must be dedicated to the Communist cause, prudent men never misled by high temper or arrogance who would test the feelings of the masses and make decisions based upon them, as Mo Tzu and Mao had both recommended in their time. The best of them were attached to regular army battalions for training, sent on maneuvers and put through political night school, and they provided an invaluable link between the local people and the local professional soldiers.

In addition to these, millions of students, intellectuals, and civil servants who were sent "down to the countryside" to learn about life in the rural raw were given basic training as auxiliaries in all the necessary arts required of the peasant-soldier, from plowing fields to pitching hand grenades. They could be seen on the roads, marching in columns thousands strong, carrying packs and water bottles, straw helmets, spare shoes, and basins that were used for everything from washing feet to carrying water and from moving earth to boiling noodles.

In ancient China, as already noted, the peasant-soldier became the soldier-peasant, manning frontier settlements within which he grew his own rations, and this tradition inspired not only the self-sufficiency of the modern Chinese static division, but the deployment of the Production and Construction Corps along China's immense boundaries. Minority peoples with inconveniently close kin on the other side of the Sino-Soviet and Sino-Mongolian borders were withdrawn into the hinterland of Sinkiang and Inner Mongolia. The frontier was then sealed off by paramilitary colonies of these armed Chinese pioneers, who were responsible for farming and forestry as well as guarding and patrolling the often desolate terrain in which they were stationed—and watching the Russians over the way.

Meanwhile, as Chinese propaganda hammered into the heads of the millions the overriding need for all to prepare against possible Soviet aggression, vast networks of underground tunnels and shelters were constructed in all cities, equipped with command posts, telephone exchanges, radio transmitters, first-aid centers, and food reserves. But few if any were proof against poison gas or flooding or fallout, let alone a direct hit by a nuclear missile, and "underground Peking" was regarded by some as no more than a gigantic mantrap.

The suspicion therefore arose in men's minds that the Chinese leaders did not fear war—Moscow would not embark on one lightly: nuclear missiles were most certainly "tools of ill omen"—but that they wished to put the fear of war into the minds of the masses ("the absence of an external enemy will lead to the ruin of the state"). The Russians had signally failed to attack China in 1960, after she had been economically crippled by the ill-timed Great Leap Forward, and again in 1967, when she had been rent by the Great Cultural Revolution. Yet they had to be depicted as treacherous, plundering murderers. For the Chinese must be conditioned to work harder, to flinch from no sacrifice, to strive to be self-sufficient patriots who would "rather have nuclear weapons than trousers."

Peking was instilling into the masses a pride and a despair that would jerk them into united action—to make more steel, dig more shelters, drill after work, study after drill, and die if need be. If half the population of China were to be wiped out in a nuclear attack, Mao had said, the other half would still survive and socialism would triumph. If Russia invaded China from the north, America from the south, India from the west, and Japan from the east, China would still be victorious, Chou En-lai told a delegation of Japanese politicians in January 1973.

The Chinese would make war from what all their philosophers had declared was an impeccable ethical position. "Allow the enemy to enter our territory," Mao wrote in an instruction published in November 1972, "so that the people of the whole world may see that we fight from the standpoint of justice." The morale of the Russians would be low, the morale of the Chinese high, for they would be "protecting the home and defending the nation." Although he had described his strategy in the words "We do not fight battles that are hopeless, and if we cannot win, we run," [2] in this context "run" meant "enticing the enemy to penetrate more deeply" into China so that he could be cut off and annihilated. For the adversary, China was to be one vast ambush. For the Chinese, it was to be one vast "death ground" from which there could be no withdrawal.

Vigorous diplomacy and propaganda designed to discredit and isolate the modern Wei north of the border nevertheless visibly demonstrated that Communist leaders in Peking were as keen to win the war without loosing an arrow as Sun Tzu himself would have been. And it can be taken that they were also honoring his precepts invisibly. The Chinese intelligence service has boasted that wherever water can go, its agents can go—and no foreign power should take a Chinese defector at face value just because he shows a few ideological scars to prove he has been maltreated by the Maoists.

However, as all great Chinese thinkers from Mencius to Mao have stressed, the security of the state depends less on the skill of its diplomacy, the strength of its army, or the cunning of its spies, than on the relations between its people and its government; not on thinking or fighting, therefore—but ruling.

PART THREE
RULING

20

The Case for Murder

The pseudo-Maoists of the West, who insist on treating the Chinese Communist leaders as if they were inhuman and pathologically incapable of sinning, trip over their own indignation when reminded of Chou En-lai's questionable activities in Shanghai. For in the late 1920's the subtle author of "smiling diplomacy" was responsible for directing an underground struggle against the Kuomintang in the course of which his killer squad committed some peculiarly revolting murders. But these would sit easily enough on many a Chinese conscience, for if aggression becomes "just punishment" when directed against the vile, murder becomes just execution when it removes evil and opens the way to good.

Assassination is cheaper than war, but like war it is sanctioned by success, and it was a weapon ruthlessly wielded by both the worst and the best of Chinese emperors. The worst are identifiable by the fact that their brutal slaughter created disunity out of unity and they lost the Mandate of Heaven. The best are identifiable by the fact that their equally brutal slaughter created unity out of disunity, and they gained the Mandate of Heaven.

Like a catalyst, the nature of the slaughter itself is unchanging and, the Taoists would say, cannot be defined as good or bad. As for the murderer, if he is a man of integrity he has no choice but to murder, for he must keep his appointment with his destiny, although it be another man's appointment with death.

Even Confucius praised the violent liquidation of the last tyrant of the Shang Dynasty by the first hero of the Chou Dynasty as a "revolutionary action consonant with the Will of Heaven and in accord with the feelings of Man." In terms of Chinese political morals, therefore, the chaotic centuries that followed the fall of Shu and Wu and the rise of the house of Tsin cried out for a little constructive killing to end the miseries of the millions.

The first Tsin emperor was not only dissolute beyond all reason, but stupid enough to revive the feudal system and to make all adult members of the imperial clan landed princes and military commanders within their own domains. In consequence, court rivalry quickly became lethal and the killing began early. As Professor Wolfram Eberhard has put it with admirable economy: "In A.D. 300 Prince Lun assassinated the empress Chia and removed her group. In 301 he made himself emperor, but in the same year he was killed by the prince of Ch'i. This prince was killed in 302 by the prince of Ch'angsha, who in turn was killed in 303 by the prince of Tunghai. The prince of Ho-chien rose in 302 and was killed in 306; the prince of Chengtu rose in 303, conquered the capital in 305, and then, in 306, was himself removed . . ." [1]

In 316 the Huns put an end to all this imperial bickering by overrunning much of China north of the Yangtse River, burning the capital at Loyang, taking the emperor of the moment prisoner and making him serve wine to their generals. The Tsin court withdrew westward to Ch'ang An, only to be captured again, and this time the new emperor was made to wash up the cups as well as serve the wine, and to act as a beater when his master went hunting. Apparently tiring of this jest, however, the Hun king finally killed him off and all the nobles seized with him. The remaining Tsin moved south of the Yangtse (the next emperor establishing his capital near modern Nanking), more nomadic tribes flooded through the Great Wall—Turkic, Mongol, Tungusic, Tibetan—and for nearly three hundred years north China was lost to the Chinese.

On the Yellow River the Hunnish empire was replaced by

a Tibetan empire. But the Chinese still retained the south, and in 383 Fu Chien, the ambitious barbarian ruler of the north, decided to end this unsatisfactory state of affairs by launching a gigantic offensive against the Tsin, arrogantly silencing the fears of his followers about the obstacles ahead by announcing: "I am the commander of an army a million strong, and it will be enough for each man to cast his whip into any river to stop it from flowing."

However, his columns were plagued by political intrigue, treachery, espionage, and the hit-and-run tactics of the Chinese as they rode southward over frustrating terrain intricately cut up by mountains and waterways which further disrupted their supply system and the synchronized timing of their advance. And when they did reach a big river, the Chinese capitalized on Fu Chien's mistakes by pulling yet another trick out of their bag of spiteful military traditions.

The Tibetan leader, having pitched camp on the north bank of the Fei with the first 300,000 troops of his scattered army to arrive, foolishly sent a distinguished captive as his envoy to the Tsin on the south bank. This man at once told his fellow Chinese all he knew, and concocted with them a ruse calculated to enable their smaller force of some 80,000 men to gain the day. He then returned to the Tibetans and reported, "The Tsin swear they will not surrender, and they call for a decisive battle on this bank. If you will but move your men back some distance, they will cross the river and engage."

Delighted at what he took to be a fatal error on the part of his adversaries, Fu Chien duly withdrew his forward troops, whereupon a fraudulent rumor at once raced through the rear of his army that the van had already been defeated, the Chinese agents responsible for it spread panic as fast as they could, and the Tsin attacked. Caught off balance, low in morale and short of supplies, the invading cavalry were twisted into one vast tangle of frightened humanity "seeing the enemy in every blade of grass and bush," and those that were not slaughtered or trampled by foe or friend were thrown into headlong flight to face death from hunger and cold. Of Fu Chien's grand army, only about 100,000 survived, and his power was broken. He had paid dearly for not "knowing his enemy," being outwitted by spies, using a traitor as an envoy, losing his initiative, and trying to pit a dispirited mob against desperate and united opponents with a river behind them.

A fit of almost aimless splintering now seized the north, but although the Tibetan empire collapsed, a powerful Tartar empire [2] rose in its place, whereas in the south a series of weaker dynasties succeeded the Tsin. Nonetheless, during the dark days that saw the capitals of both China and Rome fall to the barbarian, Chinese civilization continued to flower.

While in England the Anglo-Saxons were building themselves small wooden settlements around the log hall of their lord, the Chinese were laying down the six canons of art and six rules for cartographers, producing distinguished lacquer paintings and the first grid map, riding in sedan chairs, sipping tea, burning coal for fuel ("a sort of black stone, which is dug out of veins in the hillsides," Marco Polo was to remark with astonishment nearly nine centuries later). The days were filled with idleness and luxury, the nobles and scholars whiling away their leisure hours with singsong girls on the river and vying to cap each other's elegant verses.

But if the Chinese in the south were decadent, they were not the only champions of things Chinese, for China was demonstrating the power of her cultural metabolism, her ability to digest alien intruders one after the other. The nomadic barbarians were so effectively assimilated that in the year 500 the Tartar emperor in the north decreed that his people must adopt Chinese names, customs, language, and dress, and rewarded intermarriage. The dominant blood might still be Tartar, but the dominant civilization was Chinese. The story was to be repeated more than once. In the eleventh century the Kitan invaded China from the north, in the twelfth the Kin, in the seventeenth the Manchus. The Chinese absorbed them all, rejecting only the inedible Mongols of Kublai Khan.

They absorbed more than men. In the fifth century pilgrims and missionaries moving to and from India began to preach Buddhism widely in China. The faith spread like brushfire, and a hundred years later it was estimated that there were thirty thousand monasteries and two million monks and nuns in the country. The Taoists at first saw the foreign creed as a dangerous rival, but soon found room for Buddha among the multitudinous gods that they were by now patronizing. In the sixth century Fu Hsi, a Chinese famous for inventing the revolving bookcase, made a point of wearing a Taoist cap, a Buddhist scarf, and Confucian shoes to symbolize the union of the "three ways to one goal."

By this time, after 360 years of divisive slaughter, the moment had also come for a little constructive assassination in order to bring about the union of China herself. Almost incessant murder had been the undoing of the great Tartar empire, and more unsystematic parricide in the state of "Northern Chou" which succeeded it now brought to the top of the pile of corpses as hero of the hour the father-in-law of the latest local emperor. In 581 this Yang Chien began putting history straight by massacring his young sovereign and fifty-nine princes, and declaring himself ruler. He then subdued the south and became first emperor of the Sui Dynasty, whose writ ran from the Great Wall to Tongking. China was China again.

With the blue blood of sixty-odd royal personages on his hands, the assassin proceeded to prove himself an energetic and thoughtful administrator. For twenty-four years he ruled with vigor, prudence, and thrift, budgeting carefully in order to refill the exhausted treasury of his long-divided realm, yet cutting taxes to ease the burden on the millions, who for the first time began to know the joys of a marginal tranquillity. State granaries were built, and work was begun on a great canal system that was only to be completed a century later. The borders were fortified and the Turks, the latest barbarian challenge beyond the northern and western frontiers, were astutely played off against one another.

But murder most fair was to be followed by murder most

foul. The heir to the throne was a tolerant, weak, luxury-loving idler with no great harm in him who was regarded by his father with exasperated contempt. His younger brother, on the other hand, was a sly and scheming profligate who exploited the discontent of gentlemen unhappy about the almost miserly way in which the country was being run by forming his own faction. These friends at court spoke up for him, and he conducted himself in an ostensibly sober and filial manner until the emperor, unsuitably impressed, passed over his elder brother and made him crown prince.

However, his sober and filial manner wore thin enough to arouse the suspicions of his father when he began seducing the beauteous empress who had taken the place of his dead mother. Apprised of the affair, the sick and angry ruler cursed him for an "animal" unfit to govern, and named his eldest son the heir again. At this the younger sent troops to seize and dispose of his brother, poisoned his father, declared himself emperor, and took his stepmother for a concubine.

The reign of Yang Ti was one of despotic cruelty evenly matched by insane extravagance and ruinous caprice. He was a restless, lustful, and violent man, who kept on the move most of the time during the thirteen years that he ruled, and imposed an unbearable strain on the treasury and administration by insisting that his entire chancellery and court go with him wherever he went. He built new palaces in three separate capitals,* conscripting two million men to put up an exquisite royal abode in Loyang in which the doors opened automatically, and screens and blinds closed of their own accord when the emperor left an apartment. A device was also fitted into the floor at the entrance to the enormous library whereby at his approach a mechanical Immortal would fly down and part the embroidered curtains, which would then roll up of themselves.

In the western suburbs he created an enclosed garden covering two hundred *li,* planted with peach trees and willows and strange flowers and shrubs, and stocked with rare birds

* At Ch'ang An, Loyang, and Chiang Tu (now Yangchow) on the Yangtse in modern Kiangsu Province.

and animals. In the center of this pleasance lay an ornamental lake fed by a sinuous waterway, on whose banks stood sixteen magnificent pavilions tiled with porcelain and staffed by beautiful women. Here he would wander on horseback surrounded by a thousand concubines, drinking and singing and versifying among trees that were eternally in bloom, for when leaves withered and flowers fell in autumn and winter they were replaced with blossoms fashioned from silk, so that spring would be eternal in his illusory paradise.

Construction did not end with the building of palaces and pleasure domes. Yang Ti linked the Yangtse to the Yellow River with what was to become the Imperial Canal and to prove an immense boon for both the transportation of grain and the swift movement of troops, for the principal channel was more than 600 miles long and 40 yards wide and could take lighters of 500 tons burden. It was flanked on each side by highways, shaded along its entire length by trees, and served by nearly one hundred post stations.

But it was also served by forty sumptuous pavilions for the personal use of the emperor, who did not count the cost of this prodigious project in lives and the livelihood of the poor. In adjacent areas every male from fifteen to fifty was called up for forced labor and beheaded if he dodged the draft. Those who reported for work were discouraged from flagging with whips and cangues, and households in the region through which the canal passed were obliged to provide nearly two million children or old folk to feed and help the 3,600,000 men impressed for the main task. According to one estimate half a million unfortunates died at this ditch under vile conditions of semi-slavery during the long hot summer of the year 607 alone.

When the canal was opened, the emperor made a solemn progress along it from Loyang on the Yellow River to Yangchow on the Yangtse with his empress, his concubines and courtiers, his officials and palace guards and priests and nuns, sailing in a specially built four-decked "dragon boat" 230 feet long which was fitted with a throne room and 120 cabins ornamented with gold and jade.

This vessel was only the first of a huge fleet. Under a moving forest of banners, the procession of luxurious barges stretched stem to stern for some 60 miles, manned by 9,000 boatmen, towed by 80,000 peasants, and guarded by accompanying cavalry on either side of the imperial flagship. The country for 80 miles all around had to supply the food for this grand tour—whose announced object was to take the court to Yangchow to see the moonflowers bloom.

The Sui Dynasty was earning an enviable reputation for military prowess, for its armies had sacked the capital of Champa halfway down the Indochinese peninsula, won the submission of the Turks in the north, chased the Mongols out of the northwest into Tibet, and invaded Formosa. But the Chinese fought four costly and futile campaigns against the Koreans which, together with Yang Ti's other extravagances, emptied the coffers of the empire and beggared the people. Fields and orchards reverted to wilderness and destitute peasants were compelled to become bandits, whereupon rebel upstarts came forward to seize this or that region and proclaim themselves contenders for royal power.

Unable to stamp out the smoldering revolt, the emperor resigned himself to the eventual loss of Ch'ang An and Loyang on the Yellow River and fell back on the consolations of wine and women in Yangchow. "What an excellent head!" he is said to have exclaimed, looking at himself drunkenly in the mirror one day. "I wonder who will chop it off!" He did not have to wonder for long.

He had already had one close shave, for in 615 the Turks had launched a surprise attack and surrounded him with a vast army. He had only been saved from almost certain capture by an enterprising officer who had recommended that all available Chinese troops should be strung out thinly in a protracted line, so that in daylight the enemy would see an endless display of fluttering banners and at night hear drums beating far and near, as if an enormous relief force had somehow arrived. The stratagem worked. When an agent in the camp of the Turks spread a rumor that another tribe was also marching to attack them, they broke their cordon and withdrew.

A year later the same officer rescued a cousin of the emperor named Li Yuan, a viceroy responsible for the defense of North China, whose army had been encircled at Taiyuan by the increasingly powerful rebels. Just as all seemed lost, he led a charge of crack cavalry clad in black armor and riding black horses who cut their way through the enemy lines with a scythe of arrows and sprung the trap. He was no devoted servant of the emperor, however, and while Li Yuan still hesitated to believe that the historical moment had arrived for the Mandate of Heaven to pass, and that he should therefore join the rebels himself rather than fight them, this young man begged to differ. And he was a very young man indeed. For his name was Li Shih-min, he was Li Yuan's second son, and he was only eighteen years old at the time.

Li Shih-min's father was Chinese, but his mother had been a Tartar. He was a cultured aristocrat of the Middle Kingdom, but he had in him something of the savage spirit of the barbarian across the Wall. He grew up with a taste for belles-lettres and poetry, was a scholar versed in history and philosophy, an able administrator who had also studied the art of war and who practiced archery and horsemanship like any other Chinese gentleman.

But there was more to him than that. His sharp, piercing eyes betrayed an exceptionally quick intelligence. His giant frame gave him the strength to draw a bow that could put a bolt through a thick door and shoot arrows of twice the normal weight with frightening speed and accuracy. And he nourished an even more frightening ambition. He proposed to become emperor of China.

Events seemed to shape themselves to his will. When his father was defeated in a battle against the Turks and feared that he would be punished by the emperor, Li Shih-min seized the opportunity to press him to change sides. "The empire is finished," he declared. "The people are suffering beyond all measure. If you think that this is a time to pay heed to the niceties of conventional loyalty, you are blind to the situation. Below you are the bandits, above you the law of the emperor. There is nothing to be done but follow the will of the people and raise a volunteer army. It is a chance that only comes once in a thousand generations."

Accused of treachery and warned to hold his tongue, Shih-min returned to the attack the next day. "You have been given a mandate to exterminate the rebels," he said. "Can you exterminate them? Because if you cannot, you will have committed a crime. And if you can, your merit will not be recognized and your peril will be even greater." [3] As the ancients had said, the successful general courted a quick end once a war was won and he was no longer a necessity, but a dangerous nuisance. And the point was well taken.

In the half-light of history, Li Yuan is lost in the shadow of his brilliant son, yet he was an astute commander. It was the parched summer of 617, and the region was simmering with revolt in the heat. But he did not side with the more vociferous rebels who clamored to replace the Sui Dynasty. He set about the destruction of Yang Ti in his own way. First he made a secret pact with the Turks (while falsely claiming that his chief opponent had done so) under which it was agreed that if together they were able to take the capital at Ch'ang An, the Turks could have the money and movables as their share of the loot, while his would be the land and the people. At the same time he provoked widespread discontent, which led to a popular uprising, by conscripting all men from twenty-two to fifty years old for a new military adventure in Korea, making it clear that he was reluctantly obeying an imperial edict issued by Yang Ti in person.

A few months later he captured Ch'ang An with the aid of a Turkish army and installed a thirteen-year-old grandson of the emperor as the Son of Heaven, treating him with meticulous respect and addressing him as "Your Imperial Majesty" so that none could yet accuse him of usurping the throne. But in 618, when other rebels caught Yang Ti in Yangchow and lost no time in strangling him, Li Yuan instructed his puppet in the correct procedure for yielding the mandate to him, and assumed power himself. Within five years he had liquidated the last provincial rival to resist his dominion and ruled all China as founding emperor of the great T'ang Dynasty, which was to endure until the tenth century.

The real hero of the day was Shih-min, but it seemed that he was to be denied the fruits of his revolutionary exertions, for like Yang Ti he was only the second son, and his elder brother was heir-apparent. His father nevertheless consoled him with private promises that he would be made crown prince, and this inevitably encouraged more unedifying fratricide. The heir-apparent was confident of his claim to the empire, but the determination and drive of his able and ambitious brother made him uneasy. The first and third sons of the emperor therefore banded together against the second, forming their own clique and courting the concubines and dignitaries around the ruler, and a furtive struggle for supremacy developed.

The heir-apparent might not have enjoyed the prestige of the heroic Shih-min, but he was the lawful successor of his father, and as such he could count on a strong following in Ch'ang An. This included the imperial kin desirous of upholding the proprieties imposed by clan law, court officials and generals who automatically gave their allegiance to the rightful heir, and the imperial guard in the capital itself. Moreover, his most trusted political counselor, seeing the emperor hesitate between his sons, recommended that the eldest be sent to suppress a rebellion that had broken out in the northeast. The heir-apparent acquitted himself well, his faction grew, and his father stopped talking about favoring Shih-min.

However, if the crown prince had the ear of the palace, Shih-min had the ear of the people. He was master of a great army, some of whose officers had started life as peasants, carpenters, and weavers, while others had been drawn from eminent families. They were blooded veterans, tempered in war, and between them they captured the imagination and earned the respect of men of all estates. Shih-min himself was a capable commander, renowned for his exploits, a living talisman of victory who treated the vanquished with calculated care, winning their best generals and officials over to his side. When the Turks invaded in force in 624 the emperor and the heir-apparent were all for burning the capital and fleeing, leaving the millions to the nonexistent mercy of the enemy, and it was Shih-min who emerged as their champion, attacking the barbarians with such ferocity that they were compelled to withdraw.

The capital was saved, but the rivalry at court sharpened dangerously. Two years later the irrepressible Turks came again, and this time the heir-apparent named his youngest brother commander of the forces mobilized to repel them, whereupon the youngest brother promptly demanded that the pick of the generals serving Shih-min be transferred to his army. The pair then invited Shih-min himself to a great feast at which they proposed to do away with him in comfort, but Shih-min learned of the conspiracy and secretly memorialized the emperor, who angrily summoned his other two sons to his presence.

The tables were turned, and having suborned palace guards ostensibly loyal to the crown prince, Shih-min and his commanders intercepted the brothers within the gate of the Forbidden City itself and cut them down. The corpses were decapitated and the heads sent to the waiting emperor by hand of a general who had instructions to say that his sons had plotted an insurrection, and to demand that Shih-min be given full authority to suppress it. Two months later Shih-min compelled his father to abdicate in his favor, and then rounded off the exercise by butchering all the male offspring of his dead brothers.

"Power is like roasted meat, the more you chew it, the more fragrant it becomes," say the Chinese. "A great man cannot be without it for a day." Two second sons had hacked their way to the throne, but while the name of Yang Ti will stink to eternity, the name of Shih-min has been venerated throughout the centuries—for it is synonymous with the most magnificent page in Chinese history.

21

The Golden Rule of the Assassin

Li Shih-min ascended the throne in Ch'ang An in 627 with the reign title of T'ang T'ai-tsung, and quickly wiped out the displeasing memory of his family's earlier alliance with the barbarians across the border by carrying the war against the Eastern Turks into Mongolia, and thrashing their armies so severely that there was peace on the frontier for fifty years. He then moved on to annihilate the Western Turks, opening up the route to India and Persia. The cowed nomadic tribes along the fringes of the Middle Kingdom "heard the wind and returned to the current," their leaders flocking respectfully to the Chinese capital to offer their submission to the "Heavenly Khan."

Tolerant and perceptive, T'ang T'ai-tsung gave them a sympathetic welcome, for like Han Kao-tsu he did not judge men by their background, but by their qualities, and he knew how to use them accordingly. A few days after he had assassinated his brothers, he summoned Wei Cheng, the political adviser of the murdered heir-apparent, and sternly taxed him with sowing discord among the imperial princes. "If the heir-apparent had listened to my warnings from the outset and taken all necessary precautions," was the arrogant retort, "the ending would have been very different." The emperor recognized in this provocative counselor the loyalty that is not given merely in exchange for immediate profit, but survives even when the books show a loss. Here was a man of rare courage and integrity, and T'ang T'ai-tsung made him his closest adviser.

The new ruler had the essential impartiality of a true Son of Heaven, whose domain is the Four Seas and who must ideally show a godlike lack of prejudice rare even among well-established gods. He was not interested in where a man came from, whether circumstances had made him friend or foe (carpenter or coffin maker, as Han Fei Tzu had put it). He did not dwell on the past, but boldly employed former enemies whom lesser monarchs would have liquidated for the sake of a little peace.

He dealt with all in his court and government in an open and direct manner, laying down that when his chief minister had an audience with him, the censors and imperial historians should be at his side. The historians were to record dispassionately what the emperor said, whether it was good or bad, and to the censors and other officials he explained: "From my youth I collected bows from every quarter, but it was only when a craftsman instructed me that I realized not all were of good quality. He pointed out that in some the grain was not straight, and although they might be strong, they were not accurate. Now the affairs of empire are so numerous that it is impossible for me to know them fully. Therefore I hope that in the future you will tell me of the hardships the people may be suffering, and will draw my attention to all excesses and shortcomings, so that prejudice and ignorance may be avoided."

He had seen for himself how the extravagance and dissipation and wasteful warmaking of the second Sui emperor had led to his downfall, and he was determined to base his own power on policies that would win the approval of the many. "For if the emperor is a boat, then the people are the waters of the river," he said. "And while the waters can bear the boat, they can also sink it."

He is reputed to have ordered that all memorials submitted to him should be hung on the walls of the palace so that he could ponder them as he came and went. He accepted rebuke without rancor, and would wash his hands and burn incense before reading a written admonition from one of his ministers. When the censors took him to task for organizing lavish hunts, he banned hunting, and when surprised by Wei Cheng while petting a falcon in the imperial gardens, he guiltily hid it in his robes (where it suffocated). He had the highest regard for his forthright counselor, and once asked him how he could avoid being deceived. Let men discuss all matters freely, Wei Cheng replied immediately. Let the ordinary people criticize the government, and always scrutinize the acts of that government yourself to make sure that it is on the right path.

And by and large, the imperial administration under this parricidal paragon was on the right path. The empire was divided into ten provinces, officials were chosen by public examination, and senior inspectors toured the country to evaluate their conduct of affairs, promoting the capable and demoting the corrupt. The complex and sophisticated government, which included among its nine ministries a board for economic and financial affairs, has been favorably compared with Europcan counterparts of nearly a thousand years later. For the emperor was anxious above all to enrich the country yet provide a better life for the poor, and the board was staffed with experts who had been ordered to work out a sound economic system based on the theories of benevolent rule propounded by Mencius nearly a thousand years earlier.

Big estates were broken up, and much of the land divided equally among the peasants. Every man over eighteen received a share of the soil and became a tenant of the state, paying rent in rice—or sometimes silk, linen, or silver—and reporting for twenty days of annual forced labor on public projects when there was no work to be done in the fields. These rents and obligations were reduced in bad years, and the landless workers in the cities were not taxed at all. Merchants and artisans were not allowed to own land, but although they were obliged to pay dues on their other assets, these might also be remitted to stimulate commerce and the crafts. The revenue nonetheless accumulated, and the empire prospered.

A strong Legalist streak ran through the philosophy of T'ang T'ai-tsung, and while his realm might be administered with Confucian magnanimity, rewards and punishments were precisely defined and the law strictly applied. Death and banishment dominated the list of corrections, and a whole clan could be collectively condemned and executed in cases of conspiracy and insurrection.

Penalties were nonetheless humane compared with what had gone before. When he noticed on a medical diagram that some of the "five viscera" lay close to the back of the body, the emperor amended the provisions for flogging (which was often fatal). Where hitherto a man would have been strangled, his right foot was chopped off, and where he would have lost his right foot, he was drafted into the army instead. Ninety-two crimes for which death had been the sole penalty were transferred to the banishment list, and if the death sentence was passed the verdict had to be reviewed on three separate days, during which the judge might touch no meat and listen to no music.

Discovering—while inspecting a prison personally—that 390 condemned men were awaiting execution, the Son of Heaven set them all free to rejoin their families on condition that they swore a binding oath to return in the following autumn and take their punishment. Every one of them came back when he was due to die and the emperor, greatly moved, remitted their sentences. According to the historical records of the dynasty, only twenty-nine men were beheaded throughout the entire empire in the year 630.

China was no Utopia—a landless aristocracy was supported out of public taxes, and so much power mistakenly given to the military governors of the provinces that they would one day crack the empire apart again. But meanwhile it was ruled on the basis of "respect for the law and love for the people" by a monarch conspicuous for his energy, ability, and liberal understanding, whose ministers and counselors were for the most part honest and outspoken men of discernment. And the best of these was his old enemy Wei Cheng.

"With polished bronze for a mirror, one may correct one's

dress," the emperor remarked sadly when the great censor died. "With history for a mirror, one may know the reasons for prosperity and for ruin. With man for a mirror, one may learn the causes of success and of failure. And now that Wei Cheng is dead, I have lost my mirror." He then performed the mourning sacrifices himself, wept bitterly before the coffin, and held no court for five days.

In 1962 Lu Ting-yi, then Chinese Minister for Propaganda, commissioned a biography of Wei Cheng, personally edited the draft, wrote a preface to it, and then saw that it was widely distributed both inside and outside the Communist Party. The "Spirit of Wei Cheng," the virtue of speaking up fearlessly without regard for the anger of a superior, became a subject of study in ministries and schools, and of instructive editorials in the press. But when Chairman Mao castigated the Soviet Union, and warned the Chinese to work harder and to be ready to defend the Republic, Lu Ting-yi coined the slogan "Use the destruction of the Sui to serve as a mirror," pointing out that the dynasty had been overthrown because it was constantly imposing heavy labor on the masses and engaging in unprofitable war. "Don't we mobilize the people too much?" he asked boldly.

The implications were obvious. Four years later, he was dragged out for public trial, accused of plotting to undermine the political authority of Mao Tsetung, and dismissed from his post in disgrace. The biography of Wei Cheng was damned as a "poisoned arrow" aimed at the Chairman, a capitalist attempt "to satirize the present by borrowing from the past." The spirit of Wei Cheng was dead, it seemed, and for an obvious reason: in order to live, the spirit of Wei Cheng required the spirit of T'ang T'ai-tsung—even if he had murdered to become the monarch.[1]

As an assassin, T'ang T'ai-tsung was in any case an amateur compared with the woman who first came to his court as a winsome little concubine aged no more than thirteen. This frail creature first showed something of her mettle when the imperial grooms proved incapable of controlling a magnificent stallion presented to the emperor by a northern tributary, and the ruler sighed that although he was master of the Four Seas he was evidently not a master of these four legs.

"Why not simply have it thrashed with an iron whip and its head clubbed with an iron hammer?" suggested the Lady Wu Chao seriously. And as the emperor squeamishly demurred, she added impatiently: "Then take a knife and slit its throat. Are you afraid it will not submit even when it is dead?" When T'ang T'ai-tsung himself died, this Wu Chao contrived to become the consort of his heir, then Wu the regent, and in the year 690, Wu the reigning empress of China. Her progress was not achieved without some sacrifice, however, and her methods make gaudy reading.

Her first step was to stifle her own baby almost at birth in order to pin the killing on the empress who stood in her way, and when this failed to eliminate her rival, she framed her on a charge of conspiring with another court lady to poison the ruler. Once these two unfortunate women had been thrown into prison, Wu Chao was able to destroy them at leisure by directing the work of executioners who flogged them unmercifully, chopped off their hands and feet, flung them into a brewing vat, and cut them to pieces when they died.

Thereafter she climbed to absolute power over the bodies of three crown princes, and since she proposed not only to get to the top, but to stay there in the face of what seemed to her to be totally unreasonable opposition, other persons had to be liquidated.

Although historians are troubled by some borderline cases which would not have troubled Empress Wu herself, she is generally credited with having poisoned her sister, her niece, and one of her own sons, with obliging another son to hang himself, with having three grandsons and one granddaughter whipped to death, with ordering the execution of two stepsons plus their sixteen assorted male progeny, and with starving one daughter-in-law and disposing of three others by various imaginative means. In addition, she had fifty recalcitrant T'ang princes killed (ensuring in nineteen instances that all their kin were wiped out with them), she exterminated thirty-six senior ministers and generals (three of whom had suppressed rebellions for her), and altogether arranged for three thousand families to be slaughtered.

In time not devoted to bloody executions, however, the empress ran China with consummate ability, sacking the incompetent and corrupt, advancing men of merit (including on occasion her own critics), and never granting positions of power to her relations. During the fifty years that she ruled the empire—first through her weak husband, then as dowager empress, and finally as woman emperor—until she abdicated in 705, military spending was reduced, farming and commerce thrived, the money poured in, and the country continued to enjoy the unaccustomed measure of peace and prosperity bequeathed to it by T'ang T'ai-tsung. Between them, two killers had given the Chinese nearly a hundred years of the best government the Middle Kingdom had ever known—or was to know.

In Europe the Holy Roman Empire was to end an age of disorder, only to collapse itself. But the T'ang Dynasty was to endure for three centuries, to take the frontiers of China almost to Samarkand in the west, to Manchuria and Korea again in the north, and Yunnan and Annam in the south. In its heyday the walled capital at Ch'ang An had a cosmopolitan population of nearly 2,000,000, including Persians, Greeks, Syrians, and Arabs as well as Japanese and Koreans, and in the southern trading city of Canton lived about 120,000 Muslims, Zoroastrians, Jews, Manichaeans, and Nestorian Christians.

Religious strife might sweep the bigoted Occident, but the T'ang emperors were for the most part broad-minded until the middle of the ninth century, and the imperial verdict of T'ang T'ai-tsung on the teachings of the first Christian missionary to reach the capital in 635 was: "This doctrine does good to all men. Let it be preached freely in the empire." Yet behind the religious and racial flexibility was the Confucian ossature that gave the Chinese state its firm political shape, and in the feudal days of Charlemagne some 8,000 students would be studying to pass the imperial examinations in Ch'ang An at any one time.

A golden age of poetry had dawned—an anthology of nearly 50,000 T'ang Dynasty poems was later assembled—and it was in the pear garden of the imperial palace that the first drama was performed. Painting and music flourished, and fine porcelain, often decorated with Indian, Persian, even Greek motifs, was exported to the West. Block printing had been invented, and in the later days of the dynasty thousands of volumes were published, including dictionaries. The world's earliest printed book is a Buddhist *Diamond Sutra* put together by the Chinese in 868.

By then, T'ang China had long since had to reckon with the rising power of another faith—Islam. The son of the last Sassanid monarch was given asylum in Ch'ang An when the Muslims conquered Persia, but Arab envoys from the Caliphate who later arrived in the capital were graciously received in their turn. Chinese and Arab troops clashed at Samarkand in 751, when the Chinese overreached themselves during a period of uncharacteristic aggressiveness. But only a few years afterward Arab mercenaries were helping the T'ang emperor to crush a rebellion, and later in the century ambassadors from Harun al-Rashid came to China to conclude an alliance.

Many of the Arab mercenaries stayed in the empire, and from them sprang a Muslim minority which grew rapidly (the Muslims bought Chinese children sold by the poor in times of need, in order to raise them in the True Faith). While the West was to learn of papermaking and porcelain from the Chinese prisoners taken at Samarkand, China was opening her own gates to the cults and arts of the West. But if the case for constructive murder seemed to have been proved, the advent of the next great Chinese dynasty provided the model for the bloodless coup.

22

The Soft Touch

Insofar as one woman can send history reeling, it may be said that the doom of China's most glorious dynasty was sealed by China's most notorious minx. For the advent to the throne of T'ang Hsuan-tsung, grandson of the pitiless Empress Wu, heralded a brilliant reign blessed with nearly forty years of peace but cursed at the end of it by the Lady Yang.

The emperor was a keen patron of the arts, and the first half of the eighth century is renowned for its riches in Chinese poetry and painting and for the beginnings of the Chinese play. But as he grew older he gave himself up more and more to the pleasures of his splendid court and its three thousand women, only to fall hopelessly in love in his sixties with his own daughter-in-law. Obliging his son to surrender this statuesque beauty to him in 745, he made her his imperial concubine, and from that moment forward T'ang China was on the road to ruin.

It was not merely that Yang Kuei-fei was criminally extravagant, or that she was filled with the usual ambition of her kind and cajoled the infatuated Son of Heaven into making her brother chief minister and several hundred of her clansmen high officers of state. She was also the perpetrator of one of history's most tasteless farces.

Besotted in his palace, the emperor paid little heed to the defense of China, across whose northern borders the nomadic Kitan now posed a new threat, but left the responsibility to the garrison commanders on the ground. Some of these were themselves generals of Tartar stock who had earlier proved their loyalty to the dynasty, and among them was a huge, sweating, swag-bellied Turk named An Lu-shan. This fellow hid a shrewd, scheming brain behind much gross buffoonery, with which he so beguiled the ruler and his concubine that eventually he was allowed to sit beside the emperor when they banqueted and was formally adopted by the Lady Yang.

On the day of that ludicrous charade, the bloated barbarian was swaddled like a monstrous babe in arms in specially sewn cradle clothes, and carried by eunuchs in an ornate sedan chair to his "mother" for the customary ritual bathing of the newborn. The emperor gave a sumptuous feast, and ministers vied with each other to felicitate the "favored child" on his first bath. Thereafter the overgrown infant moved freely within the forbidden pavilions of the palace women, and showed himself most commendably filial and loving toward his imperial mama.

An Lu-shan was not a babe in arms when the arms were forged of Chinese steel, however. Harping on the Kitan menace over the border until he was given command of an army of more than 150,000 men, he waited for a suitably evil moment and marched south to seize the capital and the throne. The emperor fled incontinently with his court and the garrison of the palace. The troops—hungry, tired, outraged by the imperial fatuities that had brought them to their present pass—mutinied at Ma Wei, murdered the chief minister, and clamored for the head of his sister, Yang Kuei-fei. The distraught and terrified emperor then presented his beloved belle with a silken girdle with which to hang herself, and shortly afterward abdicated in favor of his son.

The civil war that followed lasted ten years, during which the registered tax-paying population of China is said to have fallen from nearly 53,000,000 to fewer than 17,000,000. An Lu-shan and his heir were both assassinated and the T'ang Dynasty was restored, but the damage done was irreparable. The court could no longer control the provinces, let alone safeguard the frontiers. The Tibetans sacked Ch'ang An in 763, the Chinese lost their hold on Manchuria and Korea, and Mongolia fell into the hands of the Turks.

In their extremity, successive emperors were forced to depend increasingly on the troops of provincial military governors for the defense of the realm, and these soon began to behave like independent warlords, pocketing imperial taxes in order to pay for their own private armies. A precarious unity punctuated by local revolts was preserved until 868, when it was shattered by a bloody popular uprising whose leaders took and plundered the capital before it could be put down. The fugitive emperor fell among rival commanders, and at the turn of the century the last T'ang ruler, like the last Han ruler before him, was carried off by the strongest of the squabbling generals. Observing established convention, this warlord duly killed the emperor, put a puppet in his place, and then usurped the throne from the puppet.

History, it appeared, had slipped back seven hundred years. After 906 the country was divided into a northern empire ruled by five short-lived dynasties of armed adventurers, and a jigsaw of some ten petty principalities in the south whose self-styled "kings" were the heirs of local governors that had seized power when T'ang China broke into fragments.

But the shadow was to pass quickly. In 959 an emperor of the fifth dynasty to rule over the north died, leaving a seven-year-old boy to mount the throne amid muted rejoicing. The frontiers were once again threatened by the Kitan, and having presented his congratulations at court to the infant monarch on the first day of the following new year, the commander of the imperial troops in the capital at Kaifeng led a large army out against the barbarian. He did not get far, however. For his brother and his fellow generals had other ideas about the future, and they proceeded to create their own ruler in truly Roman fashion.

Just before dawn one morning, his brother called a parade and proclaimed boldly: "The Son of Heaven is young, and even as we set out to risk our lives in battle against the enemy, there is no one at court who cares about our meritorious deeds. Therefore we shall make our commander our emperor." The conspirators then crowded into the tent of the half-awake general, thrust a robe of imperial yellow on him, pushed him onto a horse, and presented him to his army as the new sovereign. Previously primed, and keen to be rewarded for their services by a soldier who would appreciate them, mutinous officers raised their arms and swore allegiance to him. The reluctant Chinese Caesar marched his army back to the capital, the child ruler abdicated with due ceremony, and General Chao K'uang-yin became the Emperor Sung T'ai-tsu, founder of a dynasty that was to hold sway over China for three hundred years.

Reluctant? Some say Sung T'ai-tsu was monarch *malgré lui*, pitched willy-nilly onto the Dragon Throne. But others believe that he had planned this bloodless coup with his brother from the outset. Chairman Mao is known to have spoken with professional approval of the skill with which the two men won over and organized not only generals but officers of medium and low rank to ensure the success of their "revolution."

Mao himself prepared the ground with the same thoroughness when he won back the leadership of the Red Army from Chou En-lai, its chief political commissar, in 1935; when he became sole master of the Chinese Communist Party at the Seventh National Congress in 1945; and when he unleashed the Cultural Revolution to bring down his "revisionist" opponents in 1966.

The subsequent acts of the emperor nevertheless suggested that he knew he was engaged upon a slippery enterprise, in which one thoughtless move could transform him at any moment from a victor with his head above all others into a headless victim lying flat on his back. He was aware that a coup was not a popular uprising, but a bid for personal advantage, and that in consequence coup had bred coup with grim monotony during the previous half-century in North China, as each new usurper had unwarrantably decided that the day had arrived for him to overthrow his predecessor. In

China, it is understood that it is foul weather that makes friends—since men band together in adversity—and fair weather that makes rivals. The self-interest that had persuaded his fellow generals to put him on the throne in bad times might well persuade them to pitch him off it in good.

Sung T'ai-tsu was a northerner, scion of a prominent family whose forebears had been mandarins and provincial governors, a soldier of distinction with a fine edge to his mind, and his masterly solution for this problem was to draw the teeth of friends and enemies alike.

On entering the capital, he gave strict orders that no one was to be harmed, from child emperor to child beggar, and once he had mounted the throne he showed charity toward the fallen dynasty and consideration toward its officials, whom he confirmed in their posts. Then, instead of killing off his generals as mere "meritorious dogs" in the accepted manner, he invited all the powerful commanders who had proclaimed him their ruler to a handsome banquet.

Once the wine was coursing through them and laughter filled the air, he dismissed the guards and began to speak dolefully of his unenviable lot. Anxiously questioned by his mystified guests, he explained: "The whole day is spent in fear, and I am unhappy both at the table and on my bed. For which one of you does not dream of ascending the throne? I do not doubt your allegiance," he went on, when they expostulated, "but if by some chance your subordinates, seeking wealth and position, were to force the yellow robe upon you in turn, how could you refuse it?"

The generals, thoroughly ill at ease by now, protested their loyalty and asked what could be done to dissolve his mistrust.

"Man's life is but a blink of an eye," he answered. "The best way to pass one's days is in peaceful enjoyment of riches and honor, and you deserve to be able to withdraw from public duties which oblige you to put on court dress and to present yourselves at the palace at five in the morning. If you are willing to give up your commands, therefore, I am ready to provide you with fine estates and beautiful dwellings, where you may take your pleasure with singers and girls as your companions. Would that not be better than an existence filled with danger and uncertainty? We shall join our families by marriage, and with no suspicion lingering between ruler and subject, will live in friendship and tranquillity."

The generals realized that the emperor intended to gather all power into his own hands, and, thankful for his "liberality in great measure" which at least allowed them to keep their heads on their shoulders, tendered their resignations on the next day, pleading illness. The emperor then conferred titles, wealth, and estates upon each of them. He had achieved with a neat finesse over a cup of wine what others before him had killed and killed and killed again to accomplish.

Having satisfactorily rid himself of his backers and bosom friends, Sung T'ai-tsu coldly set about making himself sole, unassailable master of China by emasculating the army as a potent force within which would-be warlords and would-be emperors could organize insurrection. Trusted mandarins selected by public examination were sent down to the provinces from the capital with overriding authority in all political, fiscal, legal, and military affairs, and with strict instructions to report directly to the court and to remit to it all revenues not needed to meet essential local expenses.

As the prestige and power of the scholar-official waxed in distant prefectures, the repute and influence of the soldier waned. Provincial military governors were withdrawn. The only armed forces left permanently in provincial garrisons were made up of over-age or disabled veterans and very young or unfit recruits, and these were employed on police duties and public works. Conscription ended, and national defense was confided to a crack professional army based on the capital whose tactical units were controlled directly from the palace.

During the Sung Dynasty these imperial troops were rotated in the provinces for three-year spells of duty under different garrison commanders, but the commanders themselves did not move. By keeping the generals in fixed posts and circulating the soldiers, the sovereign made sure that no lasting links of loyalty were forged and no regional conspiracy could be mounted against the throne. (Toward the end of 1973, when senior generals of the People's Liberation Army had been commanding the same formations in the same areas for five, ten, and even fifteen years, Mao inverted the Sung Dynasty formula. He left the soldiers where they were, but cross-posted eight out of eleven regional commanders whose local authority and local allegiances had transformed them into powerful "red warlords.")

Sung T'ai-tsu was nevertheless able to subjugate most of the ten independent states in the south rapidly and with little bloodshed. Sickened by the sad, splintered condition of their civilization, the ordinary Chinese had been waiting for a leader to arise so that they could become one and at peace again under a new Son of Heaven. And although he practiced time-honored Legalist techniques, his success was also due (according to historical records) to his disarming policies and his reputation for showing a nicely calculated sense of humanity on occasion, whether he was sending his own fur robes to a fighting general on a freezing front or treating a rebel with leniency.

For in his campaign to put China together again, the emperor displayed something of the qualities of Chuko Liang. After King Liu of South Han surrendered to him in 971, he enfeoffed him as a marquis, received him in the imperial park, and offered him wine. Now this king was known for his disagreeable habit of killing off ministers he no longer favored by poisoning them, and as he took the cup from the emperor he could not stop himself from crying out in his fright, "Your subject's crimes certainly merit death, but I beg Your Majesty to spare your subject's life. Indeed I do not dare drink this wine."

Sung T'ai-tsu laughed and took back the cup. "I treat men honestly," he said, and swallowed the wine himself, teaching the abashed marquis a memorable lesson while making him a loyal friend for life.

When Ch'ien Shu of Wu Yueh, another intransigent monarch, wished to bring tribute to court as proof of his doubtful allegiance, ministers presented the emperor with numerous memorials urging him to lock the rebel up in order to avert trouble in the future. Sung T'ai-tsu gave the man a favorable audience, nonetheless, and as he left presented him with a bundle wrapped in yellow cloth, telling him to open it only when he was halfway home. On doing so, the reluctant vassal found that it contained all the memorials advocating that he be imprisoned forthwith.

While adroitly "pacifying" the southern states, however, Sung T'ai-tsu did not attempt to recapture the lands beyond the Yellow River lost to the Kitan when the T'ang Dynasty collapsed. His object was to keep the peace in and around a unified China no longer bristling with weapons and warlords, not to make war with a powerful army which might be turned against himself instead of against his enemies.

The same civilized policy was pursued by most of his successors, and after one disastrous battle and much inconclusive maneuvering thereafter, the third Sung emperor decided in 1004 that the best way to "pacify" the Kitan was to pay them tribute. By the time Ethelred the Unready of England was placating his importunate neighbors with danegeld in the West, Sung China was sending the Kitan silk, tea, and silver at the opposite end of the world, and playing them off against the other strong barbarian state to the north, the Hsia. This form of defense cost less than one tenth of the annual sum needed to maintain a large army, and it seemed cheap at the price. But it was to produce results so lamentable that the Chinese were never to forget them.

All went well as long as the delicate exchanges between Sung, Kitan, and Hsia enabled them to forgo fighting and to settle their differences amicably—or in kind. But meanwhile the Sung army became unhealthily swollen with static veterans too old to fight, and the mobile units circulating in the provinces under Sung T'ai-tsu's security system too often found themselves in unfamiliar country under an unfamiliar commander when an adversary attacked. In consequence a new, rising power—the nomadic Kin—not only wiped out the Kitan empire in 1125, but within a year seized the Sung capital at Kaifeng, capturing the emperor and his father. Their horsemen then pursued the fleeing Chinese, crossing the Yangtse River and plundering cities as far south as Hangchow and Ningpo.

Disarmed by their own diplomacy, incapable of defending themselves competently, Kitan and Sung had both fallen before the first barbarian bully to challenge them. To their terrible cost the Chinese had ignored the golden rule propounded by their philosophers and strategists since the days of Confucius—"in peace men should prepare for war, and in war men should prepare for peace." Words must be backed by weapons. Only the maze of lakes and marshes and waterways of Central China had slowed down the Kin cavalry, as they had slowed down the Tibetan cavalry nearly eight hundred years before.

The Chinese had not, of course, lacked the weapons themselves, for they were technically far in advance of the West. In the seventeenth century Francis Bacon was to write of three discoveries "unknown to the ancients, of which the origin, though recent, is obscure and inglorious; namely printing, gunpowder, and the magnet." But a Taoist book printed in the ninth century had already warned alchemists of the properties of gunpowder, which the Chinese used in flame throwers in 919, and not long afterward in bamboo grenades and incendiary rockets.

They had discovered not only polarity but magnetic variation, and by the beginning of the Sung Dynasty their armies and ships were carrying a "south-pointing fish" or "needle" to guide them. They were sailing giant junks as far as the Persian Gulf, and when men in England were fleeing before the longships of the Vikings, naval craft driven by treadmill paddle wheels were keeping the peace on China's rivers and lakes. A fleet of these, mounted with trebuchets firing explosive bombs, was to smash an invading armada of six hundred vessels on the Yangtse in 1161.

But meanwhile, as the ancients had emphasized, it was not the steel in the sword but the steel in the man that counted, and the Sung army was mercenary and soft. Porters carried its camp stores, and its soldiers demanded extra pay for serving far from their homes. The landed gentry wanted prosperity at any price, and ministers urged their emperor to capitulate to the alien Kin and buy them off rather than waste money on war and still see the rich fields of China ravaged. In 1141 the Chinese sued for peace, and purchased it with gold, horses, and oxen. The latest Sung emperor, having first ascended the throne at Nanking, had already withdrawn his capital even farther south to the gorgeous city of Hangchow.

23

Absolute Scholarship Corrupts Absolutely

The mood of the moment in Hangchow was hardly conducive to valor. Farther to the west, this was an uneasy epoch of war and conquest in which the Christians launched their often bloody crusades, Saladin was to take Jerusalem, and the merciless hordes of Genghis Khan were to ravage Asia from the Mediterranean to the China Seas. But whereas Europe was a cultural pauper when it opened, the Southern Sung Empire was a populous island of civilized and luxurious living, so that Marco Polo was later to write of its capital on the enchanting West Lake, "It is without doubt the finest and most splendid city in the world."

More than a thousand years had passed since the heyday of Han China. Hangchow was solidly paved with stone and brick, bisected by a grand Imperial Way, and veined with canals which were flanked by weeping willows and crossed by 117 decorative bridges. A public sanitation service kept the streets clean; 2,000 firemen, equipped with fireproof clothing, manned stations at intervals of 500 yards.

In the homes of the wealthy, the unsurpassed Chinese landscape scrolls of the Sung artists sometimes covered entire walls, and rooms were decorated with delicate vases and other antiques which were already being faked by experts in the thriving curio business. Big houses had their own baths, while for the more (or less) modest there were several hundred public bathhouses in the city, whose keepers (like men in every other calling) belonged to their own guild—"The Companions of the Fragrant Water."

Apart from the more obvious luxuries, shops sold rhinoceros hide, exotic fish, painted fans, artificial flowers, toilet paper, and beauty aids like tinted nail varnish, hair transformations, and liquid soap. The restaurants of Hangchow offered hundreds of dishes, including steamed dog and "two-legged mutton" (*Homo sapiens,* suitably garnished). Special agencies provided escorts, concubines, boy singers, and chair porters. Talented courtesans promised dalliance, and on the mountain-ringed West Lake, the floating fields of flowering lotus were threaded by gaily painted boats bearing gaily painted girls who sang beguilingly for the young and old exquisites of a city largely given over to pleasure and art and drink and dreams.

Men were preoccupied with all aspects of Mammon, however. The government issued paper currency backed by silver and gold, and when inflation loomed, tried to make it more attractive by printing notes made of a scented mixture of paper and silk. Cash and food were distributed to the needy, and the state ran hospitals, orphanages, and almshouses. But poverty still dogged the peasant, who might drown an unwanted baby at birth in a lean year, and many unfortunates slept in the streets of the capital. Even before the loss of the north, Wang An-shih, the great "socialist" reformer of the dynasty who had tried to narrow the gap between rich and ragged, had been unable to prevail for long against China's grasping and corrupt conservatives.

Like Sang Hung-yang before him, this much-maligned innovator, who also rose from humble beginnings to become an outstanding minister, ruled that grain and silk should be exchanged among the provinces to smooth out regional gluts and shortages (instead of being sent to the capital as tribute), and that farmers might borrow at low rates of interest before the sowing season and repay after the harvest. He fixed prices and limited profits, persuaded the emperor to publish edicts against trade monopolies, and obliged scholars who wished to become mandarins to study law and political economy as well as the Classics.

All this inevitably brought about his ears the wrath of the officials, the landed gentry, and the mercantile magnates for whom the cause of the wretched poor was no more deserving than the cause of the wretched patriots who wanted to throw away good money trying to win back the north. Moreover, die-hard Confucians denounced all innovators as moral health hazards, if only because they substituted new ideas for old, and the novel proposition that mandarins should know more than the Classics and the commentaries written upon them particularly outraged them at that juncture.

For it was a time of philosophical ferment, during which the first "Neoconfucians" were seeking to give the dry, ethical teachings of their sages a metaphysical sheen that would attract those seduced by the alien and more exotic influence of Buddhism. The ancient texts were re-examined, and conveniently yielded a hitherto unsuspected element—a *Li* that was the equivalent of the First Principle of the Taoist cosmos, in accordance with which *yin* and *yang* and the Five Virtues interacted.

This *Li* was the supreme law controlling the universe, and the Sung emperors were among the first to find it a sympathetic invention. And not without reason. Chu Hsi, the greatest of the Neoconfucians, declared, "Since *Li* is eternal, the order of ruler and subject, of upper and lower should never change." *Li* decreed that China should be a centralized state administered by scholar-officials versed in the Classics. If the system were tampered with, therefore, all would dissolve into chaos, for the cosmic ecology itself would have been upset.

The doctrine enabled men in authority to excuse everything they did themselves and to condemn the less pleasing acts of others. As one commentator put it sardonically, "Those who have influence and position are found to have *Li* on their side . . . so that even when they are wrong, they insist they are right. But if an inferior protests that he has *Li* on his side, he is denounced for insubordination." The new *Li* automatically perpetuated the Establishment—the imperial mandate and the imperial hierarchy of mandarins—and the Establishment gratefully perpetuated the new *Li*. The Chinese were beginning to turn in upon themselves, to push their way down dark and narrow alleys of stultified thinking, so that one scholar was later to write:

"When Confucius sat in the hall, he wore a belt around the waist and a double-edged sword. Of his seventy-two students some studied the rites, some played the lute, some practiced archery, some drilled with the spear, some talked humanity and filial piety, and some discussed military or agricultural or political affairs.

"But the Confucians of the Sung Dynasty wore no sword belts, and they sat in silence with downcast eyes, like clay figures. Of the students, some said not a word, some recited the Classics in low peculiar tones, some busied themselves annotating the works of Confucius and Mencius. All had a sacred and inviolable air of godlike solemnity." [1]

The robust outlook and inquiring minds of the sages were forgotten. Nothing was left but hollow, ritualistic teaching, from which was drawn in the name of Confucian "culture" a set of rigid and pernicious commandments and taboos. Of filial piety the Sung philosophers said, "If the father wishes the son to die, the son cannot but die." A woman had to be "chaste," meaning that if she were widowed she must on no account marry again—the younger she was and the poorer she became, the more virtuous her chastity. Most praised among women were those who killed themselves in the most excruciating manner possible when their husbands died—or even their betrothed. Eunuchs, opium smoking, the loathsome custom of foot binding—all were in time rationalized as aspects of *Li*.

In Hangchow the military were the lowest form of life: "You do not use good iron to make a nail, or a good man to make a soldier." The merchant was moving up the scale, and the days were gone when he was compelled to dress in coarse cloth, to wear one white shoe and one black. The scholar, however, was supreme, almost sacrosanct. Before King John signed the Magna Carta in 1215, the civil service examinations in China were attracting several thousand candidates every year from each of the empire's sixteen provinces, and the humblest could aspire to eminence by virtue of his learning. But as only a man tried and tested in the Classics was considered fit to be an official, the object of studying them was no longer to acquire propriety and wisdom, but simply to acquire public office.

"Divine instruction" deteriorated into hidebound pedantry. The examinations themselves became so stylized that before long what was required of the candidate was an empty exposition of the doctrine of the Confucian sages composed in a given form and to a given length. Personal views were not wanted, and any imaginative thinking could spell failure. A good fist with a writing brush and an ability to memorize and quote in context were the best guarantees of success, and the whole admirable, elaborate system began to produce a mandarinate packed with ignorant grinds and craven dullards.

That suited the ruler perfectly, and the scholars themselves would have been the last to change the formula. For once they had passed, perhaps come first in the imperial finals, everything was open to them—honor and influence and position, riches and land, and glory for the whole clan. Poor families pinched and scraped to put their sons on the long road to bureaucratic power, for even if they fell by the wayside, they would have earned a new respect from all others: "Go to the examination and if you only fart, you will be doing something for your ancestors," the Chinese said. A failed licentiate also commanded esteem. He had still taken the first steps toward the ultimate in prestige—and servility.

For servile they were, these mandarins—as slavish toward their superiors as they were arrogant toward their subordinates and scornful of the rest of society. If the emperor slapped a minister lightly on the shoulder as a sign of approval or benevolence, the man would rush off to have a dragon's claw embroidered on his robe where the Son of Heaven had touched it. But when banqueting with inferiors, he would keep all others waiting, and then make the longest and most platitudinous speech.

The corruption of the mandarinate continued through the dynasties so that the Director of the Central Propaganda Section of the Chinese Communist Party was to be quoted in the Peking *People's Daily* of July 24, 1957, as saying: "Cadres in the Communist Party are divided into three categories: the highest level—privileged, fatuous, conservative, ignorant, uncultured people who obstruct progress; the middle level—illegal local emperors who pretend to obey but do not, whose political enthusiasm has faded, whose only idea is to clutch at enjoyment; and finally the lower level—a herd of stupid and ignorant clots without regard for law or morality, who shit and piss on the heads of the people, enjoying their authority and good fortune, all 'yes sir, yes sir' to their superiors, playing poker and not giving a damn about performing their duties."

He could have been describing the civil servants of the Sung Dynasty, in whose day it first became the fashion for Chinese to call themselves "smooth subjects," submissive and loyal to the nearest authority. Their own emperor was a vassal of the Kin, and their more docile descendants were to fly flags and banners proclaiming them "smooth subjects" of the invading Mongols during the Yuan Dynasty, of marauding Japanese pirates during the Ming Dynasty, of the usurping Manchus during the Ch'ing Dynasty. And when foreigners from the West carved up their country for the concessions it offered, they became "smooth subjects" in turn of the Russians, the British, the Americans, the Germans—according to the particular slice of China in which they lived.

But while the Sung emperors may seem to have ruled over a bloodless society of timid sycophants, for every *yin* there is a *yang*, and even in the environs of Hangchow men were to erect a temple to the revered memory of the heroic Yo Fei.

24

The Hero Worshippers

In the ideal society, the Taoists had said, there would be no "filial sons" or "loyal subjects," for the simple reason that all would be filial and loyal. To the Chinese, therefore, the advent of an outstanding "hero" is a sure sign of evil times in which most men are being complaisant, cowardly, or corrupt in the face of disaster or dishonor. It was thus inevitable that the soft Southern Sung Dynasty should produce a blood-and-iron champion on the battlefield who was to become one of the most famous figures in the Chinese military pantheon.

The record of the Sung could not be solely one of shameful surrender in any case, for when the Kin first overran much of the empire, they refused to negotiate with the Chinese at all, and meanwhile their callous treatment of the millions they had already subjugated aroused the indignation of many of those still free in the south. In consequence, the Chinese living in semi-bondage in the north organized a "loyal and righteous army" of rebels, the war party at the Sung court in Hangchow won a temporary victory over the peacemakers, and, as usual, the moment for action found its man waiting in the wings.

Yo Fei had been born into a farming family, but he had read his Sun Tzu, he rode like a barbarian, he could bend a three-hundred-pound bow, and his philosophy of life was tattooed on his back—"Absolute Loyalty to the Country." He became a soldier at the age of twenty and proved so able that within a few years he was commanding a powerful army with a bad reputation among the Kin for winning its fights.

He himself attracted loyalty. He was wiry and vigorous and bold, lively of eye and quick of wit, never arrogant, self-indulgent, or idle. He always led his men into action personally, and he had discovered a fatal weakness in the "iron horse," the basic battle unit of the Kin cavalry which had hitherto panicked the Chinese foot soldiers.

This "iron horse" was formed by binding together three mounts ridden by men wearing heavy armor and helmets, and once it was launched full tilt at the enemy its sheer mass and momentum made it irresistible. Yo Fei's defense was the "star scatter." As the Kin charged, the Chinese broke ranks and dispersed, leaving the frustrated enemy striking at nothing until he was exhausted. Formidable in the advance, the "iron horses" were clumsy to maneuver and vulnerable during the withdrawal, when Yo Fei would throw fresh reserves of picked veterans against them. These would not confront the mounted Kin, but attack low and from the flank, slashing at the legs of the nearest horse with a heavy sword. As soon as one horse fell, all three went down in a helpless tangle, and the rest was easy slaughter. (Lin Piao adapted Yo Fei's "star scatter," introducing into the Red Army the "three-thirds system" whereby whole battalions would suddenly break up into independent fighting squads of only three or four men which would then attack in an irregular wave, reconcentrating and dispersing again unpredictably.)

The one ambition of the single-minded Yo Fei was to reconquer the north for China. As a farmer's son he sympathized with the destitute peasants stripped of their lands by the Kin, and as a soldier he appreciated their potential as allies. He therefore sent men deep into Kin territory for secret talks with the leaders of the "loyal and righteous army," exchanging intelligence and synchronizing operations with them so that when he attacked, the partisans would cut the Kin supply lines. He began to score heavily and repeatedly against the enemy until, to the joy of the Chinese populace, he and his son had taken their army to within fifteen miles of

Kaifeng, and his successes north of the Yellow River were threatening to force the Kin back toward their original homeland in Manchuria. But before he could win a decisive victory at the front, the war party in the rear suffered a decisive defeat.

The Sung emperor in Hangchow was the younger brother of the ruler who had been captured when Kaifeng fell to the Kin. He was a peaceable, artistic man who did not want more war and was in particular uninterested in a victory that might procure the release of his elder brother and so lose him the throne. Moreover, his chief minister was a great landowner named Ch'in K'uei who led a glib peace party of powerful grandees at court that simply wrote off their unhappy compatriots in Kin hands as nationals of another state. "Southerners belong to the south, northerners to the north," as Ch'in K'uei put it, anticipating by more than eight hundred years those who would complacently regard two Koreas, two Vietnams, even two Chinas as natural geopolitical phenomena.

Despite the opposition of the dignitaries behind Yo Fei, the Sung court reached a covert agreement with the Kin, and as they were about to mount a new expedition against the north, the general and his son were summoned to the palace, where Ch'in K'uei ordered that they be thrown into prison and there secretly dispatched. The heroic struggle against the Kin which had begun in 1131 ended exactly ten years later with a sordid double murder in Hangchow. It is said that Yo Fei's last words were "Return us our mountains and rivers," but all that he had won back was given up again. The body of China was now formally cut in two and divided between the empires of Northern Kin and Southern Sung, with the Chinese vassal paying annual tribute to the Kin suzerain.

Yo Fei and his son were not to be forgotten, however. Their bodies were smuggled out of the palace and buried beside the West Lake, where even now the imposing Temple of Prince Yo provides the setting for a curious tableau (unless it has been changed recently). On one side of the steps are the tombs of the hero and his son, on the other their statues. Below these, Ch'in K'uei and his wife and two henchmen kneel with bound hands, four battered iron figures scarred and discolored by centuries of reproachful pilgrims who have showered them with abuse and stones and beaten them with their wooden shoes, as is the custom. "The green hills have the good fortune to hold the bones of the loyal," read the words of one protesting graffiti artist, date unknown, "but guiltless iron is cast in the form of a treacherous minister."

The temple symbolizes a Chinese truth that makes the character of the Chinese hero required reading—that in the minds of the millions the ghosts of the past are the gods of the present. And the process may be self-perpetuating, for in part the very real Yo Fei of the Sung Dynasty belongs to hallowed legend because he can be identified with another, earlier legend—Chang Fei of *The Romance of the Three Kingdoms.*

Chang Fei, who swore the oath of brotherhood in the peach garden with Liu Pei and Kuan Yu, was an improbable myth of a man, but so vividly portrayed that to most Chinese he is at once recognizable when met today. He had a head like a leopard, round and staring eyes, a pointed jowl, and stiff whiskers. His nature was fierce and bold, his voice like thunder. He never took thought for himself or counted the enemy in front of him, but when convinced he was right, would speak and act without any hesitation—or reflection. He was the personification of loyalty and impetuous courage, and he hated evil.

This foible prompted him to drag a corrupt high official off by the hair one day, bind him to a hitching post, and, once he was defenseless, flog him to within an inch of his life. For when he hated there was no pity, just as when he loved there was no limit. He would shout an enemy army off the battlefield, curse his sworn brother Kuan Yu for a traitor when he joined Ts'ao Ts'ao (not understanding the motives involved), and then round on Liu Pei for pausing to think before sending troops to avenge Kuan Yu's death.

When Liu Pei could not at first coax the Sleeping Dragon into receiving him in his thatched hut, Chang Fei's formulas for bringing the elusive sage to his beloved brother were to "take a rope and bind him" or "go behind the house and set fire to it." Fiery, fearless, totally inflexible, and sometimes maddeningly obtuse, Chang Fei was finally murdered by his own soldiers. But for Chinese conditioned to be pliant and to justify connivance with subtle casuistry, his is the unyielding, uncompromising spirit that alone saves men in times of terror.

However, he is still not Kuan Yu—the "God of War" who accepted the gifts of Ts'ao Ts'ao when he was cornered, but did not let them shake his loyalty to Liu Pei once he could escape. Countless temples were to be raised to "Lord Kuan," and even today a strict ritual must be observed by actors in non-Communist Chinese communities who play the role in operas inspired by *The Romance of the Three Kingdoms.*

They must abstain from eating meat for ten days before the performance, and bathe and sleep alone. Before going on the stage, they must burn incense and bow to a picture of the hero stamped on a piece of yellow paper, which they then put into the military headdress they wear. Once made up for the part, they must conserve their energies, and not chat or joke with others. After the performance, they must take the paper likeness of Kuan Yu from their heads, kowtow to it, burn it with incense, and wash their faces. Only when they have removed their make-up and costume may they talk freely, eat, and defecate.

These taboos are not just part of the mumbo jumbo of a notoriously superstitious profession. A sophisticated senior business executive playing Kuan Yu in amateur Peking opera in Singapore in the early 1970's would go through the same motions. They do not imply worship of a deity, but reverence for the sacred principles that he personifies, the principles of the *hsieh,* or knight.

It was no coincidence that the Chinese who rebelled against the Kin during the Sung Dynasty called their band the "loyal and righteous army," for the two ideograms *chung* and *yi* express the virtues that the Chinese venerate in the *hsieh,* and to which they also pay homage when they bow to the great image of Yo Fei in his temple at Hangchow, or to the images of Kuan Yu to be found in temples from Malaysia to San Francisco.

Chung is accurately translated as "loyalty." *Yi* is usually translated as "righteousness," but it is made up of the characters for "sheep" and "I," and since in the Chinese context "sheep" does not denote docility, but sacrifice, the combination carries the sense of a man offering himself up to Heaven for what is right. *Yi* therefore means honorable conduct, moral duty, chivalry, to do without fear what is seemly.

This is not a digression. Restless under the rule of the Manchus, the Chinese expressed their angry nationalism by worshipping Yo Fei and Kuan Yu, and their alien emperors found it expedient to deflect popular hostility by honoring the cult of Kuan Yu themselves.They ennobled him posthumously as the "loyal and righteous, divine and martial great sovereign," and so turned those perilously evocative Chinese monosyllables to their own account. For the successful Machiavelli must be sensitive to the psychological touchstones by which he will be judged, and in China the touchstones were the heroes of the past.

They were all the more dangerous because they might so easily belong to the realm of the rebel rather than the realm of the ruler. The Chinese *hsieh,* like the Christian knight, defended the country against the enemy, the weak against the wicked, the poor against the proud. But he was no gentleman by virtue of noble birth or royal favor. The down-at-heel Liu Pei may have been of imperial ancestry, but Chang Fei was a wine seller and a dog butcher, and Kuan Yu was on the run for killing a man when the trio swore their oath in the peach garden. In other societies he would hardly have been considered "parfit" or "gentil," an exemplar of "honorable conduct" and "moral duty." He was a wanted murderer. But he had slaughtered a bully, no matter how or why. And in China that gave him a valid claim not only to respectability but to respect.

25

The Living Dead

Subjected to much misery and misrule in their long history, the cheated Chinese learned to scrutinize all authority for flaws and forgeries before taking it seriously, and for them a crime committed in the name of justice was no crime where there was no justice. In a corrupt society the honest man too often found himself an outlaw, while the rogue was a reputable member of the Establishment. The meanings of words were inverted, so that the bestial killer might be called "emperor" and the benefactor he sought to slay "bandit."

For redress, therefore, the millions looked not to the magistrates, but to delinquent do-gooders who became the savage watchdogs of the community. "Do not prate to me of justice and humanity," said the Chinese. "The man who does me a good turn is a good man." The *hsieh,* for whom to uphold the "right" was to punish the corrupt, the cruel, and the rapacious, and to protect the downtrodden and the victimized, was the hero of his day whatever the price on his head.

But a wider company of Bad Samaritans grew from this tradition—the "men of the rivers and lakes" who did not settle and marry and accumulate the duties and dependents that made others cowardly, but who were forever on the move. Idealistic vagabonds or fugitives from injustice, their "rivers and lakes" meant the whole world of China, a world within which all men were brothers, and which had its own code ("while the court has its laws"). They were impulsive ruffians, careless of Confucian injunctions that violence was a vice, "nature's gentlemen" at their best, and bound by their loyalty to each other. They would say what most men would not dare to say, and do what most men dared not do, they challenged tyranny whenever they met it, and their rough justice was too often the only kind available.

In the twelfth century a worthy named Sung Chiang gathered around himself a band of these "fine fellows" who had flouted the law, and set up a nest of brigands in the inaccessible, marsh-bound mountains of Shantung—a process characteristically known in China as "forming a righteous assembly." Raising an apricot banner on which were inscribed the words "Performing the Way on Behalf of Heaven," Sung Chiang rustled horses, built fighting vessels easy to maneuver in the water-logged country below the prodigious peaks of Liang Shan P'o, and trained his men until they were the scourge and the salvation of ten surrounding counties—robbing the rich, helping the poor, and harassing the iniquitous local administration. Their numbers multiplied rapidly, and they were able to defy and defeat the imperial troops sent to exterminate them, although few had learning or wit and most were crude if muscular peasants who could "support people on their fists and horses on their shoulders."

The exploits of this Robin Hood of the Orient inspired the great classical novel *Shui Hu Chuan—Water Margin* [1]—in which the epic story of 108 villains who flee from the abuses of Sung justice to become the heroes of Liang Shan P'o is related. Sung Chiang is called by his real name, and heads a hodgepodge of fictional drifters, deserters, monks and merchants, ruined peasants and benevolent landlords and threadbare aristocrats who have been grievously wronged by authority or hounded by the magistrates (because they have killed off a venal mandarin or two in the heat of the moment or given way to some similar impulse).

They are impeccably "loyal and righteous," their fraternal allegiance is as binding as the oath sworn in the peach garden, their crafty tactics smack of Sun Tzu, but the peculiar niceties of their philosophy are also well brought out. Wu Sung (who slew the tiger with his bare hands) escapes to Liang Shan P'o because he has also butchered his sister-in-law, after failing to get her convicted in the corrupt Chinese courts for poisoning his brother. It is not his crime that disgusts other members of the brotherhood like Li Kuei, alias "Iron Ox," however, but his appeal to the magistracy for redress in the first place.

This Iron Ox is a rude, murderous, damn-the-consequences giant with a black skin and yellow hair, for whom recourse to the law is not only a ludicrous waste of time and effort, but an unhealthy habit that undermines men's instinct for rebellion. He is contemptuous of the entire imperial establishment, and the only weapon with which he is prepared to fight injustice is not justice, but his great steel ax: "Smite first and discuss things afterward," as he would say. He kills without blinking an eyelid, but those he kills are overbearing officials, and when he catches a thief trying to rob him, he sets him free and gives him money on learning that he is the sole support of an eighty-year-old mother.

Men like these were usually impatient, undiscriminating, without restraint. They could only fight crime with more crime, and once they had struck an undeserved blow, they could not make good the wound. They could only create chaos, and they could not live in society. Yet they reflected the real sense of right and wrong among the ordinary Chinese, their ingrained suspicion of published codes, the knowledge that human society is flesh and blood, not edicts, and the cynicism that says that when the law is not corrupt, it is too often sterile. For a people hungry for common compassion but bereft of faith in the mercy of prefects, the bravo who stepped in and evened the score by hacking someone's head off there and then represented swift and divine retribution, "the Way of Heaven" itself.

He was also a glimpse of an alternative, especially if the emperor was a foreign usurper. During the Ch'ing Dynasty, when China was ruled by the Manchus, conspirators not only turned to Yo Fei and Kuan Yu for inspiration, but quoted from *Water Margin* to incite the rebellious to band together in secret societies against the alien. The societies had—and have—their own "Hall of Loyalty and Righteousness," and one of them modeled its oath on that sworn on Liang Shan P'o—"Yesterday separated, today joined in one hall, with the stars as our brothers, Heaven and Earth our father and mother . . ." Chinese thugs exploit and twist the ideals of *chung* and *yi* for their own ends in these freemasonries, which have now degenerated into criminal gangs of thieves, pimps, extortioners, and murderers. But their members still sacrifice to Kuan Yu, swear solemn pledges of loyalty, and vow to face death rather than reveal a secret or betray a brother. For some Chinese, therefore, they seem to offer a haven in a soulless bureaucratic universe in which the towns are too large for men to know one another, and the records so voluminous that no one can expect more than a glance from the government for his grievances and sorrows.

Sung Chiang and his merry men live in the minds of Chinese even where no secret societies are allowed to exist—in China itself. Mao Tsetung is said to have carried *Water Margin* in his knapsack when young, and the parallel between the 108 heroes in their aerie above the swamps of Shantung and Mao with his first guerrillas in the mountain fastnesses of Chingkangshan needs no checking with a protractor.

Mao's followers were also "bandits" fleeing from the "justice" of Chiang Kai-shek who set out to rob the rich and succor the poor and to strike ruthlessly at the existing order and its minions. But Communism and the Communist Party offered a brotherhood with a *yi* and a *chung* that could evoke an instinctive response from the Chinese masses. So Mao became the "emperor" and Chiang Kai-shek the "bandit." Wu Sung and the tiger changed roles.

The Communists have been very conscious of the influence of *Water Margin* and it has, in consequence, touched off ideological fireworks in Peking. The book was published again in China in 1972, whereupon hundreds queued every day to buy it until it was sold out. But the new Communist edition ended with the "fine fellows" safe in the marshes and still in the ascendant, whereas the original version went on to relate how Sung Chiang and his heroes, lured into the open by an imperial pardon, were treacherously destroyed after they themselves had somewhat shamefully put down another rebellion on behalf of the Son of Heaven.

It was a mistake to cut that, some Maoist commentators protested. The betrayal of the heroes by the corrupt imperial regime taught that "unless revolutionaries are resolute, they will be exploited," and proved that "in the struggle between oppressed peoples and the ruling class there is no room for compromise." Wrong, countered their opponents. The obnoxious suggestion that a great rebel like Sung Chiang would not only accept a pardon but agree to suppress a popular revolt started by someone else had to be thrown out. The book had to show that leaders of peasant rebellions did not betray their class or surrender to their rulers, so that its revolutionary importance would be enhanced.

In the summer of 1975, Chairman Mao himself reputedly issued an "instruction" urging the masses all over the country to discuss and criticize the grievous errors of Sung Chiang, in what the Communist press described as "a new struggle of great significance on the political and ideological front." The devious medieval bandit had "pushed a capitulationist line" which was "in the interests of the landlord class." He had sabotaged the peasant rebellion by submitting to imperial authority, just as backsliding "revisionists" in China of the 1970's were prepared to pander not only to bourgeois tradition at home but to the "new tsars" across the border in the Soviet Union.

Mao—who has been heard to identify distinguished veteran cadres around him with characters from *Water Margin*—knows that the eternal image of the *hsieh* is not to be torn from the Chinese retina in one generation. Nevertheless, the Party is the only brotherhood that may now exist, and in the future all heroic inspiration must be associated with the regime itself, not with rebellion against it. The old images must therefore be overstamped with those of newer idols.

The Communists are accordingly creating their own revolutionary gods, not only from among the arthritic septuagenarians of the Long March, but from among young men and women whose acts of courage are flashed across the country and whose names are repeatedly imprinted on the minds of all by the great ubiquitous Chinese propaganda machine.

These have only one composite loyalty—Chairman Mao, the Communist Party, and the Chinese people. And when the masses readily compare some comrade to Hsu Kuo-p'ing (who tackled a bear in 1969 armed only with Mao's Little Red Book) rather than Wu Sung (who tackled a tiger without it), the Chinese Communists will have begun to win their battle against the sticky fingers of their own national mythology.

Somehow the stereotype of the turbulent past must be transmuted into the stereotype of a Communist present, and the "hero nature" that kills for *yi* and puts loyalty before law transmuted into the "party nature" that will make any sacrifice for the Communist cause. For the Chinese spirit (obverse—prudent Oriental prevarication; reverse—impulsive quixotic courage) is the basic currency in which the modern ruler must deal, and which he must display himself if he is to enjoy credit with the masses.

Both sides of this coin were much in evidence in the last days of the Sung Dynasty when, the Kin having swooped down on the Kitan, the Mongols swooped down on the Kin.

Genghis Khan was a brilliant soldier, and the standards of savagery he demanded of his terrifying hordes of unwashed, drunken, yet superb cavalry can be compared to advantage even with those set by the First Emperor of Ch'in. If the defenders of towns in his path did not submit to him at once without loosing a single arrow, their inhabitants were butchered down to the last babe in arms. And when, having ravaged and massacred their way through Russia and the rest of Asia, his horsemen annihilated the Hsia empire in 1224, they reduced its cities to flattened boneyards and left only one man in a hundred alive.

The sinified Kin, who had earlier lost Peking[2] to the Mongols, thereupon begged the Chinese to come to their aid, if only in their own selfish interest ("We are to you as the lips are to the teeth; when the lips are gone the teeth are cold"). But the myopic mandarins in Hangchow saw this as a chance to strike at their old enemies in the north, and allied themselves with the new and pitiless invader against them. Kaifeng fell in 1233, and with the Kin vanquished and China isolated, the Sung ministers committed the final idiocy of ordering an attack on the Mongols themselves.

The Mongols swept south to find the going harder—and sometimes disconcertingly softer—than anything they had encountered in Western Asia or Europe. The wetlands hampered their cavalry, the maddening tangle of waterways in some parts of Central China forced them to take to boats which stubbornly refused to handle like horses, they were laid low by disease, and they were more than once routed with explosive bombs and rockets. But there were Chinese fighting on both sides, and many of the Chinese gentry, hoping to keep their estates and official posts, threw in their lot with the Mongols and gave their loyalty thereafter to the Yuan Dynasty founded by Kublai Khan in Peking. By 1276 the Khan's cavalry were outside Hangchow, the emperor was a child, and although many Chinese were in a pugnacious mood, the court favored surrender.

It was at this moment that a prefect in South China named Wen T'ien-hsiang, a wealthy aristocrat still in his early thirties who had much admired the ill-fated Yo Fei, sold his estate and hastily raised an army to fight the advancing horde. With no time for training, he force-marched 10,000 volunteers to the capital, where they received a tumultuous welcome, and almost at once threw himself into battle against the Mongols at the head of 3,000 cavalry. Half of his men were killed, none surrendered, but the day was lost. The chief minister at court fled, and Wen was appointed in his place—with instructions to negotiate a peace.

Refusing to regard any talks with the Mongols as a prelude to capitulation, Wen T'ien-hsiang took a high tone with the enemy commander when he reached his camp, berating the barbarian for invading Chinese soil at all. The Mongol general protested that the Sung Dynasty was decadent, and that Kublai Khan merely wished to replace it with a just and benign government. "In that case withdraw your army and then we can discuss a settlement," riposted Wen, and shrugged off threats against his person with the words "If the country exists, I too shall exist; if the country dies, I too shall die."

However, less obstinate ministers quietly yielded the city to the Mongols, who promptly took the emperor and most of his court to Peking. Wen escaped en route, disguised himself as a beggar, and raised a force to recapture the Central Plain, only to be defeated again. The Mongols then pursued him until, his army smashed in a final battle in Fukien Province and his commanders dead, the indefatigable patriot withdrew into the mountains of Kwangtung to rally men around him once more. But he was surrounded and made prisoner by a turncoat Chinese general, and when he tried to poison himself, he was prevented.

Meanwhile, the brothers of the captive Son of Heaven had been compelled to withdraw southward, and the day came when the youngest of them all found himself ruler of China with little more land to call his own than the desolate, rocky island of Yaishan off the Kwangtung coast. Seeing that the situation was now hopeless, a courageous minister took the eight-year-old emperor on his back and jumped into the sea with him from a high cliff so that he would avoid the disgrace of falling into enemy hands.

Wen was escorted to Peking, where Kublai Khan received him with great ceremony and promised him high honors if he would show to the Yuan Dynasty the same loyalty he had shown to the degenerate Sung. Wen stoutly refused to "acknowledge a bandit as his father" and was thrown into prison to think things over. But his unwavering answer to all further offers was that to live on one's knees was shameful, only to stand up and die was glorious, and after four years the Mongols, losing all patience, duly executed him.

Although he consistently lost his arguments and his battles, Wen T'ien-hsiang is for the Chinese the personification of dignified, uncompromising patriotism. His "Song of the True Spirit," composed in his cell, is pasted up on doors by the superstitious to keep out all manner of evils, and it is of gallant figures like his that they say, "Some people now alive are already dead, but some who are already dead still live."

None knows better than a Chinese, however, that a man needs both his soft tongue and his hard teeth—and which will last longer. Yo Fei was the hero and Ch'in K'uei the villain of the piece, and nothing can detract from the glory of the one or the dishonor of the other. Nevertheless, it was the laudable eagerness of the war party at court to fight the Kin that later led Sung ministers into the cardinal error of joining the Mongols against them—and then trying to take on the Mongols alone when the Kin had been eliminated.

Wen T'ien-hsiang is a legend, his steadfastness symbolized by the small, highly polished knife that Chinese Nationalist generals carry—not so that they can defend themselves if cornered, but (in theory) so that they can kill themselves rather than be captured. Yet it was not the teeth of Wen T'ien-hsiang that took the edge off the Mongol invasion of China, saving millions of lives and preserving an entire civilization that might otherwise have been put to fire and sword. It was the tongue of Yelu Ch'u-ts'ai.

Yelu Ch'u-ts'ai was a distinguished Kitan, deeply imbued with Chinese culture and Confucian ideals, who was made prisoner by the Mongols and thereafter became a trusted adviser of Genghis Khan. Now on first reaching the Celestial Empire the Mongols, disgusted to find no good pastureland for their horses, rather typically suggested that it "would be better to exterminate the Chinese and let the grass grow." But Yelu Ch'u-ts'ai was quick to point out to the Great Khan that he would reap far greater profit if, instead of destroying this immensely rich realm, he simply taxed it. And when his captors took Kaifeng after a long and bitter resistance, it was he who discouraged them from massacring the million-odd people within it as a matter of course by reminding them that all the skilled Chinese craftsmen and engineers of the entire region had fled into the city, and could be put to good use if allowed to live. Kaifeng was spared, and China was not laid waste. Never had the Mongols shown such mercy—for the very good reason that the astute Kitan had not appealed to their mercy, but to their greed.

Circumstance is the key to the contradictions in Chinese character, and therefore to the course that their leaders will take at any one time, for even their inflexibility is flexible. And while all Chinese might appreciate that only the tongue of Yelu Ch'u-ts'ai could soften the impact of the Mongol when he invaded, they also knew that only the teeth of another Yo Fei could rid them of the creature.

26

The Tongue and the Teeth

China was now part of a much vaster Mongol empire. Alien influences crowded in, but things Chinese also spread to the ends of the known earth. The Polos arrived, merchants of Venice who stayed to become diplomats, and they were followed by Genoese traders and by Franciscan envoys from the Pope at Avignon. In 1321 a Russian won first place in the imperial examinations. Cloisonné came to Peking from Byzantium, and strange musical instruments from elsewhere in Western Asia.

Meanwhile, Chinese printed textiles appeared in Italy, Chinese playing cards in the Mediterranean; there were Chinese engineers in the Middle East, and Chinese quarters in Novgorod and Moscow. It is believed that the West may first have learned about printing from imperial paper money that was now being turned out not only in Peking but in Tabriz. And one day in 1287 the people of Bordeaux flocked to greet a strange figure who had arrived to seek an audience with King Edward I of England. The visitor was Rabban Sauma, a dignitary of the Nestorian Church who had been born in Peking and had traveled across the entire Mongol empire on a safe-conduct from Kublai Khan.

But the Chinese who constructed the marvelous astronomical instruments intended for the new observatory at Peking, and who invented the prototype of modern telescope mountings, was one of a mere handful entrusted with work of real importance by Kublai. For the object of the khan in employing men of all creeds and countries was to administer China with as few Chinese as possible.

There was little love between the ruler and the ruled. The people were divided into four categories, and the Mongol was the lord of creation. If a Mongol murdered a Chinese, he was simply fined. If he hit a Chinese, the Chinese was not allowed to hit back. By 1325 one man in six was starving, and the population—100,000,000 during the Sung Dynasty—had fallen by half. Officials were corrupt and callous, and the seventh Yuan emperor even revived the idea of massacring the natives, but proposed to do it in batches, killing everyone of the same name at the same time.

However, the aptitude of the Mongol for degenerating from mounted butcher into soft voluptuary was quite exceptional, sporadic uprisings began to break the skin of China, and less than a hundred years after the khans had conquered the Sung, armies raised by a wandering Chinese mendicant called Chu Yuan-chang had not only chased the invaders right out of the country, but had sacked and burned Karakorum, the remote cradle of their immense transcontinental empire.

Although this hero has been described as a repulsively ugly monk, his portraits contradict one another and he certainly had no pretensions to piety. He was born of a miserably poor peasant family, and when a plague of locusts left him orphaned and hungry at the age of seventeen, he took vows in order to be able to eat. But in a poverty-stricken China under the Mongol boot, the temples were in turn to become destitute, and he was soon forced onto the road—a filthy beggar in a ragged robe fated to become the revered ancestor of three centuries of emperors.

Was he worth a second glance? It is said that he killed off obtuse artists who ill-advisedly depicted him as he really looked, while presenting to his princes "likenesses" painted by crafty fellows who gave him a firm chin and a lofty, almost supernatural air. These spoke of him as "Lord of wealth and honor, whose five features face the sky" for the same reason that his enemies called him the "pig emperor"—he had a turned-up snout of a nose.

Yet his face was at least part of his fortune. For when he came before the "marshal" commanding the rebel army that was defying the Mongols in his native region * (after prudently casting lots to discover which camp he should join), the marshal was struck by his appearance and bearing, and not only kept him at his side but made him his son-in-law.

The episode is reminiscent of the marriage of the village headman who had become Han Kao-tsu, the founding emperor of the Han Dynasty fifteen centuries before. And the parallel does not end there. The "Fragrant Army" of this Marshal Kuo Tzu-hsing, who had risen against the Mongols in 1352, belonged to the hallowed tradition of semi-mystical Chinese societies like the Red Eyebrows and the Yellow Turbans. Its followers wore red headdresses, and belonged to the esoteric White Lotus sect of Buddhists, and it was also known as the "Red Army" or the "Turban Army." But once the man who was to found the Ming Dynasty had assumed command of it on the death of his father-in-law, he discarded most of the mumbo jumbo, declared war on the tyranny of the Mongol, and called on all Chinese to help him wipe out their country's shame.

In thirteen years of hard fighting he proved himself a courageous, winning general, but it was his plausible benevolence, his sly common sense, and his "revolutionary" concern for the poor and the downtrodden that enabled him to turn semi-anarchy to advantage and gain an empire. Like other perceptive Chinese from Ts'ao Ts'ao to Mao, he knew that the true leader did not beat swords into plowshares, but used both to beat the enemy. Where he fought well, he made sure that men farmed well. When he moved forward, therefore, he moved forward from firm and well-fed bases in which he enjoyed popular support.

The other rebel chiefs killed and looted for quick profits, but like Han Kao-tsu he coaxed the best among them into

* In modern Anhui Province.

joining him with fine pledges and much high-principled talk, while drawing the people themselves to his side with a shrewd display of clemency. As he advanced he asked the populace for no compromising heroics but only a passive and sympathetic welcome, in exchange for which he promised that his soldiers would not slaughter or pillage, steal women or kill cattle. He announced that he alone would bear the responsibility for uprooting the Yuan Dynasty, and that all men who rallied to him—Chinese, non-Chinese, even Mongol—would thereafter be treated on an equal footing. And like Han Kao-tsu he ensnared those with talent, whatever their origins, and sensibly took their advice.

What should be his grand strategy for overthrowing the usurper—and then making sure that he himself was supreme? he asked the scholar Chu Sheng. "Build high walls, store large quantities of grain—*and be slow to adopt the status of emperor,*" was the canny reply. And six hundred years later, amid mounting warnings that the People's Republic must be ready to resist Soviet aggression, Chairman Mao urged the Chinese: "Dig deep shelters, store large quantities of grain, *and do not lord it over others.*" [1] Revolutionary China was to avoid being identified as a would-be superpower, just as the "revolutionary" monk had avoided revealing his imperial ambitions prematurely.

The monk spent ten years smashing the armies of his more obstinate rivals south of the Yangtse, and only afterward turned north again to drive the last Mongol ruler out of Peking. But from 1368 he sat enthroned in his own chosen capital of Nanking as Ming T'ai-tsu, first emperor of the Ming Dynasty. For the mendicant, the moment had arrived when the tongue must give way to the teeth, when the intelligent contender for the realm must shrug off the easy manner and noble air that won him friends and influenced people on the way up, and reveal the dispassionate ruthlessness beneath that alone can keep him on top, the "ruffian spirit" without which no man can be a real leader, say the Chinese.

The "revolutionary" rebel was forgotten, and the emperor set about stamping out all opposition and concentrating all power in his own hands. He abolished the Secretariat, which supervised the civil service and could be an effective curb on a restive ruler, and prescribed the death sentence for anyone who suggested that it should be restored. He divided the government into six boards responsible directly to himself and headed by scholars whom he treated as little more than clerks, and personally controlled the administration of the provinces through three imperial departments—for internal affairs, military affairs, and punishments.

Dangerously sensitive about his lowly origins, he ran a ruinously magnificent court but was correspondingly miserly with his authority. Where hitherto the Chinese ruler and his counselors had conferred in an open manner, Ming T'ai-tsu laid down that when he held audience, his great officials should crawl to the foot of his throne, knock their heads on the floor in the kowtow, and then kneel before him. If one word of a memorial was not in accord with the emperor's intentions, the hapless imperial secretary responsible would be dragged out and flogged, or even decapitated.

As he left for court each morning, it is related, a mandarin would bid a solemn farewell to his wife and children, and if he returned safely in the evening, all rejoiced and congratulated him. When the emperor appeared with his jade girdle fastened tightly around his waist, it was a sign that he was in good spirits and few might die, but when his girdle was hanging loose, all those present would pale.

For Ming T'ai-tsu was a born and barbarous killer. He massacred countless innocents when he dispatched his enemies, and he inveigled the leaders of the influential cliques that had supported him into murdering one another. He had no further need of "meritorious dogs," for "when the fleet deer is caught, the hounds are cooked," as one minister had astutely remarked during the Spring and Autumn era.

He not only eliminated prominent men who had given him their backing, but buried them under a mountain of corpses. His record far outdistances that of Han Kao-tsu. When he executed Hu Wei-yung, his last, loyal chief minister, on a trumped-up charge of treason, 30,000 people were implicated and slaughtered—twenty of whom he had himself ennobled for their services—and the liquidation of one general cost another 5,000 their lives. The victim was not always lucky enough to be beheaded. If his crime was grave, his hands and feet would be chopped off first, his throat would be pierced, and he would then be carved up systematically with more than 3,000 cuts of the knife. During the Ming Dynasty, culprits were also strangled or banished or beaten with bamboos (although fifty strokes could be fatal, twice that number were sometimes administered).

The heir-apparent remonstrated with his bloodthirsty father, but the emperor replied by throwing a prickly branch before him and asking him to pick it up. "You are afraid of the thorns on it and you cannot," he sneered as his son hesitated. "Would it not be better, then, if I trimmed it for you? Similarly, those I have killed were a danger to the empire, and it is your good fortune that they have been cut away."

It has been argued that Ming T'ai-tsu scoured his realm for ambitious villains and venal mandarins before he died, just because his son was weak and vulnerable. On the other hand, many Chinese feel that no such excuse need be made for him, for in China it was recognized that a powerful nobility could prove a terminal growth on any new dynasty.

And corrupt bureaucracy could prove a wasting disease. A Chinese fable recounts that a man of Ch'i, respectably dressed like an official in cap and gown, walked into a crowded shop, seized some gold, and made off with it. "How did you come to take another man's gold under the eyes of so many people?" he was asked when apprehended. "I did not see the people," answered the man of Ch'i. "I only saw the gold." Most of the powerful and privileged in China did not see the millions around them, but only the spoils, and by the fifteenth century the empire was being administered by 100,000 mandarins in a civil service that was very largely the captive of wealthy and acquisitive families, although it was open to all.

In consequence, the imperial censorate was popular with

the ordinary man, for a commissioner on circuit who traveled "secretly" from province to province (as one Spanish chronicler [2] put it) could seize and punish junior officials, and would afterward report to his superiors "in summe all such things wherein he hath found them culpable." The laws further provided that anyone could lodge a personal complaint in the capital itself against a local mandarin who abused his authority, and the mandarin might come to an excruciating end. Next to the government *yamen* in every county was a "skin temple" in which the hides of officials flayed alive for greed and extortion were displayed, cured with lime and hung on a mannequin of rice straw stuck on a bamboo pole. One of these "men of straw" would also be set up in court when justice was dispensed, in order to put the magistrate in a proper frame of mind.

The prisons of China during the Ming Dynasty have been described as so vast and crowded that they looked like walled cities, and the Legalist principle of collective guilt whereby families were grouped in tens and hundreds was practiced. The chronicler records that any householder learning of a misdemeanor must "giue the iustice to vnderstand thereof, that the fault may be punished." A man failing to report a transgression "is allotted the same punishment yt the offender should have." But this was not new, and it was part of a wider system which also confided to close-knit clans and small village communities responsibility for gathering their own taxes and settling their own legal squabbles, without constant interference from some local judge or other jack-in-office.

The millions, therefore, did not call the rebel who ruled them monster, but "Capable Lord," for he enabled their pleas to be heard, he chastised those who preyed upon them, and he encouraged all races to intermarry and live together in peace within the empire. But neither the village-pump praises of a peasantry far removed from the palace, nor the need to keep mandarins and nobles in their kennels when they were not handed over to the butcher, could justify the unbridled cruelty of Ming T'ai-tsu or the execrable tradition of treating men like "straw dogs" that he so meticulously honored.

It was a cruelty that the Chinese nonetheless accepted, part of the natural process in a ludicrously imperfect world which the left-wing historian Ts'ao Chu-jen has compared to a pool full of all kinds of unlovable creatures: "Leeches, worms, water snakes, frogs, centipedes, I eat you, you eat me, we all eat each other. Appeal to Heaven, and what does Heaven do? Does it determine right from wrong, crooked from straight? No, the sun shines and the pool dries up, but after a few days it rains again, another pool collects, leeches, worms, water snakes, frogs, and centipedes appear, and the war of all against all begins once more." Last year's bandits may be this year's officials, and last year's rebel this year's emperor—which only means, say the Chinese, that they will enjoy bigger and better opportunities to kill and to rob.

The measures taken to establish the "power" of the throne and to keep that power safe from the traditional hazards presented by women, eunuchs, and royal rivals were not all lethal, however. The Ming emperors deliberately took their consorts from families of no consequence, and then shut them up in their own quarters where they were strictly forbidden to meddle in the affairs of court or state. Ming T'ai-tsu also had set up at the gate of the palace a metal plaque three feet high that read: "Eunuchs may not interfere in political matters. Any that disobey will be beheaded." But he was slow to curb the power of the princes, and they still commanded big armies on China's borders.

It was his heir, the Emperor Hui, a grandson in his teens, who took steps to strip them of their potential to make trouble after posing the pertinent question: *quis custodiet ipsos custodes*—"If the barbarians rebel, the princes will resist them, but if the princes rebel . . .?" This aroused the righteous wrath of Ming T'ai-tsu's capable younger son, the Prince of Yen, who quickly mounted a revolt before he could be deprived of the means to do so. The emperor dispatched a large army to crush him, but palace eunuchs in the pay of the rebel sent him word of the expedition, which had left the capital empty of troops.

The prince struck southward from his headquarters in Peking, and after a wearisome and bloody war seized Nanking, burned down the palace, and massacred his sovereign's supporters. The second Ming emperor escaped, to pass the next forty years of his life as the first Ming emperor had passed his youth—disguised as a Buddhist mendicant. The usurper proclaimed himself Son of Heaven with the reign title of Yung Lo, and moved the capital back to Peking.

He also promptly put into effect the measures that his predecessor had so angered him by even contemplating. After 1402, princes of the imperial clan were barred from all military and civil posts in the government, their affairs were run by mandarins responsible to the ruler, and they could neither marry nor leave the provinces allocated to them without his permission. For most of the dynasty, control of the army was split among five commissions directed by civilian bureaucrats in the palace, and the commanders appointed to coordinate large-scale operations were career officials rather than generals. No mere military insurrection was going to overthrow the Ming—and no mere military insurrection did.

The plaque putting the eunuchs in their place was now destined to be stolen, however, for while bolting one door that his father had left open the Emperor Yung Lo made the fatal mistake of opening another that his father had safely closed. He did not treat the palace eunuchs who had secretly helped him to win the throne as meritorious (if doctored) dogs, but rewarded them for their part in his victory and looked upon them as his trusted confidants. Ming T'ai-tsu would have known what to do with them. He had kept the number of his womenfolk and his eunuchs to a ceiling of one hundred of each. But the Emperor Yung Lo unwisely exceeded these quotas, and it is said that by the end of the Ming Dynasty there were not only 10,000 women in the imperial palace, but some 70,000 eunuchs—since, paradoxically, eunuchs multiply faster than women.

The Ming Dynasty is renowned for its splendid architecture, for fine porcelain and enamel, for the development of the Chinese novel, for a great encyclopedia and a comprehensive *materia medica* and many other marvels. But it is also renowned for the despotism of most of its monarchs, for the slavishness of most of its mandarins, and for the evils and calamities brought upon the long-suffering Middle Kingdom by its legions of imperial geldings. Twenty-five years after his death in 1425 a successor of the Emperor Yung Lo was foolish enough to make a favorite eunuch named Wang Chin commander in chief of an expedition against the Mongols, although he was entirely without military experience. The Chinese army was surrounded and cut to shreds not fifty miles from Peking, the neighbors recognized the symptoms, and thereafter Tibet defied China, Annam seceded, the Japanese invaded Korea, and the empire lost Manchuria.

Increasingly corrupt and exacting, the eunuchs beggared the provinces with extortionate taxes, and the government was flooded with the resignations of mandarins who dared not squeeze the peasants further. At the beginning of the sixteenth century one of these emasculated overlords named Liu Chin assumed the power to issue imperial decrees, and immediately used it to order the execution of three hundred personal enemies. Having thus cleared the court, he filled all important palace posts with members of his own clique and went on to wring the empire dry, confiscating and taxing wealth until he had acquired for his private purse gold and silver and precious stones worth more than the annual revenue of the entire Chinese realm.

But even he pales before the image of Wei Chung-hsien, who lived a hundred years later. Having first gambled his way to penury, this loafer had himself castrated in order to obtain a post in the inner palace, and thereafter so insinuated himself into the confidence of the infant heir-apparent that when he ascended the throne, Wei was able to treat him as no more than the chop required on his own abominable edicts. He then lost no time in murdering all his adversaries with or without testicles, including every scholar of the Tunglin College on whom he could lay his hands.

The college was a center of eloquent opposition to the "Castration Clique" that now misruled the empire, and when he was finally able to close it and drive its terrorized members underground, Wei converted it into a "living shrine" to himself. His effigy, dressed in the cap and robe of the emperors of antiquity, was set up in the main hall, and all who failed to kowtow to it were put to death. It was the first of many temples raised to the neutered scoundrel, who was ceremonially greeted everywhere with the cries of toadies wishing him "nine thousand years" of life (which he disdainfully ignored).

The grim comedy reached its climax when the Emperor Hsi Tsung, engrossed in his carpentry rather than his court, decreed that Wei Chung-hsien should be honored equally with Confucius—which meant that he himself had to kneel and knock his imperial head three times on the ground before the figure of his own household slave, when sacrificing to the sage in spring and autumn. Censors and other officials who memorialized the throne in protest against these abuses were so hideously silenced in the torture chambers of the palace that their corpses were often unrecognizable. "If he were chopped into mincemeat, his sins would not be expiated," wrote one of these brave men.* In the event, the emperor died in 1627, and Wei, having hanged himself to escape retribution, was savagely torn to pieces.

Although the puppet emperor was uninterested in affairs of state, and passed his days happily enough working with wood and lacquer, Wei and his minions have been accused of feeding him aphrodisiacs and smothering him in girls, on the principle that if one man's political urge can persuade him to accept physical castration, another man's physical urge can beguile him into accepting political castration. For throughout the history of imperial China, presumptuous eunuchs and ambitious mandarins and empress-regents anxious to keep their hands on the levers of power have methodically de-

* Yang Lien, imperial censor. He was seized, nails were driven into his ears, and then sacks of earth were piled on top of his body until he was crushed to death.

bauched weak rulers, young and old, so that in their pursuit of pleasure they would exhaust their energies and leave the business of running the empire to others.

The Chinese Machiavelli is as aware as the next schemer that a bed can destroy as effectively as a bullet, and to make the best possible use of such weapons he disposes of traditions in Chinese secret police work which were established above all during two periods—the brilliant era of the Ming Dynasty and the long and prosperous reign of the Empress Wu.

In her tireless search for enemies to execute—and for men she could trust with the task—the famous T'ang Dynasty empress had a special "mailbox" set up in the capital for the convenience of informers keen to accuse others of treachery. She also decreed that officials in the provinces should send up to the palace at once any person who told them that he had something disagreeable to confide to her, on pain of being charged with conspiracy themselves. She not only gave an immediate audience to every public-spirited gossip who came to her, but would almost automatically confer rank on him (while those he denounced were strangled or beheaded). In this way a whispering pastryman became a general, and a village rowdy was made a judge, for most of these talebearers were recruited as permanent agents or even officers in a new hierarchy of terror dominated by a dozen grand executioners.

A training school was opened in which all the relevant skills were studied, from espionage to the art of arm twisting, and it was said that no unfortunate who passed through the "Gate of the Beautiful Vista" into the headquarters of the secret service was ever seen again. Most victims confessed to their crimes, imaginary or real, for to induce them to be frank those in attendance might push bamboo spills under their fingernails and hot mud into their ears, turn them on a revolving rack, suspend them by their hair, singe their eyes, pour vinegar into their noses, and then boil up a cauldron in which to cook them alive.

Men were hunted down, tortured, and executed indiscriminately, often without the knowledge of the empress, whose judges might in their turn find themselves starving in a stinking cell with a stone hammer banging rhythmically at their skulls if they acquitted a suspect that the headsmen wanted put away. There is little doubt that Wu Chao sanctioned the purges in which they obliterated 3,000 families between 688 and 691, but she did liquidate their sinister organization toward the end of her reign.

Nothing quite like it was seen again until Ming T'ai-tsu created an instrument of fear picturesquely called the "Brocade Gown Guard" which operated outside the jurisdiction of the normal courts. The Emperor Yung Lo then added another dimension to terrorism by allowing his eunuchs to establish the "Eastern Factory," whose less attractive title correctly implied that all human consignments checked into its workshops were raw material for mental and physical processing. Finally the Castration Clique under Wei Chung-hsien expanded and rationalized the system by opening a "Western Factory" and bringing the older Brocade Gown Guard under its control.

Eunuchs were originally employed in the imperial household not only because they were impotent, but because in theory their impotence meant they were also without standing, without morals, without families, and without any fortune but that deriving from the ruler himself. For the same reasons they were now made masters of the entire network of spies and executioners responsible for smelling out dissent and treachery, arresting a culprit even in the inner precincts of the palace, screwing a confession from him, and imposing upon him the horrible penalty for his alleged perfidy. Armed with these prerogatives, the Castration Clique falsely charged and then struck down innumerable upright court officials, accusing any man that stood in their way of mythical misdemeanors, and swiftly disposing of both him and his family without regard for the protocol which demanded that when a mandarin was detained, the Son of Heaven must be memorialized.

The pattern of power during the Ming Dynasty was not solely that of an autocratic emperor satisfying his whims through a vicious conspiracy of eunuchs, however, nor solely that of a conspiracy of eunuchs satisfying their whims through a negligent emperor. Other corrosive influences were at work. For if the fatal, civilized softness of the Sung court had provoked a return to despotic savagery, the ignoble subjection to the Mongols to which that softness had led had also provoked a fierce Chinese cultural chauvinism which was, in its turn, to destroy the empire.

27

All Chinese Are Brothers

The Confucian tradition was restored, the emperor performed the ancient sacrifices, the qualification for the mandarinate was narrowed once again to a knowledge of the Classics and the Neoconfucian commentaries. "The Truth has been made manifest to the world," declared one scholar. "No more writing is needed." After the trauma of rule by Mongol khan, Ming China was showing withdrawal symptoms.

This was not only the day of the tyrant and the court capon, therefore, but of the eighteen grades of mandarin upon whom the whole Confucian system rested. The princes had been denuded of real authority, the military had been made subordinate to the scholar-officials, and the willful emperor himself was obliged to express his very willfulness through the bureaucratic forms and the moral content of a Confucian society, and to suffer the admonitions of his bolder censors (even if the eunuchs quietly disposed of them afterward). For a killer may be a king, but he cannot hope to kill with impunity if he casts aside convention and stalks his victim through the streets naked.

Properly clad, on the other hand, he may murder unchecked, and in his Confucian dress the emperor wielded absolute authority—moral and immoral. The different elements of society did not contend with each other for power, for he held all the power himself. In consequence, most mandarins were still as servile and hidebound as they had been under the Sung. They dared take no decisions without imperial approval, and the ruler was daily inundated with memorials phrased in odiously sycophantic language. On his side, he treated the mandarins like slaves, making them grovel for days on end in his outer courtyards and demanding their heads for trivial offenses. Mencius had described them as "concubines" nearly two thousand years before. And now they were not so much courtiers as courtesans.

Chinese civil servants were not always to be so, yet the basic theme was to be repeated in Peking within the Communist Party under Chairman Mao, if with variations—the palace struggle for favor among official cadres loyal to a single source of power that dominates all on the basis of one philosophy, rather than a clash between warring elements with diverse ideas inside and outside the administration.

By the time the Jesuit Father Matteo Ricci reached China at the end of the sixteenth century, the empire had receded into Neoconfucian isolation. Government of the barbarians along the borders was left to their own chiefs, who were placated with resounding Chinese titles. Vassal kings were expected to do little more than seek investiture by the Ming emperor when they mounted their thrones, to adopt the Chinese calendar, and to send tribute to Peking from time to time as a token of their homage.

The Chinese were no longer ready to go out and meet the foreigner halfway, and Ricci wrote of them that although they "could easily conquer the neighboring nations, neither the King nor his people ever think of waging a war of aggression. They are quite content with what they have, and not ambitious for conquest."

Chinese ships kept to coastal waters, and Chinese subjects were forbidden to leave the country. The Portuguese, who by now had arrived on the scene, were regarded as little better than pirates and were confined to the tiny peninsula of Macao in the far south, from where they traded with the Celestial Empire through nearby Canton like hawkers at a back door. Firsthand knowledge of the West was replaced with a compost heap of fancies, and the Middle Kingdom kept the white barbarian at bay in an age that gave birth to Da Vinci, Copernicus, Tycho Brahe, Kepler, Galileo, Newton.

When Father Ricci was able to penetrate into the interior of China in 1598, he found that the astronomical instruments so beautifully executed during the Yuan Dynasty, and designed for use near Peking, had been standing neglected on a terrace in Nanking for two centuries. The scholars on the Board of Mathematics did not understand them, and were ineptly calculating the calendar from outdated tables. Chinese mandarins, whose studies, as Ricci noted, were confined to "moral philosophy," were so astonished at his grasp of astronomy and mathematics that this self-confessed amateur was to remark, "They are persuaded I am a phenomenon of scientific knowledge . . . which causes me no little amusement." Some even wanted him to correct the calendar, on which the efficiency of the emperor's sacrifices and Heaven's goodwill so heavily depended.

That task was ultimately confided to Father Adam Schall, one of the Jesuits who followed in Ricci's footsteps and captured the imagination of a small number of influential officials at court—sometimes of the sovereign himself—by introducing them to Western learning and such desirable wonders as telescopes, clocks, and cannons. But once the emperor became aware that Catholic missionaries were loyal to a rival Vicar of Heaven in Rome, they were treated as craftsmen rather than counselors, and their science was not widely studied or applied.

The beginning of the slow process whereby the empire was to sew itself up in its own shroud of jade had nevertheless been obscured by its livelier contacts with the outside world during the early reigns of the Ming Dynasty, by alien acquisitions like spectacles, maize, peanuts, and syphilis, by the reconquest of Annam, and above all by the seven maritime expeditions of the great Ming admiral, Cheng Ho.

Cheng Ho was neither soldier nor merchant. He was a Muslim eunuch, a court official dispatched by the Emperor

Yung Lo to impress barbarians overseas with the power and prestige of their Ming suzerain, and to shop for curiosities (which would be classified as tribute) for the amusement of the palace. He first set out in 1405 with a fleet of 63 seagoing junks—the biggest a four-decked flagship 444 feet long—carrying gold, silk, lacquer, and a force of nearly 28,000 men. On a stele erected thirty years later he recorded: "The barbarian countries we have visited are Champa, Java, Sumatra, Siam, crossing straight over to Ceylon, South India, Calicut, and Cochin; we have also gone to the western regions of Hormuz, Aden, and Mogadishu . . ." Cheng Ho took back to Peking a prince and a king who defied him, and within ten years of his initial voyage sixteen states from Malacca to Hormuz had sent tribute to the emperor of China. The Chinese had reached East Africa more than half a century before the Portuguese were to sail into the Indian Ocean.

However, jealous Confucians at court persuaded the next emperor to curtail these expeditions as too costly. Cheng Ho was ignored despite his achievements, and the Chinese lost their mastery of the Indian Ocean to the Arabs (who lost it to the Portuguese). But then they were soon to lose their mastery of their own shores. During the sixteenth century Japanese pirates raided ports up and down the China coast at will, took their fleets up the Yangtse to burn and pillage cities further inland, and by 1555 were laying siege to Nanking. Their luck was not to hold, however, for in the same year a Chinese patriot who was to earn renown as "Tiger Ch'i" undertook the defense of the Chekiang coast, just south of the estuary of the great river.

The son of an impoverished general who said sadly when he died, "All I can bequeath to you is the territory of our country to defend," Ch'i Chi-kuang took his father at his word, and soon showed such a talent for novel tactics, brutal discipline, and exterminating alien marauders that his fame reached the court in Peking. By the time he had destroyed the main Japanese pirate stronghold in Foochow by a brilliant stratagem (and executed his own son for disobeying an order to attack) he had become the obvious man to chasten the pugnacious Mongols who were once again threatening the dynasty at the other end of the empire.

On arrival in the far north, Tiger Ch'i found the Great Wall alarmingly dilapidated and the morale of the garrison troops low. He therefore set them an example by immediately ordering his own men to throw up new defenses and build lookout towers, working in all weathers with almost no rest, and to reinforce the Chinese positions further he invented the "wagon camp." The wagon camp was a fortified laager consisting of a square of carts mounted with cannon, behind which he packed his cavalry and infantry. When the barbarian horsemen charged, the cannon continued firing until the Mongols were almost upon them. The foot soldiers then fanned out from inside the square, thrusting in front of them long-handled multi-pronged forks of iron, and as the horses reared and turned tail in fright before this advancing wall of spikes, throwing the enemy into confusion, Tiger Ch'i's cavalry counterattacked and cut their riders down.

But once the danger on the frontier abated and he could be withdrawn, this imaginative commander fell victim to the envy and hostility of corrupt ministers at court who slandered him in memorials to the emperor. He was finally dismissed from office, and returned to his home to pass the rest of his days in melancholy solitude.

By now dynastic history was once again on the down curve. The Manchus replaced the Mongols as the menace in the north, and as the fabric of the state rotted away in the hands of its venal guardians, the empire was rent by local rebellions and Nemesis appeared in the shape of Li Tzu-ch'eng.

Born a simple peasant in North China, Li was intoxicated by astrological predictions that he would "be king hereafter." Confident of success, he began his career as a bandit in Shensi, raised his own standard of revolt against the decadent Ming, and carved up the slovenly imperial troops sent to quell him. He then declared himself emperor, and in 1644 marched on Peking. He entered the city without difficulty, and in despair the Son of Heaven strangled himself with a silken girdle, although a Ming army of 200,000 men under a general named Wu San-kuei was still stationed on the Great Wall. General Wu would not attack the rebels, however, because they now held prisoner in the capital a round-faced singsong girl with whom he was infatuated.

Wu's first move was to offer his allegiance to the rebels in exchange for the girl, and when they rejected this deal, he asked the Manchus beyond the Wall to help him annihilate them instead. The rebels then surrendered the girl, whereupon Wu began conspiring with them against the Manchus. But when he refused to return the girl to them as a hostage, they killed off his family in Peking. So Wu switched sides again and entered the capital with the Manchus, who seized the city and established their own dynasty on the throne of China. Li was hunted down and killed. Wu subsequently decided to attack the Manchus after all, but he died during the campaign, and they massacred his entire clan. Shakespeare could hardly have contrived it better.

The frivolous young profligate who had inherited the Ming throne had meanwhile moved his capital to Nanking, where he consoled himself with the pleasures of bed and board and shut his eyes to all urgent memorials warning him that the formidable Manchus, having robbed him of the north, had struck across the Yellow River in readiness to overrun the south of his empire. He himself was more concerned with the dearth of good drama than the defense of the realm, and his nobles were all for appeasement. The commander in chief, who alone had the bad taste to suggest that the Chinese offer a spirited resistance to the barbarian, was cold-shouldered at court, and a prominent member of the ever-powerful Castration Clique contrived to siphon off the supplies he badly needed for his army.

But this latter-day Yo Fei was not to be discouraged so easily. Short, dark, and masterful, an eminent scholar born of a family of landlords and distinguished mandarins, Shih K'o-fa was the epitome of the great Confucian and had been a dedicated member of the Tunglin College which had opposed the depredations of the eunuch Wei. He was also a tough and energetic commander of austere habits who shared the sufferings of his men like Wu Ch'i long before him, renouncing winter furs but sleeping fully clad in the field, ready for action. Although despotic in the cause of discipline, he had earned the trust of his subordinates, and he now decided to make the city of Yangchow, the northern gateway to Nanking, the pivot of his defense against the oncoming enemy.

The dice were loaded, however, and they were cast against him. While Shih K'o-fa flatly rejected the fulsome blandishments of the Manchus (who knew that if only he could be suborned, Nanking would fall like a worm-eaten apple), ministers at court not only opened negotiations with the invaders behind his back, but secretly engineered the assassination of generals who were keen to fight on, and recalled their armies to the capital. In consequence, the Manchus jogged easily down to the walls of Yangchow, whereupon commanders of all neighboring garrisons were forbidden to move to its relief. The betrayal was complete.

Shih K'o-fa was compelled to hold a city packed with nearly a million people at the head of 40,000 troops who had passed a thin winter deprived of essential supplies. He nonetheless ignored all calls to capitulate, and the Manchus attacked with the fury of the frustrated this first major obstacle to their smooth progress south. It took them ten days to breach the walls, and as they poured through the gap, Shih tried to cut his throat. But he was seized by two loyal subordinates and hurried out of the eastern gate toward safety, only to be intercepted and led before the Manchu commander—a bloody, black-avised apparition of arrogant middle-aged mandarin that steadfastly declined to serve the adversary.

The Manchus killed him in cold blood, slaughtered the citizens of Yangchow, and pressed on to Nanking, where the Chinese commander defending the capital prepared to offer his surrender personally, as had already been agreed, and summoned a common soldier to accompany him. But it was as if the spirit of Shih had entered into the peasant. The soldier cursed the general roundly, and when told to hold his ignorant tongue, howled that he for one would not give himself up, ran swiftly to the banks of the Yangtse, flung himself in, and drowned.

Chinese resistance did not end with the death of Shih K'o-fa and the fall of Nanking in 1645, for a pirate named Cheng Ch'eng-kung but known to the West as Koxinga rallied to the last Ming emperor when he had already been driven to the far south of his realm like the last Sung emperor before him. The Ming fleet was rebuilt, a powerful force of infantry and cavalry recruited, and by 1659 the pirate and the prince were at the gates of Nanking. Their army was defeated, however, and Koxinga was forced to fall back on the island of Formosa, where he threw out the incumbent Dutch and, like Chiang Kai-shek three hundred years later, established his own Confucian court. He died in 1682 while planning "to return to the mainland," crying out, it is said, "How can I meet my emperor in Heaven with my task unfulfilled?" The Manchus only won the submission of this last corner of the Ming empire in 1683—nearly forty years after they had entered Peking.

The lone, hysterical soldier who drowned himself at Nanking has no memorial, and all that was found of Shih K'o-fa was a boot and a few garments, but the other "hard-bone" heroes have their tombs—and temples. Should they? It may be argued that much misery might have been avoided if this splendid company of scholar-soldiers and sailors had been less stiff-necked, that 800,000 lives would have been spared at Yangchow alone if Shih K'o-fa had only yielded instead of yelling defiance.

But the Chinese say that there is a time to live and a time to die, and that according to moral circumstance "death may be as heavy as a mountain, or as light as a goose feather." Mencius once remarked: "Fish is my delight, and so is bear paw. But if I cannot eat both, I must forsake fish so that I may have bear paw. Life is my desire, and so is righteousness. But when I cannot have both, my only course is to forsake life in order to hold fast to righteousness."

Success is not the object of the exercise—the resistance of Wen T'ien-hsiang against the Mongols was notable for a long string of defeats, and he could hardly have expected to crush them outside Hangchow with 3,000 cavalry recruits force-marched from South China. But the dynasty itself was on "death ground."

Reward is not the sole aim. The Chinese distrust for authority is only sharpened by memories of the sorry fate of valiant men and of the perfidy of the ingrates who destroyed them—the murderers of Yo Fei, the slanderers of Cheng Ho and Tiger Ch'i, the poltroons who cynically trapped Shih K'o-fa in the net of their own treason.

Nor, therefore, does the subject sacrifice himself because the sovereign is righteous. Good Chinese and true have throughout history been the victims of weak, treacherous, greedy, or foolish emperors, yet have been ready to give their lives for the decadent dynasties they personified—when the enemy has also been an alien. For there was never any lack of heroes and villains who would defend the Devil himself against all comers, provided the Devil was Chinese, China itself was at stake, and the moment had come not to do what was expedient in the flexible traditions of Sun Tzu, but simply what was "right." The Mandate of Heaven might be removed from an unworthy ruler, but it could only legitimately pass to another Chinese.

Popular hatred of the Ming Dynasty—with its cruel and despotic monarchs, its Brocade Gown Guard, its Eastern Factory and Western Factory of neutered torturers, its corrupt mandarins and pusillanimous nobles and rapacious eunuchs—became popular loyalty once the Manchus had usurped the throne. Even the vacillating, lovelorn Wu San-kuei, who had invited the barbarians into China in the first place, was to mount the biggest and most dangerous insurrection of the century against them thirty years later.

The threat of foreign aggression, real or invented, has always been a court card in the Chinese power game, whether held by foreigners or by China's rulers. And this is all the more true when there are 800,000,000 Chinese (give or take the population of Spain), and even the pursuit of the ideal classless and selfless Communist society is inspired by a specifically Chinese socialism.

28

Barbarians in Perspective

Perhaps nothing illustrates the importance of being Chinese more than the life of the scholar Huang Tsung-hsi, who was born under the Ming and died under the Manchus. His father was treacherously "executed" by the Castration Clique, and he himself went to Peking to exact personal revenge for the killing at the age of eighteen. But once the Manchus invaded, he took office and led troops against the barbarians in a forlorn attempt to save the last maggoty vestiges of Ming rule. And when they established their alien Ch'ing Dynasty on the throne of China, he refused all offers to serve the court, although the usurpers swept away the hated eunuchs and sought out the scholars they had so viciously victimized, awarding many of them high posts in the administration.

Instead, he composed a withering denunciation of the modern monarch, describing him as no more than a parasitic despoiler of the people. "The great scourge of the empire is its sovereign," he concluded. "In ancient times, people loved and supported their ruler, looking upon him as a father. And so he was. Today, the people resent and hate their ruler, regarding him as a thieving enemy without any right to claim their loyalty. And so he is."

Huang did not plot rebellion, however, but passed his later years in retirement, writing and teaching. For it was not yet "time to die." When subjugated, the Chinese would tolerate the importunities of barbarians as long as they brought benefits and the books therefore balanced, and the heavily outnumbered Manchus were wise enough to show a scrupulous respect for Chinese culture, to employ Chinese officials, and to recruit eight Chinese "banners" to match the eight Manchu "banners" that garrisoned the empire. During the first prosperous century under the Ch'ing, imperial troops annexed Tibet, reconquered Mongolia and much of Turkestan, defeated the Gurkhas in Nepal, and once more added Korea and Annam as well as Burma to the list of China's vassals.

But the honeymoon was not to last. As a population explosion threatened to shatter the very well-being that had been provoking it, and misery and poverty crept over the country like a dull stain, extravagant emperors and corrupt courtiers began digging their hands deep into the coffers of the realm and frittering away its riches on palaces and temples and lavish living. The dynastic rot had set in again. The Chinese saw the debit side of Manchu rule in a clearer light, and in doing so saw red.

For the list of entries made mortifying reading. The conquerors had compelled the conquered to cut off their hair and wear pigtails as a sign of their subjection. Chinese men were obliged to wear Manchu clothes, Chinese women were barred from the imperial harem, and marriage between Chinese and Manchus was forbidden. The Manchu bannermen were the absolute masters of the empire, privileged drones who might hold civil or military posts, but were not required to take examinations or to do any work. All drew fat pensions from the state, and many were awarded fiefs and enclosed domains in which to play the rapacious landowner with the Chinese peasant as foil. Their principal occupation was to behave like overlords, and this formula for converting a once wiry and well-knit nation into a loose cluster of lazy and incompetent idlers proved so effective that they came to be regarded by hostile Chinese as no more than gluttonous cuckoos in the nest.

In 1775 the White Lotus sect rose against the dynasty and was only suppressed twenty-seven years later after an orgy of killing. A second uprising followed in 1813, to be brutally crushed in its turn. But worse was to come, for in 1851 a man describing himself as the younger brother of Jesus Christ founded the "Heavenly Kingdom of Great Peace," and half of China was plunged into the all-consuming furnace of the great Taiping Rebellion.

The hitherto unknown member of the Holy Family responsible for this insurrection was a disgruntled schoolteacher from South China named Hung Hsiu-ch'uan, who had failed the imperial examinations so consistently for fifteen years that he felt sure he had been floored solely because he was a southerner, and from a clan with a reputation for being anti-Manchu. A normal, intelligent, hard-working scholar in straitened circumstances, he had nevertheless seen strange visions in his youth, and when he later read a Chinese tract on the teachings of Christianity, he became convinced that his sickbed fancies had been a revelation from God.

Refused baptism because his "thinking was not clear" (as the Protestant missionary giving him guidance objected), Hung made himself independent of all existing churches by the simple method of founding his own. The Taiping creed acknowledged the Ten Commandments, recognized the Holy Ghost, and preached sound Christian intolerance of other religions (but not love). There was more to the movement than a new view of the Almighty, however. Hung was organizing yet another secret society to fight against injustice and poverty and the foreign rulers who must inevitably be held responsible for those evils.

He taught that inequality must be uprooted, so that hunger and want would vanish and "the empire become one family" in which all men—including all barbarians—must bow to the one true deity. Mo Tzu had said that just as the ministers were above the people, and the monarch above the ministers, so Heaven was above the monarch, and Hung saw that a politico-socio-economic god was the ace which alone could trump a king. He did not challenge the Ch'ing in the name of the Ming, therefore, but in the name of the Maker.

From his headquarters in an inaccessible region of soaring peaks in Kwangsi Province ironically called the Judas-Tree

Range, Hung set out in 1851 with a snowballing army of wretched peasants and half-starved miners that accumulated fortunetellers and quacks and vagabonds, gamblers and monks, acrobats and merchants and Chinese deserters as it rolled forward. Chopping their way through the soft, pusillanimous imperial banners sent against them, the Taiping hordes marched north, overran the cities of the Yangtse, and in 1853 took Nanking, where Hung, now the self-styled "Heavenly King" of a new dynasty, made his capital.

For nine years this visionary ruled half China, and wherever his soldiers went in the south, pigtails were docked, Ch'ing bureaucrats were hunted down and killed, and their local *yamen* burned by cheering mobs. The Taiping made bonfires of title deeds and IOU's, slaughtered grasping landlords, stripped powerful gentry of their estates, their chattels, and even their clothes, and split them up among the astonished poor. And as government troops took their revenge, killing and burning indiscriminately in their turn, the ranks of the Taiping became further swollen with the bitter and desperate survivors of their savagery.

The rebellion was more than a major insurrection. It was a "cultural revolution," the forerunner of the Communist upheaval that was to come a century later. The Heavenly King urged the masses to seize political power by force. He promised to end all distinctions between rich and poor, and he published a plan for communal land and communal production that anticipated the "people's communes" which Mao was to introduce in 1958. Peasants were incited to wreak vengeance on village dignitaries who had abused their power. Women could own land and become officials or soldiers. Prostitution was abolished, foot binding forbidden, opium smoking and girl slavery outlawed and made punishable by death, gambling and drunkenness and looting pitilessly discouraged. As in the Cultural Revolution of the 1960's, superstition fell under the ax, Buddhism and Taoism were proscribed as idolatrous, and shrines razed or wrecked.

Once enthroned in Nanking, however, the behavior of the Heavenly King became less heavenly, and he began to show some of the morbid symptoms earlier observed in the first Ming emperor. The "equality of man with man" was forgotten in the pursuit of wealth and luxury. Troops were levied for work on a new royal palace, and those who caviled were executed. Special robes were tailored for the divine if ill-tempered monarch, and a complicated ritual invented to emphasize his divinity. When he went out, his palanquin was carried by sixty-four bearers, and he was followed by the lesser "kings" who were his lieutenants, each in a sedan chair borne by forty men. A guard of honor a thousand strong accompanied the cortege, and as it passed, the common people would scurry to the side of the road to shout, "May He Live Ten Thousand Years!" No Ch'ing emperor demanded more.

Moreover, Hung now made the mistake of settling down in the "Holy City" of Nanking, only dispatching small evangelistic forces to the north which failed to win converts as they advanced and were unable to capture Peking. Most northerners did not warm to these crusaders from the south, who regarded their Buddhist and Taoist temples as heathen abominations and incinerated them wherever they found them. He also neglected to build a fleet to protect the flank of his Jerusalem-on-the-Yangtse, he neglected to garrison the territory the Taiping occupied, and he neglected to suppress a regicidal struggle for supremacy that broke out among his lesser "kings" at court. He could have taken Peking away from the degenerate Manchus in 1854, but by 1864 they had taken Nanking away from him. The Heavenly King committed suicide, and the Heavenly Kingdom came to an end. The dream of a Chinese Eden had been destroyed by a Chinese serpent.

Men called Tseng Kuo-fan "the Python" because, it is said, he was covered with ringworm. But he looked sound enough to scholars and peasants alike in Central and North China, for he was a Chinese and a Confucian, he was mustering men to turn the rising tide of the iconoclastic and sacrilegious Taiping, and he paid them punctually and well for their work.

Persuaded that the spineless generals commanding his

banners were more concerned with fudging their pay sheets and ration requisitions than fighting the rebels, the Ch'ing emperor had commissioned Tseng to raise a special force in his native Hunan. Tseng recruited a militia officered by mandarins, manned by peasant volunteers, imbued with Confucian ideals, and trained in the unorthodox tactics of Tiger Ch'i. Fine-sewn with clan loyalties, it was to earn renown as the "Hunan Army," for every man in it was a Hunanese. The principle of setting barbarian to fight barbarian had been reversed. The Manchus had set Chinese to fight Chinese—and to add to the irony, while both sides were indeed fervently Chinese, both were compromised with foreigners.

Like the Communists in the 1970's, the Taiping also denounced Confucius and Mencius as false gods, tore their precepts apart, and smashed their images. And even as they were patriotically clamoring for the overthrow of the Manchus, they were propagating a barbarian faith, welcoming foreign missionaries, calling the aliens from the West "coreligionists" with whom they were eager to trade and to whom they wanted to open up all China. In short, the Taiping "nationalists" were jettisoning Chinese culture for an imported creed and imported customs. Tseng Kuo-fan could therefore pose as the champion of all things Chinese and the guardian of the Confucian doctrine that he believed to be the soul of Chinese civilization. In territory under the Taiping, he declared, "scholars cannot read the works of Confucius, and all of China's propriety, morality, human relations, poetry, and laws of the past several thousand years are utterly swept away in one day."

It was true that in pursuing his sacred task of wiping out the anti-Confucian rebels (and killing thousands of fellow Chinese in the process) the Python was acting as the servant of the oppressive Manchu usurpers whom the Heavenly King was so courageously trying to evict. Moreover, in spite of all claims to their brotherly consideration advanced by the Christian Taiping, the self-righteous Western powers not only fed guns and ammunition to their heathen enemies, but lent them a barbarian general—Charles George Gordon—to help them fight the good fight against these Chinese "Worshippers of God."

The Python could still retort, however, that in serving the Ch'ing emperor in Peking, he was defending the interests of the Chinese gentry by defending the entire Confucian fabric itself. For there were barbarians and barbarians. The Manchus had venerated Confucius even before they poured through the Great Wall. They had continued to preserve Chinese culture, if only to keep the monstrous Chinese dragon docile. They had religiously maintained the mandarinate and the imperial examinations in the Classics. And the Ch'ing ruler observed the rites and prayed at the temple of Confucius in the north, while the followers of the Heavenly King hammered his effigy into fragments in the south.

The Taiping were anxious to let the foreigner into the far corners of the empire, but the Manchus adamantly insisted that he must be kept in quarantine on its fringes. The centuries were creeping on and alien influences creeping in, but the seepage was slow because Ch'ing fears of a changing China acted as an effective damp course against capillary action. And here was the heart of the matter: the Manchu might not marry Chinese women, but he had married Chinese civilization. This barbarian had been digested.

The Middle Kingdom was not called the Middle Kingdom for nothing. China was the center of the world, the sole repository of the universal Confucian truth. The emperor was the vicar of Heaven, and all other lands—"All under Heaven"—his vassals. As we have seen, the Chinese concept of empire was not one of colonial dominion but of cultural suzerainty over the benighted barbarian, of very literally "civilizing the natives." The Chinese did not seek to conquer, but to absorb.

The absorption might be mutual, but since there was no question of equality between China and other nations, there could be no question of a fair exchange. The Christian missionaries who brought the Gospel to the Pacific Islander and clapped a muumuu over his wife's brown bosom may have learned from him the knack of spearing fish and even dabbled in his quaint pagan beliefs, but they declined to bow down before his grinning idols. Similarly, the Confucian scholar-soldier might ride in Mongol cavalry boots and read the Christian Bible, but he would not sell his birthright for these baubles.

The Heavenly King was rejected not because he was Christian, but because he denounced Confucius and fired Buddhist and Taoist temples in a holy war fought to stamp a foreign faith on China. His crime was that he tried to convert absorption into saturation. He sacrificed the Chinese cultural tradition to the interests of Chinese nationalism, and he lost out to men who subordinated Chinese nationalism to the Chinese cultural tradition.

Their superiority complex was to persuade many Chinese that they could pick and choose among the offerings of the West—accepting here, rejecting there—without betraying their own way of life. It explains how one egregious, self-styled "Confucian scholar," * who had traveled widely in Europe and translated Western works into Chinese could defend the binding of women's feet, and dismiss the prevalent form of government he had found among the Anglo-Saxons as "demo*crazy.*" When asked why polygamy was allowed in China, but not polyandry, this enlightened cosmopolitan replied: "One teapot serves four teacups. How can four teapots serve one teacup?"

In 1860 another Chinese scholar could remark disdainfully that the Celestial Empire had nothing to learn from the Occident but making "solid ships and efficient guns." It was therefore not surprising that the Confucian Python, Tseng Kuo-fan, should buy Western weapons and Western expertise for his Hunan Army, while his colleague Li Hung-chang enlisted the support of England, America, and France against the Taiping.

They must nevertheless have been haunted by misgivings. For the Western powers spurned the rebels and supplied the Ch'ing commanders with the ships and guns they wanted

* Ku Hung-ming (1857–1928), author of *The Spirit of the Chinese People.*

purely in order to win more time in which to pillage the empire. The Taiping were militant, socialistic, revolutionary, and therefore a menace. The Manchus were effete, decadent, cowed, and therefore compliant. The West had compelled them to sign humiliating treaties which promised much profit, and it was anyway easier to exploit a weak China under an alien emperor than a strong China under a nationalistic Heavenly King.

The Ch'ing generals were aware of this, and when one of them, called Hu Liu-i, first saw a steamboat on the Yangtse, he fainted. "The Taiping are no problem; it is the foreign ships already sailing up our rivers that are the real danger," he said bitterly when he came to. "Tomorrow's catastrophe is something that we cannot even imagine."

29

Democrazy

Neither the Ming nor the Ch'ing could be blamed for their distrust of the barbarian. In 1517 the Portuguese sailed up the Pearl River to Canton, ostensibly to trade, and almost immediately won themselves a sound reputation for compulsive plundering and killing. The Dutch came next, indiscriminately looting and murdering up and down the China coast. In 1637 Captain John Weddell, armed with a Royal Commission from a needy Charles I, reacted to passive obstruction from the Chinese by bombarding and assaulting one of their forts, stripping it of thirty-five cannon, and burning down the quarters inside its battlements. A century later the Chinese repaired the *Centurion* of Captain George Anson, only to have the importunate fellow sail back and demand provisions after he had dangerously goaded the Spaniards by seizing the treasure-laden Acapulco galleon.

By this time the emperor had confined foreign traders to Macao and to waterside "factories" at Canton, where they were compelled to conduct all their business through a small cabal of grasping Chinese officials and merchants bent on squeezing the last ounce of silver out of them. Commerce was grotesquely lopsided, with the barbarians from the West purchasing mounting quantities of tea, silk, lacquer, and rhubarb and paying for them in cash, since the Chinese wanted to buy little or nothing in return.

This self-sufficiency not only encouraged Ch'ing ignorance

of the outside world, but a complementary arrogance to which Europe somewhat fatuously pandered. For men were so entranced by the rosy reports of the Celestial Empire and its philosopher-kings put about by the Jesuits that in seventeenth-century England Sir William Temple described China as a paradise beyond Plato's imagining, and in eighteenth-century France Voltaire declared that the Chinese administration was "the best the world has ever seen."

The illusion that the Son of Heaven was lord of all he did not survey was therefore kept intact. In 1816, one year after the battle of Waterloo, the British envoy Lord Amherst was accordingly refused an imperial audience and dismissed from Peking with an edict which condescendingly informed the Prince Regent that his "tribute" was accepted, but provided he recognized "our sovereignty" there was no need for him to dispatch further ambassadors with gifts "to prove that you are indeed our vassal." Later a senior court mandarin, memorializing the Dragon Throne on how to bring foreign dogs to heel, wrote of Queen Victoria: "It seems it would be best to start by sending instructions to her."

These lofty assumptions were by then anachronistic, however. Leaning heavily on stiff Confucian tradition in order to hold the loyalty of a mandarinate mentally mummified by its own ritualistic studies, the alien Manchus instinctively rejected all innovation. Behind a gorgeous façade the administration decayed, the empire atrophied and shriveled. There was flagrant corruption at court once more, and in the provinces the despicable Manchu bannermen had long since been seduced by easy living—and opium.

European and American traders in Canton (the British first among them) had discovered that their acute imbalance-of-payments problem with a China too proud to import their wares could be solved if they financed their purchase of silk and tea by smuggling opium into the empire. In 1821 some 5,000 chests were peddled to the Chinese, and in 1836 more than five times that number, containing perhaps 1,500 tons of the drug. The emperor tried to close his realm to this discreditable traffic, while the British became increasingly determined to crack it open to general commerce, and one incident after another was added to a tragicomedy of cross-purposes which inevitably ended in war.

China lost, and in 1842 was forced to open five ports to British merchants, the Queen acquired Hong Kong, and white Anglo-Saxon Protestant missionaries eagerly seized their first chance to convert the heathen along the China coast. The wedge was in the door. The Middle Kingdom was compelled to sign a series of humbling agreements with formidable powers that were by definition inferior—"unequal treaties" still upheld today on the basis of a narrow Western concept of "law" that the Chinese dismiss as iniquitous and morally invalid.

In 1857 Britain went to war with China again, France joined the fray just for the loot, and three years later Lord Elgin captured Peking and burned down the Summer Palace. China was obliged to sign the Treaty of Tientsin. More ports and the Yangtse River were thrown open to Europeans. The British were allowed to buy land and could be tried only by their own consular courts. Missionaries were free to move into the interior.

Seventy years of ad hoc surgery on China's sovereignty followed. A second expeditionary force marched on the capital to lift the siege of the Legation Quarter during the Boxer Rebellion in 1900, after the Dowager Empress Tzu Hsi had deflected the fury of the xenophobic "Society of Harmonious Fists" from the Manchus to the other aliens in China. Another treaty was signed, more ports were opened. The Chinese customs and postal services were now directed by a European, foreign warships could navigate on Chinese rivers, foreign troops were stationed in foreign enclaves.

The "red-haired barbarians" and the Japanese "dwarfs from the east" carved the empire into spheres of influence, the British taking the Yangtse Valley, the French the southwest, the Germans Shantung, the Russians Manchuria. Vast tracts of land in Central Asia and north of the Amur had already been acquired by the tsars, the Chinese tributaries in Southeast Asia by Britain and France, Formosa and the

Korean protectorate by Japan. In 1898 the young Emperor Kuang Hsu himself, echoing alarmed reformers among the Chinese, had insisted that if China was to survive there must be "careful investigation into every branch of European learning appropriate to existing needs." But he had been imprisoned in his own palace by the die-hard dowager Tzu Hsi, who was supported by Confucian scholars still as scared of change as their Manchu mistress.

The empire threatened to disintegrate, a strong undertow of progressive thinking now ran through the younger and angrier Chinese, revolution broke out, and in February 1912 the last emperor renounced the throne and declared China a republic. The Ch'ing had no choice, for their most able general had refused to commit his crack troops to their defense—and the crack troops were loyal only to the general. The dangerous legacy of the private army left by Tseng Kuo-fan was to cost the Son of Heaven his own inheritance.

Once pitted against the Taiping rebels, the Python had personally recruited, trained, and led 120,000 Chinese soldiers who owed not a grain of their rice rations nor a round for their rifles directly to Peking, for the Hunan Army was paid and fed and armed out of the provincial purse. It was matched by the Huai Army of Li Hung-chang, the Python's brother-in-arms, yet so sturdy was the net of allegiances within each force that neither man could have assumed the other's command, and the court had little control over either. But whereas the Hunan and Huai armies nonetheless fought and subdued the enemies of the emperor, the "Peiyang Army" * that succeeded them sold out to the rebels. For "the Toad" was no Python.

They called Yuan Shih-k'ai the Toad because he was a squat fellow not quite five feet tall, with a big head and a thick, short neck, who flung his legs and arms out stiffly as he strutted up and down. He came of a rich and powerful family, and he led a life of unashamed luxury surrounded by ten winsome concubines. As a youth he had been impatient of

* "Peiyang" (North Sea) included the littoral provinces of Liaoning, Hopei, and Shantung.

study, and he had burned his books when he failed his examinations at the age of eighteen. But he was not to be underestimated. His ambitions lay elsewhere, and he is said to have exclaimed: "A man should have great dreams and not be restricted to paper and pens. With ten thousand good troops I could be master of the empire."

He had the right qualities. He was malicious, tricky, light on loyalty, hungry for power, and he has been compared to Ts'ao Ts'ao. Like Ts'ao Ts'ao, he was also an able and bold commander, and after China lost the Sino-Japanese War in 1895, the Dowager Empress commissioned him to organize a modern Chinese army, for he himself had crushed a rebellion in Korea and fought well against the enemy.

Yuan started with a contingent of seven thousand men. He hired German instructors to train them, their officers were drawn from among Chinese students who had attended German military academies, all ranks wore "German" uniforms, and the Toad wore a Teutonic mustache. The Ch'ing court, watching the embryo develop into a formidable "foreign" force, slowly grew afraid. In 1909 Yuan Shih-k'ai was relieved of his post. His patron, the conservative Dowager Empress Tzu Hsi, had died, and Yuan was deeply distrusted by many at court, as he had connived at the suppression of the reformers. But he could not be stripped of his ambitions, or of the allegiance of an army that secretly regarded him as its sole master. A second struggle was soon to develop, this time between the temporal heir of the Python and the spiritual heir of the Heavenly King.

If Yuan Shih-k'ai was created in the image of the ambitious warlords of China's turbulent past, Sun Yat-sen was the product of China's turbulent present. Born into a farming family near Canton but educated in Hawaii, he was a Christian, a doctor, and a democrat. But although his environment had been Western, his blood was still Chinese. He was to use the secret societies, with which the Taiping had flirted and fought, to further the cause of socialism. He upheld the Confucian ethics of filial piety, loyalty, and righteousness even as he appealed for liberty, equality, and fraternity. He demanded a republic, but a republic based on an alloy of American and European concepts recast in a Chinese mold and embodied in his famous "Three Principles"—Nationalism, Democracy, the People's Livelihood.

His goal was that of the Russian Communists, but while their creed called for an explosion of proletarian violence, he preached a slow-burning socialist revolution in which none need be fatal casualties. "Marx's research into social problems revealed only the flaws in social progress, not its principles," he contended. "It may therefore be said that he was a social pathologist, but not a social physiologist." In a China burdened with few really big landlords or capitalists but cursed with almost universal poverty, the class struggle and the curing of social ills by bleeding the rich to death were irrelevant. The minority of magnates could be cut to size by breaking up great estates and dividing them among the land-hungry, and by nationalizing the larger industrial enterprises. The object must be to level, not to liquidate. A steep scale of taxes could take care of the rest.

Democracy would be practiced in accordance with the principles not of Marx but of Montesquieu—*Il faut que le pouvoir arrête le pouvoir.* The people would have the right not only to enact and revise laws, but to elect and dismiss at will the members of five separate organs of state which would "hold each other by the leg" and limit each other's power. Why five instead of three? Because Sun Yat-sen characteristically sinified his version of the constitution by providing not only for a legislature, an executive, and a judiciary, but for two more organs that were to inherit the functions of the Imperial Censorate and the Examination Board in China's traditional system of government. He did not cry out for instant democracy, moreover, but for a transition to popular government in three therapeutic phases—first, the destruction of the old regime; then, limited exercises in political liberty, taken under strict supervision from above (while the stumbling millions learned how to wield their power); and finally, full freedom of action.

After a false start in Canton in March 1911, the revolution

gained momentum and shifted into high gear toward the end of the same year.[1] Most of the cities of the south and many in the north went over to the republicans, and as the rebels slaughtered their Manchu garrisons, frightened provincial governors rallied to the new cause. In November the panic-stricken Ch'ing court hastily recalled Yuan Shih-k'ai, proclaimed a constitutional monarchy, and appointed him Prime Minister. On December 29 the revolutionaries in Nanking countered by electing Sun Yat-sen Provisional President of a Chinese Republic, and on February 2, 1912, the Manchus in Peking riposted by declaring China a republic on their own, quite different terms. Faced with a choice of Chinese "republics," each too weak to overcome its rival without the weight of his modern Peiyang Army behind it, the Toad could jump either way. And since he saw no future for his own imperial ambitions in supporting the Ch'ing Dynasty further, he aligned himself with the revolutionaries.

For the sake of republican unity, Sun Yat-sen ill-advisedly yielded his place to this turncoat, who was formally elected President in October 1912. But in 1914 the incorrigible Yuan had the constitution amended so that power was concentrated in his hands, a few months later he contrived to become President for life, in 1915 he announced his reign title as first emperor of a new Chinese dynasty, and in 1916 he died—on the eve, some say, of being abruptly eliminated by his outraged opponents.

The Toad had tightened his grip on the provinces by making many of his trusties military governors, and it was their agents who had moved across the country urging the gentry and merchants and beggars and monks and anyone else who would listen to accept him as the "True Dragon Son of Heaven" and their future emperor (while revolutionary newspapers in Shanghai abused him so harshly that, as the Chinese put it, "the dog's blood dripped from his head").

However, it was not long before the military governors themselves began to make demands and assume prerogatives not accorded them by their overlord in Peking. The army in Yunnan openly challenged his imperial status, and other provinces pronounced themselves independent. Just as Sun Yat-sen in Nanking had become the prisoner of the military power of the Toad, so the Toad in Peking had become the prisoner of the military power of a new litter of warlords. He had tripped on the snag that the first emperor of the Sung Dynasty had so adroitly avoided: if one general could become emperor, why not another?

At his death, Vice-President Li Yuan-hung succeeded him in the capital, and the revolutionaries set up an opposition government in Canton. The two republics which had briefly become one were two again—with "Generalissimo" Sun Yatsen in the south dependent on the favor of swaggering local soldiery far more interested in plunder than principles, and the President in the north little more than a puppet pulled this way and that by four powerful generals who held down huge regions of China with their private armies.

Typical of this breed was Chang Tso-lin, a short, swarthy, foul-mouthed horse thief who rose to be "Grand Marshal" and the master of Manchuria. A rapacious opium-smoking despot who made up the rules as he went along, Chang demonstrated his belief that lawlessness must be fought with lawlessness in 1927 when he ordered troops to raid the Soviet Embassy in Peking. The troops strangled most of the Chinese they found there, illegally arrested fifteen Russian diplomats—and seized incontrovertible documentary proof of a Communist plot to take over all China. But it would be wrong to imagine that the Grand Marshal was regarded as a disgrace to his profession. On the contrary, he was widely admired for his astute diplomatic maneuvering and his jealous and skillful defense of Manchuria in the face of insidious Japanese encroachment.

His political subtlety was nevertheless exposed to the profane when he summoned leading scholars to his palace before thrusting south through the Great Wall to dominate North China.[2] The assembled intellectuals were made to stand in a courtyard and wait to "hear his instructions," ringed by guards who trained their guns upon them as if they were common criminals. Heavily escorted, the Marshal then took his place behind a lectern and gave them the benefit of his analysis of the current situation in a sustained bellow, expressing himself (roughly speaking) in these words:

"Do you know what's happening beyond the Pass now? Fuck your mother, it's just like a whorehouse. So I'm off there tomorrow. You know there are good pickings to be had down there? Well, they're going to be ours—I won't take them all myself, but hand them out free and for nothing. But, fuck your mother, last time I went through the Pass I heard that you all started mucking about on the quiet back here. Now I've got to go through again, but I won't have any mucking around—and I dare you to try anything on. I've got guns all over me. Fuck it, do you think I'm scared of anyone? That's it." Upon which he turned around in a dignified manner and left the courtyard.

Feng Yu-hsiang, the famous "Christian General" who baptized his men with tap water, once shouted at his troops: "A cavalryman rides a horse, whereas an infantryman has to march, and supply troops have to carry things. What do you think we should do for the sake of equality? Should we sell the horses and all go on foot? Or should everyone ride a horse?" And when an uncomprehending soldier automatically replied "Right!" the great warlord yelled: "Revolution is not chaos. Muck around with words like 'equality,' and you can't get a damn thing done."

These men had no time to waste on the Three Principles of Sun Yat-sen, any more than the Python had had time for the socialistic message of the Heavenly King, or the Toad for the ideals of the republicans. But they had all been masters of the situation as long as they could challenge rebels with rifles. And it was only when Sun Yat-sen and his followers could begin to act in accordance with the eternal truth that Mao Tsetung was to enunciate in the well-known words "Political power grows out of the barrel of a gun" that they could begin to win.

In the Chinese context of their day, moreover, there was a second disagreeable truth with which they also had to come to terms: if the gun was power, democracy was perdition. Yet another warlord,* mystified and irritated by a modest democratic institution in his fief in the shape of a provincial assembly, marched into a heated session one day with an armed escort and propounded his own solution for its problems. "You stupid lot wrangle from morning to night, squawking without stopping in this sparrow cage," he bawled. "There's absolutely no meaning to it, so why does the Assembly have to meet at all? I'll pay all your wages, and that will be that."

Even republicans ruefully had to admit that the bully was being logical. Shipped to China and let loose in an alien, exotic political climate, Western democracy had quickly turned into an ugly, twisted, and vicious beast—"a monkey dressed in the robes of a duke." As C. P. Fitzgerald has noted,[3] parliament presented a shameful picture of irresponsibility and corruption, "votes were openly sold and openly quoted on the market" and "members, when they met, devoted all their time to appropriating large salaries to themselves." If democracy was simply a matter of dollars, why should not a poor struggling warlord rationalize the situation and buy it up?

Accordingly, Sun Yat-sen's "democratic" Kuomintang (KMT) was reorganized with the help of Russian advisers as an authoritarian party of cellular structure which the Communists could also join as individuals.[4] China was now stuck fast in the second phase of his revolution—the period when the party would educate the people until, at some time in the distant, unforeseeable future, they could outgrow its dictatorship and run their affairs for themselves.

In 1924 the Whampoa Military Academy opened in Canton with Chiang Kai-shek as commandant and Chou En-lai as chief political officer. The KMT was teething at last. Sun himself died in the following year, but in 1926 Chiang Kai-shek was able to launch his "Northern Expedition" to suborn or subdue the warlords in a bid to unite all China, and by the summer of 1928 he had reached Peking. Accustomed to the brutish soldiers of the Grand Marshal, the northerners

* Chang Huai-chih.

greeted the "barbarian army" from the south first with misgiving and then with relief, for these strange troops with outlandish accents wearing broad-brimmed rain hats of oil paper and bamboo, short breeches and straw sandals, proved as friendly to the anxious natives as the anxious natives were prepared to be friendly to them.

China was still not to know national unity or democracy, however, let alone the security and prosperity and social justice promised under Sun Yat-sen's third heading—"the People's Livelihood." Chiang Kai-shek had treacherously massacred his urban Communist allies when he captured Shanghai on his way north. By the time he reached Peking, therefore, Mao Tsetung was already defying him from his first red guerrilla base in the border mountains of Kiangsi Province. And the Japanese had meanwhile landed an army in Shantung.

The Japanese were to have the dishonor of proving themselves the most ruthless and greedy of all the foreign nations that had been tearing at the sick flesh of China for the past century. They had defeated the Chinese in 1895, when they forced upon Peking a stringent treaty that gave them Korea and Formosa, and in 1915—to the fury of Chinese nationalists—they had managed to impose on the Toad most of their notorious "Twenty-one Demands," which cut severely into China's sovereignty and gave Tokyo dangerously powerful prerogatives in Manchuria and Shantung.

Temporarily balked in Shantung in 1928, they occupied Manchuria in 1931, annexed part of Inner Mongolia, destroyed much of Shanghai in fighting against the Chinese, and shortly afterward bombarded Nanking. By 1935 Japan controlled most of North China, and in 1937—if somewhat belatedly—war between the two countries became official. The Japanese overran the eastern half of the Republic from tip to toe, setting up puppet governments in Peking, Nanking, and Canton, and Generalissimo Chiang Kai-shek was obliged to withdraw to Chungking in the west.

The Generalissimo had expended much of his energy on a futile attempt to exterminate the Communist guerrillas, whom he drove out of their mountain fastnesses in the southeast only to see them march to new mountain fastnesses in the northwest. In 1937 the Chinese suspended hostilities among themselves and gingerly joined forces to resist the Japanese, but once the invaders had gone, they fell upon each other again. In 1949 the defeated Chiang Kai-shek fled to Formosa, and the quondam "bandit" Mao Tsetung was then able to take up his quarters in the Imperial City in Peking.

Another rebellion based on the long-suffering peasantry had overthrown an administration corrupted and broken by inner weaknesses and outside pressures. The Mandate of Heaven had passed once more—as all the lessons of history had dictated that it must.

PART FOUR

ANALYZING

30

Past for Consumption

Some might argue that China's past had little to teach about China's present by 1974, when small children all over the People's Republic were chanting:

Lin Piao and Confucius are both scoundrels.
They talk about benevolence and righteousness—a bag of tricks.
They urge you to restrain yourself, to act with propriety, to restore the past.
Damn them!
Little Red Soldiers, let us go into battle and carry out relentless criticism.
Little Red Soldiers . . . (repeat)
Hey!

But if the Chinese young were being taught to scent a humanitarian a mile off, their very piping proved that history was alive and kicking in Chinese minds. For it was part of a gigantic campaign of hatred directed against the image of a man who had lived 2,500 years before and all that his name had stood for across the intervening centuries.

China was not repudiating her past. She was scrutinizing it through the prism of Communist values, translating it into the idiom of Communist dialectic, but nonetheless acknowledging it as her own youth. China yesterday and China today were one. What the propagandists kept and what they rejected from her formative years therefore revealed the shape and nature of an essentially Chinese mentality, clad only in the coarse stuff of Maoist jargon.

Confucius? "Confucius was stubborn, fierce, but very weak; sinister, cunning, and rotten to the core," was the considered verdict of Peking and Tsinghua universities.[1] The *Li* he so venerated had been concocted to perpetuate the "reactionary, dark, and rotten system" of the declining Chou Dynasty, whose riches came "from the blood of multitudes of slaves." The so-called rites, music, benevolence, and righteousness he taught his students were nothing but the "fossilized old culture of the slave-owning aristocrats," and these had not treated slaves as human beings at all. "A horse plus a skein of silk could be exchanged for five slaves. Sometimes as many as a hundred were ruthlessly killed or buried alive to accompany the corpse of a slave owner in the tomb." *Li* "meant hell for the slaves and paradise for the slave owners," yet for Confucius "everything about the system was perfect and sacrosanct."

Everywhere—even in a popular series of lurid cartoons which appeared on wall posters during 1974—the antique sage was depicted as an ultra-reactionary monster frantically trying to preserve an outworn society founded on vicious exploitation, and mercilessly suppressing the progressive element of the age, the "new emerging landlord class." His appeals for filial piety, for loyalty to the prince, and even for leniency toward the inferior were all strands in the same iron mesh of servitude within which the wretched Chinese masses were trapped in his time. As for Mencius, headlines in the authoritative *Red Flag* (for, like Confucius, he was making the headlines by then) described him as "A Trumpeter for Restoring the Slave System" who cozened men into going backward to more bondage instead of forward to freedom by "learning from the ancient kings." These—and all that followed in their infamous footsteps—were the scoundrels who had presented China's decadent emperors with a traditional framework for their tyranny.

The Legalists, on the other hand, were sympathetically portrayed. Shan Yang, who regimented all Ch'in for agriculture and war, disciplining the people with pitiless punishments and prompt rewards, was an "outstanding exponent" of the "progressive" school. He denounced the Confucian precepts of benevolence and righteousness, and correctly substituted the rule of law for the rule of *Li.* His decrees "smashed the obsolete political structure in the state of Ch'in" and were "his indelible merits in history." Those who considered his conduct a little savage should remember the words of Engels: "Without violence, without unrelenting harsh means, nothing in history would succeed." Shan Yang had "made full use of his revolutionary role in this respect." In consequence, the reactionaries had ordered him to be torn apart by chariots, and "he died a martyr at his post, laying down his life in the cause of reform."

He had proved, the *Red Flag* emphasized in another article, that "it was possible for a backward state to advance by leaps and bounds and become a developed one, provided it moved with the tide of history and firmly adhered to the Legalist line." Shan Yang, Hsun Tzu ("Men are born evil"), and Han Fei (who united the principles of "law," "power," and "technique") were all hailed as teachers who "reflected the progressive nature of a new vigorous class bent on carrying out social changes" and had "stood in the van of the tide in their day."

They had also inspired the heartless conqueror who made himself First Emperor of the Ch'in Dynasty, the despot damned by posterity for burning the great body of Chinese literature and burying alive all scholars caught hiding any relic of it. But in 1974 the *Peking Review* protested that the First Emperor had been grossly misrepresented. He was a giant who "accomplished the stupendous task" of welding China into one centralized empire for the first time. He had only been able to complete this work, however, after a "serious struggle against the clique of aristocratic slave owners" that had continued to "wildly vilify" the rule of law as a pretext for punishing and killing, and to slander the centralized state as the misshapen child of his personal "greed for power."

Given that venomous opposition, "burning the books and burying the Confucian scholars alive was a necessary measure of dictatorship," an "inevitable development of the class struggle of that era," and a "self-defense measure which the First Emperor was compelled to take . . . Progressive thinkers in Chinese history generally hailed this revolutionary action." Furthermore, of seventy royal academicians at the Ch'in court, only sixty-two were among those buried alive. The emperor was not a cruel man, and he loved literature, the commentators concluded.

Moving down the long gallery of Chinese history, the Communists paused to pass ideological judgment on many of its now-familiar heroes. The wily village headman who founded the Han Dynasty was praised as a sound Legalist, whereas Hsiang Yu, the blue-blooded butcher whose downfall he encompassed, was dismissed as a reactionary Confucian—one had promoted according to merit, the other had favored his own kin. During the period of the Three Kingdoms, Chuko Liang had followed "a strictly Legalist line" in Shu, promoting the worthy, fostering agriculture, building a strong army, and hitting out at rebellious aristocrats "who worshipped Confucius." But honors were even, for in the eyes of the Maoists his enemy Ts'ao Ts'ao had done precisely the same, "enforcing the Legalist line" and unifying Wei by suppressing nobles and "Confucianists who were bent on sabotaging the new regime from within."

Economic reformers like Sang Hung-yang and Wang Anshih, who introduced "socialist" measures during the Han and Sung dynasties, had also been Legalists, but the effete Neoconfucians had "fanatically worshipped" the old sage, and the doting, artistic T'ang emperor who lost his heart to the Lady Yang and his capital to the gross Turkish general who was her "adopted son" had deserved his fate, for he had exalted Confucius as the "king of culture."

Every peasant uprising provoked by poverty and tyranny was interpreted as an explosion of fury against the abominable Confucians, and the Red Eyebrows, the Yellow Turbans, the bandit Li Tzu-ch'eng (who seized Peking from the Ming, only to have the Manchus seize it from him), and finally the formidable Taiping were all stamped progressive by the Communist press. The disreputable aura of Christianity around the Heavenly King was tactfully ignored by publications like *China Pictorial* and *China Reconstructs,* and readers were told instead that he had invented a fictitious anti-Confucian "god-king" who was "a personification of the revolutionary peasants fighting for liberation." The Python, needless to say, was stigmatized a ringleader of reactionaries.

A major political campaign in China can generate even more ferment than a parliamentary or presidential election in the West, for every man must take a public stand on the issue of the moment or be condemned by his own silence—there is no funk hole like the secret ballot. All sensible Chinese were therefore seized, not by the urge, but by the sudden need to pulverize a philosopher who had long since become powder. And this violent exercise in historical reappraisal was only part of the "Criticize Lin, Criticize Confucius" movement, which related the ills of the past to the perils of the present by depicting the pro-Russian renegade Lin Piao as a man poisoned by the pratings of the pre-Christian philosopher.

Chairman Mao had declared that "political power grows out of the barrel of a gun," and this "thoroughly negates the reactionary and hypocritical concepts of benevolence, righteousness, and virtue preached in the doctrines of Confucius and Mencius, and proclaims the bankruptcy of Confucian humbug that he who relies on virtue will thrive and he who relies on force will perish," argued the *Red Flag.* Yet Lin Piao had remained a "devout disciple of Confucius." He had supported the Confucian concept of compromise implicit in the philosophy of the "Golden Mean" in a treacherous attempt to "reconcile contradictions and abolish the struggle between the proletariat and the bourgeoisie." At the same time he had denounced the First Emperor for burning the books and burying the scholars, and had criticized his other progressive measures with the "sinister aim of distorting history and creating counterrevolutionary public opinion to subvert the dictatorship of the proletariat and restore capitalism."

The Russians were also castigated for "picking up the filthy weapons of the Confucian school in a vain attempt to vilify our great state by attacking Shan Yang. But this only shows to what degree these renegades to Marxism-Leninism have degenerated!" They had even hastened "to confer on Mencius such laurels as 'democracy' and 'humanitarianism.' " The Chinese millions were reminded that the conflict between the Legalists and the Confucians was part of the unending class war in which the "proletarian revolutionary line" of Chairman Mao was now pitted against the "bourgeois reactionary line" of the enemy. By criticizing Mencius, men could learn to see more clearly "the counterrevolutionary nature of Lin Piao and other political swindlers," and the truth of the objective law that just as the Legalist landlords eclipsed the Confucian slave-owning aristocracy, the socialist system would eclipse the capitalist system.

Lin Piao was not the only "meritorious dog" to give Mao uneasy moments, however. The Chinese Communist armies assembled to overthrow Chiang Kai-shek in the forties had grown unevenly out of guerrilla bands recruited in widely separated red strongholds during the twenties and early thirties, and their generals had been spinning their own webs of personal and regional allegiances from the earliest days of the revolution. Once China was in their hands, therefore, senior commanders and political commissars dominating the provinces of the enormous empire they had so quickly conquered inherited the taint of the warlords, and several were soon looked at askance from Peking as dangerously independent masters of their own "mountaintops."

In consequence, Maoists who were anxious that the Party should command the gun and not the gun the Party regarded the loose, decentralized system of feudal states* upheld by

* The Chinese Communists call the Chou Dynasty a "slave-owning society," and reserve the word "feudal" for the period that followed, beginning

Confucius as doubly accursed, and the tight unified Ch'in empire, in whose capital the ruler held all the strings of power, as a worthy archetype. The Legalist formula conferred absolute authority upon the leader in his palace or politburo, and made his slightest Thought law, while in the provinces "all chiefs of prefectures were appointed by the center and could be transferred at any time."

The targets of the collective mudslinging, the ancient Confucius and the modern Lin Piao, personified the persistent "revisionist" evils in China—timeserving bureaucrats, bourgeois university examinations that held back proletarian students, books and operas that did not bear the correct social message. They were combustible effigies of the "olds" that all good Communists execrated, the ancestral customs and superstitions and habits of thought that must be swept away if China was to become a clean and classless society. The magnitude of the campaign as it rolled forward month after month reflected the importance of China's history in the minds of the perceptive Maoists—and the importance of China's traditions in the minds of the stubborn masses.

The Heavenly King of the Taiping had made the mistake of attacking old Chinese culture in the name of a new Chinese nationalism. But Mao had "used the past to serve the present" by glorifying the good in order to uproot the bad (as he saw it), justifying today in the light of yesterday and yesterday in the light of today, preserving for the Chinese millions their proud sense of continuity and cultural heritage, and appointing the Communist Party to be the guardian of that heritage—and thus its warder.

Unlike the Heavenly King, moreover, the Communists could set about smashing Confucian idols with impunity. For in the eyes of many the idols were by then too tarnished and battered to merit a place of honor. The practice of Confucian principle had been brought into disrepute by corrupt scholars and despotic emperors, by the absurd rigidities of

---

with the First Ch'in Emperor. In this book, however, "feudal" has been used to describe the Chou Dynasty, in accordance with accepted Western practice.

the mandarinate under the later dynasties, by the "Confucian" Toad, by "Confucian" warlords, and by those "Confucian" Nationalists who quoted piously from the *Analects* of the Master while robbing and raping the nation with a thoroughness and ingenuity that were beyond criticism. Finally, the Confucian society, based on feudal patronage and loyalty, was an anachronism.

The May 4 Movement, a hot blast of enraged nationalism that ripped through China in 1919, was provoked by the contemptuous cynicism of foreign powers, but it struck at the whole basis of a seedy state that had degenerated from a geopolitical giant into a geopolitical joke. According to the Communists fifty-five years later, it was "uncompromising in its opposition to imperialism and feudalism. It raised the slogan 'Down with the Confucian shop!' and opposed the worship of Confucius and the study of the Confucian canon. It was the prelude to China's new democratic revolution." The last three words are in the ideological vernacular, however, for although the students of the May 4 Movement who demonstrated in the streets yelled "Down with the old ethics and up with the new," not only was "old" Confucianism discredited but "new" Western democracy also.

Two years later the Chinese Communist Party was founded with a controversial professor from Peking University named Ch'en Tu-hsiu at its head. But, the first of many a Mao manqué, Ch'en was to prove a man for no seasons in China, even given five instead of the usual four, for he was frank, stubborn, upright, and democratic. The Communists expelled him from the Party and later accused him of praising Confucius and Mencius. The Nationalists threw him in jail because he had been a prominent Communist. He never abandoned the stand that he was a true Marxist, however, and he gave no party secrets away to his Nationalist inquisitors.

When he was let out of prison he was an old man, and he had had time to think things over. He was nevertheless resolute and unbending when passing judgments that continued to lose him friends in both camps. "If Germany or

Russia wins," he said during the Second World War, "mankind will enter upon at least a century of great darkness. If victory goes to England, France, and America, and bourgeois democracy is saved, then the path will be open to mass democracy." But democracy, whether bourgeois or proletarian, must rest squarely on certain fundamental liberties and rights. Only the courts should have the power to order arrests, only parliament should have the power to levy taxes, opposition parties should have freedom of action, people should have freedom of thought, workers the right to strike, peasants the right to till the land.

Ch'en was sharp-tongued and a quick thinker, possessed of an exceptional intellect and an inquisitive mind. He talked animatedly, his eyes flashing, and he laughed without restraint. But he was strictly honest, ever ready to admit an error. In his old age he refused help from friends, and when he died his wife went to work in a factory rather than live on charity. "You must not sell my corpse for money," he had told her.

He might have fetched something dead, but he fetched very little alive. There was no place in China for a man who believed in fundamental democratic principles under which a bourgeois system could give way peacefully to a proletarian system with the passing of time. It was a country in which Mao Tsetung would not only urge upon his followers the vital importance of realizing that "whoever has an army has power, and war decides everything," but would add: "In this respect both Sun Yat-sen and Chiang Kai-shek are our teachers"—just in case anyone should think there had ever been a valid alternative.

Conservative by instinct, most Chinese will stick to the same drastic remedy, whether for constipation or corrupt government. Mao prescribed the mixture as before—bloody revolution based principally on an army of land-hungry peasants, a band of "loyal and righteous" rebels in the tradition of Liang Shan P'o, exercising their ancient prerogative to rise against a bad ruler and change the Mandate of Heaven.

Sun Yat-sen and his followers had freed China from the

Manchus, but they had not purged her of foreigners or feudalism. Ch'en Tu-hsiu had emulated the Russians and incited the workers to strike in the cities, but the strikes had been brutally broken. All elections, all assemblies, all peace, morality, and talk of democracy were part of a malefic illusion. China was ruled by the gun, and must be liberated by the gun. If a child has ringworm, you must shave its head even if it cries bitterly, Han Fei Tzu had said. How can you rid it of ringworm if you do not shave its head? And only revolution could cure China's ringworm now.

China had been dissected and humiliated by a motley crew of barbarians. The Chinese had starved by the million, sold children and even eaten them to survive, worked day and night for a pittance in bitter cold, shivered in rags and watched their wives kneel half-clad by the wayside when strangers passed, in obedience to someone's haughty ukase.

Mao gave them a formula for revenge whose ingredients were nationalism and class war, and as the years passed he also gave them food and clothes and homes and medicines and schools and work and a unified China cleansed of the alien and respected throughout the world. He even gave them the right to risk expressing their personal views at the wellhead or on a wall poster. But he did not give them freedom and democracy. These might be the subject of many fine phrases in the constitution (qualified by much fine print in the contract of everyday life), but his was a Chinese diet designed for a Chinese patient afflicted with a Chinese sickness.

The Chairman began "sinifying" Marxism-Leninism itself when he first confided the main role in the revolution to the peasant, and in 1942 he launched a campaign of political education to recycle the thoughts of those who could only echo the Word as preached in Moscow. As we have already seen, he drew heavily on the wisdom of China's own past, founding his authority as the Red Sun of Heaven on Legalist "power," "technique," and "law," and using men objectively while remaining above them. His military infallibility was established in rewritten history which proved that he had routed the immense armies of Chiang Kai-shek by remote control, in spite of the bungling and treachery of his incompetent field commander, Lin Piao. His was always, by definition, the "correct line." He, therefore, was the ultimate judge of right and wrong.

The Communist cadres were indoctrinated mandarins imbued with the "party nature," and since the masses were the sinews of the state they were treated with calculated benevolence. All but the most incorrigible among the wicked and the blasphemous were coaxed back into the fold rather than consigned to oblivion. But the chastening institutions that had served the Ming Dynasty so well—the system of collective responsibility and the all-pervasive secret police—also served the new socialist China.

However, history had taught Mao that dynasties decayed like aging teeth (even Stalin's Russia had degenerated into a revisionist superpower). The first great emperor of a new line could not perpetuate the heroic spirit of his reign, for heroes needed trouble "as the soaring dragon needs the wind," and once the tumult subsided and the empire was at peace, the state did not want messiahs, but mandarins.

Mao was the messiah. His favorite parable was of "the Foolish Old Man who could move Mountains" simply by getting his family to dig away at the job with hoes, generation after generation, until it was done. He believed that the human will could conquer all. "Imagination can open Heaven," he cried. "One day is equal to twenty years." His challenging words rang out over the land, inspiring a stupendous revolution. But when he threw China into the crash program known as the Great Leap Forward in 1958 in a disastrous attempt to convert his backward republic into a self-reliant modern state almost overnight, the pragmatists in the Party looked at him with pursed lips and began to interpret the "Thought of Mao Tsetung" to suit themselves.

Mao's gospel was successively trimmed to justify the "revisionism" of the disgraced ex-President Liu Shao-ch'i, the "right-opportunism" of Lin Piao, the "smiling diplomacy" of Chou En-lai. But if this created contradictions, contradictions were part of Mao's prophylaxis for the decline of dynasties. For to prevent the state from petrifying in the hands of a bourgeois leadership in Peking and a bureaucratic mandarinate in the provinces, there must be perpetual revolution. Before concord lulled China into political inertia, it must always be shattered by further "contradictions" which would make "one divide into two" again, and so keep the class struggle alive.

When the moderates appeared to be betraying his revolutionary ideals, the Chairman's left-wing lieutenants urged upon the masses their "right to rebel," "to go against the tide," and as he moved into the eighties six years ahead of the century, Mao tried to make sure that his radical supporters would be strong enough to face up to the pragmatists when he himself was gone—for in Chinese history the death of the founder of a dynasty had more often than not been the signal for a fratricidal battle for power among his immediate successors.

The romantic concept of the infatuated T'ang emperor and the Lady Yang that they were as two one-winged birds which could only fly when joined together nevertheless applied to the Chinese Communist Party, for the equilibrium and stability of China were also maintained by means of constant and delicate adjustments between the contending left and right wings of the politburo under Mao. It could not be otherwise. Whatever their differences, all factions were the heirs of an essentially nationalist revolution, and in a chaotic world their first instinct would be to "respect the king and repel the barbarian."

A British historian [2] has suggested that since liberal democracy and free enterprise have failed the West, and Moscow has no better answers than Manhattan or Manchester to the difficulties prophesied by the doomologists, the Chinese may yet teach the world how to live in unity and solve the problems of fuel and food and pollution and peace. The Confucians spoke longingly of the *Ta T'ung*, the Universal Commonwealth that had supposedly existed in an ideal age in the past. The Communists believe in a world revolution that will supposedly lead to an ideal age in the future, and they welcome the multiplication of international evils which they in their turn need to arouse the masses "as the soaring dragon needs the wind."

But Confucian or Communist, the Chinese remain the Chinese, and their impact on the other three billion members of the human race will depend not only on what their preceptors have taught them to think during the past three thousand years, but how differently from the rest. This is not a comparative study, and we cannot run the gamut of Western philosophers, soldiers, and kings from Aristotle to Zog. However, two figures stand out from the pages of history as the major political and military influences on Mao and the modern Chinese—Han Fei Tzu, the master of Legalism, and Sun Tzu, the master of strategy. Han Fei Tzu has been described as the Chinese Machiavelli, Sun Tzu as the Chinese Clausewitz. It therefore seems logical to ask at this stage just how "Chinese" Niccolò Machiavelli and Karl von Clausewitz were—or were not.

31

Western Approaches

The Italian world of Machiavelli was a distorted miniature of the Chinese world of Han Fei and Sun Tzu—a jigsaw puzzle of warring states that formed a single culture rather than a single realm, within which all foreigners were looked upon as outer *barbari.* Cesare Borgia strutted across the scene like a treacherous and unprincipled hegemon, "maintaining such relations with kings and princes that they have either to help him graciously or go carefully in doing him harm." He pacified the unruly Romagna by appointing a callous but efficient minister to cow it into obedience, and when his unpopular severities were no longer required, won the people over to himself by having the scapegoat cut in two and the bits left out in the piazza at Cesena for all to see. As ruthless as the First Emperor of Ch'in, he killed off the ruling families of the cities he seized, so that they could not plot against him.

Machiavelli himself was a pragmatist, a "persuader" guided by expediency who believed that it was often kinder to be cruel and the end always justified the means. Not surprisingly, therefore, Legalism fits at least one of his fine Italian hands like a glove. If the prince wants to maintain his rule, he writes, he "must not flinch from vices which are necessary for safeguarding the state," for virtues may ruin him, while "some of the things that appear to be wicked will bring him security and prosperity." Rulers must learn to be "great liars and deceivers," and the prince should not put himself at a disadvantage by honoring his word, but merely appear to keep his promises, to be "guileless and devout . . . a man of good faith, a man of integrity."

He should show no misplaced compassion, but while making sure that he incurs neither popular hatred nor popular contempt, remember that "it is far better to be feared than to be loved." Since men are more prone to evil than good, he should distrust them all and bind them to him with the threat of prompt penalties, punishing and rewarding in a "striking" fashion that will "set everyone talking." For "the bond of love is one which men break when it is to their advantage to do so, but fear is strengthened by a dread of punishment which is always effective." The judgment of the prince must be irrevocable, his policies must be carried out meticulously, and his patronage must make ministers feel that they are totally dependent on him, so that they consider only his interests and never their own.

Like Han Fei Tzu, Machiavelli warns his prince against the motives of those who curry favor with his subjects by doing good, and against "gentry who live in idleness on the abundant revenue from their estates, without having anything to do with their cultivation or with other forms of labor essential to life" (in Ch'in they were relieved of their domains and enslaved, it will be recollected). Machiavelli emphasizes that the conduct of all—including princes—must be regulated by the rule of law, for "princes begin to lose their state the moment they begin to break the laws and"—an interpolation of *Li* here—"disregard the ancient traditions and customs under which men have long lived." Almost paraphrasing Hsun Tzu, he explains: "Men never do good unless driven by necessity; when they are free to do as they like, confusion and disorder reign everywhere. Therefore it is said that hunger and poverty make men industrious, and laws make them good."

Machiavelli wanted a strong and ruthless prince capable of uniting all Italy, "a ferocious lion and a sly fox" who would "contrive to be alone in his authority," and there is no doubt that he would have spoken approvingly of the First Emperor of the Ch'in Dynasty. Would he have agreed that there was "A Case for Murder"? Bloody fratricide had enabled not only the excellent Emperor T'ang T'ai-tsung to ascend the throne of China, but the legendary Romulus to found Rome. "Many perchance will think it a bad precedent that Romulus should first have killed his brother," Machiavelli remarks, but "it is a sound maxim that reprehensible actions may be justified by their effects, and that when the effect is good, it justifies the action. For it is the man who uses violence to spoil things, not the man who uses it to mend them, that is blameworthy."

He admires those who are generous on the way up, but mean when they reach the top. He cautions the prince against ambitious warlords, and of "meritorious dogs" he writes: "It is impossible that the suspicion aroused in a prince after the victory of one of his generals should not be increased by any arrogance in manner or speech displayed by the man himself." The general must either give up his command, therefore, so that the pacified prince will reward him "or at least refrain from harming him"—or else he must attack him. For he cannot escape the "jaws of ingratitude." Most generals hesitate between the two courses and are lost, says Machiavelli. On his side, the prudent prince strikes first and wipes out all those who may conceivably conspire against him while he is still consolidating his power, so that they cannot destroy him later. ("Kill him now or you will be sorry," as so many Chinese counselors told their masters. "Only evil can come of it if you spare him.")

Machiavelli's "Chinese" cross-references are legion. He advocates the study of antiquity, but his admonitions against blindly worshipping the past would have pleased the Legalists: "The whole truth about the ancient times is not grasped, since what redounds to their discredit is often passed over in silence, whereas what is likely to make them appear glorious is pompously recounted in all its details." Nations are victims of vicious cycles. The heroic founder of a dynasty is followed by degenerate heirs, whose fear of the growing hatred of their subjects goads them into perpetrating increasingly hideous acts of tyranny until they are overthrown by a new savior. This man triumphs precisely because the government is corrupt and the people are disaffected (the soaring dragon needs the wind), but the day will come when his line will suffer the fate of its predecessor.

Familiar streaks of Taoism also color the thinking of the Florentine, so that he describes ruling princes of the Church as possessing states yet not defending them, having subjects yet not governing them. "And as their states are not defended, they are not taken away from them; and their subjects, being without a government, neither can nor hope to overthrow it in favor of another. So these principalities alone are secure and happy."

All human affairs are fluid, and a prince is often driven by *necessità* to behave "like a beast as well as a man" in order to maintain his position, turning "as the winds of fortune and the changes in the situation dictate." His prosperity or ruin depend on how adroitly he adapts himself, and the wisest remain unmoved by their fluctuating destinies: "Dictatorship did not elate me, nor exile depress me," he quotes the renowned Roman censor Camillus as saying. ("I have no joy when I win, no anxiety when I lose," as the Taoist *Book of Lieh Tzu* has it.)

But Machiavelli is also a military philosopher. Arguments must be supported by arms, and in peace a prince must be prepared for hostilities: "The first way to lose your state is to neglect the art of war." He advocates respecting the king and repelling the barbarian when he cites the case of Germany, where, "though the emperor has no power to enforce his will, the states are united because the enemy without would overrun them if they quarreled among themselves." With Mencius, Machiavelli implies that a country with no external foe is on the road to ruin: "Discord is usually due to peace, unity to fear." Appeasement only evokes demands for further concessions ("like smothering fire with wood," as the Chinese said).

Once launched, a campaign should be short and crushing. ("There has never been a protracted war from which a state benefited," Sun Tzu declared.) All decisions must be taken promptly, and when the safety of the realm depends upon them, the ruler must not pause to consider whether they are just or unjust, kind or cruel, "praiseworthy or ignominious," for in such circumstances "no decision the king takes can be shameful." ("Do what your enemy would be ashamed to do," Shan Yang urged.)

Like the flexible Chinese, Machiavelli warns commanders against wasting men and time on long sieges or the defense of difficult positions, and counsels them either to bypass walled cities and fortresses or to persuade those within to surrender by promising that "no attack is being made on the common good, but only on a few ambitious citizens." ("The army does not punish the common people, but only those who mislead them," observed Hsun Tzu.) Machiavelli recommends a tactical leniency worthy of the Chinese masters of war, and he is a firm advocate of Sun Tzu's principle of "death ground"—the wilier generals of history always obliged their own troops to fight, but never those of the adversary, he points out. They "left open to the enemy a route they might have closed, and closed a route to their own soldiers which they might have left open."

Did Sun Tzu stress: "All war is based on deception"? Machiavelli declaims: "It is a glorious thing to use fraud in the conduct of war" and "a prince who wishes to do great things must learn to practice deceit," for while force by itself never suffices, fraud may. When the enemy appears to make a colossal blunder, therefore, distrust him. Like Chuko Liang, Machiavelli knows that armies can be thrown into confusion by "unfamiliar cries" and "strange sights." The "Sleeping Dragon" frightened off a formidable but wary enemy simply by leaving city gates open and unguarded, and Machiavelli recalls that when the Gauls found the gates of Rome open and unguarded they also "waited a day and a night without entering, for they feared a ruse."

Hsun Tzu spoke scornfully of mercenaries as "hired laborers"—"for if men do something only for the sake of benefit, they will abandon an undertaking as soon as it appears unprofitable or dangerous." "Mercenaries and auxiliaries are useless and dangerous," echoes Machiavelli. "There is no loyalty or inducement to keep them in the field apart from the little they are paid, and this is not enough to make them want to die for you. They are only too ready to serve in your army when you are not at war; but when war comes they either desert or disperse."

Like most Chinese from Mo Tzu to Mao, he emphasizes that the soldiers themselves are the sinews of war. "It was not that the walls were low . . . but that the *men* abandoned the city," Mencius said nearly two thousand years before him. "Good armies without fortresses are adequate defense," writes Machiavelli, "but fortresses without good armies are no defense at all." The prince, therefore, must "arm himself with his own subjects," for without faithful, disciplined, and efficient troops, gold and terrain and allies are of no avail. In his *Art of War* he argues that security lies in a trained militia inspired by loyalty to prince or republic, and talks of artillery as the gadgetry of mercenaries much as Mao talks of the megaton bomb as the gadgetry of imperialist "paper tigers."

Clausewitz, born into an age in which the great levies of Napoleon were to sweep across Europe, fired by the sense of purpose and patriotism that the Little Corporal and the ideals of the French Revolution had put into their veins, was also a passionate champion of the citizen army and the "people's war," and it is not difficult to find points of contact between the author of *Vom Kriege* (*On War*) and Chinese strategists ancient and modern.

"Men proficient in battle do not easily grow angry or lightly instigate war," said Lao Tzu, and in his great military classic Clausewitz writes: "War is not a pastime, no mere passion for venturing and winning. It is a serious means for a serious object." It must not be undertaken recklessly, and reason must always prevail over courage. The country must be fully prepared for hostilities, which should be conducted with dispatch: "No conquest can be finished too soon." Speed and surprise, secrecy and good information about the enemy are of paramount importance. Commanders must be mathematically minded, and think only in terms of expediency. They should not fight against a superior army or be drawn into battle on the enemy's terms, but avoid fortresses and attack weakness, concentrating their troops so that they can outnumber their opponent "at the decisive point."

Clausewitz defines war as an instrument of politics (Mao: "War is a political action"). Power is the ability to destroy the adversary, but the army must be subordinate to the state (Mao: "Power grows out of the barrel of a gun," but "the Party must command the gun"). The object is "complete victory," since "moderation in war is an absurdity" (Mao: "If the Kuomintang fight, we will wipe them out completely; wipe out some, some satisfaction; wipe out more, more satisfaction; wipe out the whole lot, complete satisfaction." [1]). So far, so Chinese.

Appearances are deceptive, however. *Vom Kriege* presents the brutal antithesis of most Chinese military thinking, and in reality the cold, professional ruthlessness of its German author has almost nothing in common with the cold, professional ruthlessness of Sun Tzu or Mao—or Machiavelli. For Mao the end was the "liberation" of China, and armed struggle was the means. For the rest: "War, this monster of mutual slaughter," must be abolished, he insisted.[2] Unfortunately, "war can only be abolished through war, and in order to get rid of the gun it is necessary to take up the gun," he continued, but "the only ones who crave war and no peace are certain monopoly capitalists in a handful of imperialist countries which depend on aggression for their profits."

Clausewitz would have regarded this as mindless blasphemy, for he had the highest possible regard for war. There could be nothing monstrous or unnatural about "mutual slaughter," since the interests of nations inevitably clashed, and conflict was therefore a normal condition among them. Its ideal form was "absolute war," in which the material hindrances and human annoyances he called "friction" were removed, and all combat built up into one great, glorious, final battle, just as the sun's rays are focused by a magnifying glass "in a perfect image, in the fullness of their heat."

Almost as if he were directly refuting the subtle strategies of Sun Tzu, he remarks disdainfully in his writings: "Philanthropists may easily imagine there is a skillful method of disarming and overcoming an enemy without causing great bloodshed, and that this is the proper tendency of the art of war." Some had already put about the unhealthy and erroneous idea that "only those generals were to deserve laurels who knew how to carry on war without spilling blood," he complains. Sun Tzu may have laid down that "to subdue the enemy without fighting is the acme of skill," but Clausewitz retorts: "The acme of strategic ability is displayed in the provision of means for the Great Battle" in which alone "the overthrow of the enemy is to be achieved." Painless shortcuts to victory like breaking up the enemy's alliances are not valid substitutes.

All war is based on deception, Sun Tzu taught. "War is an act of violence to compel our opponent to do our will," Clausewitz announces uncompromisingly, and he goes on to assert that tricks and ruses and false plans and reports have usually had little effect on the outcome of a battle: "A correct and penetrating eye is a more necessary and useful quality for a general than craftiness." Stratagem may "offer itself as a last resort" to the "weak and small," but it is "he who uses force unsparingly, without reference to the bloodshed involved" who carries the day.

Clausewitz does not hesitate to put the enemy in "death ground": "The danger of having no line of retreat paralyzes movements and the power of resistance," he claims. Nor does he warn commanders against chasing a seemingly beaten enemy with limited forces in hazardous circumstances: "When the conqueror can continue the pursuit throughout the night, if only with a strong advance guard . . . the effect of the victory is immensely increased."

It is easy enough to discover where Machiavelli also parts company with the Chinese. Unlike Mencius, he thinks the state should be enriched for the public good, while the citizens are kept poor, and unlike all Confucians (but in agreement with the Maoists), he puts his faith in extremes rather than the "Golden Mean." But—cupboard humanist or not—he also differs on a dozen questions with Han Fei Tzu, for he argues for clemency against cruelty, republic against principality, man against matter, and he does not treat the people as expendable straw dogs whose nonexistent souls may be manipulated by the next Legalist Pavlov in line.

It is nonetheless the shadow of Clausewitz, not Machiavelli, that darkens the minds of the military strategists of the West and divides them from the minds of the East. It was his grim figuring that could still be discerned behind the meat grinding in Flanders, the disastrous "Great Battle" at Dienbienphu, and the American steamrolling in Vietnam—where Sun Tzu and Mao could be sensed behind the elusive guerrilla strategy of the Vietnamese Communists. Clausewitz may believe a state must reconquer territory it has lost to an adversary, just as Mao believes a people must "liberate" territory they have "lost" to the class enemy. But there the parallel ends. For the rest, when they appear to speak in unison of "citizen armies" or "people's wars" or "mutual slaughter" as instruments of politics, Clausewitz is always talking in terms of attack, Mao in terms of defense.

32

From the Top

When the Chinese hurled wave upon wave of close-packed infantry against the withering fire of the Americans in one roaring human sea during the conflict in Korea, they seemed to have thrown their own parsimonious principles to the dogs of war, and to be "using force unsparingly, without reference to the bloodshed involved," as Clausewitz had advised. But Sun Tzu had said, "When you outnumber the enemy five to one, you may attack," and to attack in Korea was to defend China herself, for the two countries were "as the lips to the teeth; when the lips are gone the teeth are cold."

Taking it from the top again, the lengthy opus of Chinese history has this one recurring theme, to which foreign forays and "punitive" expeditions abroad have been mere counterpoint. The first instinct of the Chinese is to deploy forces to "repel the barbarian," and to this end they can normally be expected to conform to their long traditions. They will prepare for war when there is still peace, and while refraining from all rash acts, will avoid "smothering fire with wood" by giving in to their adversaries—unless they are compelled to appease now in order to punish later. As far as possible, they will skirt strength and strike weakness, seize no territory they cannot hold, fight by "attacking the enemy's strategy," and so forestall a major armed conflict.

"Repelling the barbarian" does not simply mean sitting on the Chinese border, or even rushing military aid to friendly neighbors threatened with aggression, however. It means refusing to withdraw "historical" claims that the Russians are illegally occupying 600,000 square miles of Chinese soil, publishing an official map that includes within the frontiers of the People's Republic almost the whole of the South China Sea down to offshore Borneo, sinking an intrusive South Vietnamese gunboat off the "Chinese" Paracel Islands (and so, incidentally, warning off the Seventh Fleet—a case of "killing the chicken to scare the monkey"). And if the Russians threw their armor across the northern border in a surgical blitzkrieg whose object was to amputate Manchuria, it could mean a Chinese counterthrust toward the exposed Soviet nerve-centers of Vladivostok and Khabarovsk.

Every time the Chinese have exploded a nuclear device, they have nevertheless assured the world that it has been "entirely for the purpose of defense," for "ultimately abolishing nuclear weapons," which "at no time and in no circumstances" would China be the first to use. The offensive task of preventing war by "attacking the enemy's strategy," disrupting his alliances, and sapping his will to fight may primarily be confided to the instruments of Chinese diplomacy and Communist subversion. If in a nuclear age China's ultimate deterrent must also be nuclear, it should still be regarded as no more than a deterrent.

Antique counsel not to hit out at the masses, not to make more enemies than friends, still applies today when the object of the Chinese is to undermine a Soviet regime dominated by a "revisionist renegade clique," not to annihilate the multitudinous Russians in a series of super-Hiroshimas. "The army does not punish the common people, but only those who mislead them." It pays better to go for the hearts and minds of the millions than for their throats.

Furthermore, Sun Tzu and Mao have taught the Chinese to avoid battle with a superior enemy, and China cannot hope to match the two superpowers in the radioactive field. If the Chinese fight, they want to "shape" the adversary to their requirements, to fight "downhill," not with a slender stock of nuclear warheads but with their almost inexhaustible supply of ordinary mortals.

And even that flood of men must be seen above all as a deterrent. Peking wishes to dissuade the Americans and the Russians from contemplating any kind of military mischief against China by arguing that the logical consequences of swapping dead with 800,000,000 Chinese would be lamentable. If this consideration does not discourage the enemy, the Chinese will be geared to fight a "people's war" against him with a three-million-strong regular army backed by a huge militia, and prove the accuracy of their arithmetic.

Their intransigence in all border talks with the Russians during the mid-seventies, like the stream of provocative abuse they poured out upon Moscow, showed that political leaders in Peking were not as afraid of the Soviet challenge on the ground as their almost hysterical propaganda suggested. At the same time their very inferiority dissuaded them from dropping their voices and sitting down quietly with the superpowers to negotiate nuclear differences. For a lord does not go abroad unescorted, even to conclude a treaty of peace, and wherever possible the Chinese only play from strength—whether they are striking bargains or smiting barbarians.

Yet it was their nuclear deterrent that gave them confidence. For their missile delivery systems might be sketchy, but they were widely dispersed, and if the Russians wanted to mount a pre-emptive strike big enough to knock out all the installations in China—silos and airfields and stockpiles and atomic plants—they would have to expend so much of their own hitting power that they would face their American rivals suddenly and seriously weakened themselves (and vice versa).

Neither Washington nor Moscow knew, moreover, at just what point the Chinese would feel compelled to press the button and send their own rockets smashing into preselected enemy targets if they were attacked—and so tip the scales further against the aggressor, leaving the leaders of the "third kingdom" with the game in their hands. Peking therefore had enough atomic leverage to persuade each of the giants that it would only be sacrificing the indispensable weight it needed to counterbalance the other if it tried to neutralize the People's Republic.

While thus using barbarians to pacify barbarians, China officially welcomed proposals before the United Nations for nuclear-free zones in Latin America, the Middle East, and South Asia, but opposed any move to ban atomic tests and so keep the membership of the nuclear club exclusive. All attempts to stop other nations from making their own multiple-megaton warheads, the Chinese protested vigorously, were merely designed to leave a vulnerable world at the mercy of bullying superpowers already armed to the teeth with them. Russia and America were bent on using their formidable nuclear armament to "act the overlord," and China called for nothing short of the total prohibition and destruction of all atomic weapons.

This nuclear policy fitted harmoniously into the already familiar score, for it served to play America off against Russia and simultaneously helped to alienate both from the angry young states of the Third World, among which Peking was sedulously fostering a new nationalism of the have-nots. By 1970 the Chinese had overtaken the Soviet Union to become the most generous philanthropists in the Communist camp, and were giving backward countries three times as much aid as their Russian rivals. China was by now the self-appointed champion of the underdog nations, which were the victims of shameless "blood-soaked exploitation and plunder" by the imperialists—despite the fact that by withholding their raw riches in oil, rubber, and non-ferrous metals they could bring the affluent West to its knees.

In their campaign to isolate the U.S.S.R., the Chinese not only opened a diplomatic offensive to win friends and influence people's republics in Eastern Europe, but at the other extreme courted all four members of CENTO, the anti-Communist Central Treaty Organization which included Britain, Iran, Turkey, and Pakistan and was sponsored by

Washington. Nor—to recapitulate—did they neglect the still-transparent two-dimensional "Europe" that might one day materialize as the "distant" super-ally in Russia's rear that their forebears had sought for centuries.

But above all they pursued a policy of disconcerting one government by flirting with another, playing hard-to-get here and come-hither there. For the Chinese had known for 2,500 years that in power politics the most important thing was not to be committed, but to stay aloof—not to be caught on one side, but to be courted by all.

Most of China's careful smiles were directed at Washington. The Chinese wanted the Americans to keep a foothold in the Far East and were ready to welcome their continued presence in South Korea and Japan and even Taiwan (if in modest numbers and for a short season only). Their military umbrella would remove any justification for the expansion of the Japanese armed forces to be converted into an explosion, and they would act as a counterpoise to creeping Soviet influence in Tokyo and elsewhere in the region. If thereafter a closer Sino-Japanese understanding cut the Russians out of the running, the Americans would also "go home," for as Tokyo and Peking drew together, the security treaty between Japan and the United States would degenerate from a valid defense pact into an invalid and indefensible anachronism. Meanwhile, the vestigial *affaire* between America and Taiwan prevented the Russians from pushing their way into Taipei, although they had been flirting with the Chinese Nationalists for more than ten years, it was said in Peking.

But Premier Chou En-lai, quoting Lenin at the Tenth Congress of the Chinese Communist Party in 1973, warned his audience to distinguish between those who helped outlaws in order to share in the loot and those who bowed to the exigencies of the moment by compromising with them "in order to lessen the damage the bandits may do and to make it easier to capture and execute them in the future."

The message was loud and clear. China was not going to turn away irrevocably from the United States, and so sacrifice the "big advantage" of an American counterbalance to the

Soviet Union for the sake of "small gains." On the contrary, she would tolerate Washington's importunities on the Chinese periphery for as long as necessary, "swallowing the teeth and the blood," biding her time—and giving no key positions away. If any American "bandit" read more than that into the smile of the Chinese Prime Minister, he was simply the victim of his own naïveté.

Some might accuse the Chinese of misleading them by saying one thing and doing another—treating American imperialist fiddling in the affairs of the Third World to indigestible heaps of hostile Communist syntax, yet giving Dr. Kissinger a warm welcome in Peking. But "all war is based on deception." The Chinese themselves never confused appearance with reality, or their hot-gospeling with the cold facts. "Friendly foreigners" might arrive in Hong Kong from a conducted tour of China, brimming over with flattering impressions vastly at variance with the tales of refugees (who did not openly return to capitalist bondage by train, but secretly swam to liberty across intervening waters well stocked with sharks). The truth usually lay down the middle. But the foreigners had been left free to delude themselves, and the greatest delusion of all was to imagine that somehow Peking had gone soft on international socialism.

In the mid-seventies visitors to China were shown not only how magnificently she was developing, but from what depths of poverty she had still to rise. It would take her half a century to catch up with the West—the West of October 1, 1974—said one senior cadre. "Feign inferiority," Sun Tzu had advised, and it did not all have to be feigned. True to their traditions, the Chinese had set out to win allies and sympathizers on the way up as fellow victims of a rapacious Soviet-American hegemony, and since they would be able to "forget the good that men had done" them once they were on top, they were extending a friendly hand to all and sundry abroad, including reactionary premiers and right-wing military juntas.

This "vertical policy" tempted some analysts to insult the Communist leaders in Peking by inferring that they had abandoned the cause of revolution. But to assume that the

Chinese had renounced their socialist mission in favor of the tactical friendships they now fostered with kings and capitalists against the Kosygins of the world was to mistake the lap for the race.

They were exploiting the "contradictions" between the submerged continents and the superpowers, the have-nots and the haves, and provoking a conflict that looked remarkably like the first phase in some global version of the two-stage Russian Revolution. It was as if a hundred bourgeois political personalities from Manila to Mexico were being groomed to play the interim role of a composite Kerensky opposite the tsars of Moscow and Washington, bringing more "social justice" into international relations before they in their turn were overthrown by the proletarian forces within their own states.

"Just wars" would still be supported, but China's policy was founded on the flexibility demanded by a constantly changing political cosmos, and the problems of the capitalist world were themselves evolving and multiplying in a manner that might one day make it possible to demonstrate Sun Tzu's "acme of skill" and "subdue the enemy without fighting." And from that could come the new *Ta T'ung*—unity and peace in a Communist universe purged of dissent, of which China would once again be the spiritual center.

Machiavelli, who believed that *necessità* was the mother of decision, that blind fortune was the counterpoise to human *virtù,* told Lorenzo de' Medici that the success men enjoyed depended only on "the extent to which their methods are or are not suited to the nature of the times." The Chinese, pursuing an erratic course of their own in conformity with the flow of history, would not quarrel with this proposition. If their ultimate goal seems ludicrously distant, so was the prospect of creating a Communist Chinese superpower when Mao Tsetung took to the hills like a beaten bandit with a few hundred followers in 1927—and evolved his theories on "protracted war." Their ambitions may appear no more than idle dreams today. But it is the dreams of today that become the realities of tomorrow.

Notes

CHAPTER 2

1. Ssu-ma Ch'ien, 145 B.C. to 86 B.C. See Bibliography.
2. In *The Chinese Looking Glass* I wrote that Mencius was the early authority for the principle of the "Mandate of Heaven." Although the *Book of History* and Confucius specifically condoned the killing of the last Shang Dynasty ruler, who was reputedly unworthy of his title and therefore of his role, it was Mencius who propounded the general precept that the will of the people was the Will of Heaven, and if the people deposed a king, it was self-evident that he had lost Heaven's approval. (D.B.)
3. The *Tso Chuan*.

CHAPTER 4

1. Lao Tzu has been identified both as a sage named Lao Lai-tzu and as a certain legendary Lao Tan, who has in turn been confused with a real person of the same name who was archivist of Chou in 347 B.C., 105 years after the death of Confucius.
2. *Water Margin* (*Shui Hu Chuan*) was written by Shih Nai-an (1296–1370) and has also been translated as *All Men Are Brothers* (see Bibliography) and *Men of the Marshes*, the title I used in *The Chinese Looking Glass*. *Water Margin* is now the most widely accepted of the three. (D.B.)
3. For Chi-hsia see pages 66–70. Leading scholars of this school were Shen Tao (fl. 300 B.C.) and Huan Yuan.

CHAPTER 5

1. The Duke of Wei's general was Wu Ch'i (see pages 89 et seq.). The King of Ch'i's general was Sun Pin (see pages 99 et seq. and note 1, Chapter 10).
2. Meng K'o (c. 386–312 B.C., but historians differ). Mencius was a student of Tsen Tzu, who had in turn been a student of Confucius. See also pages 50–51.

CHAPTER 6

1. Joint editorial in the Peking *People's Daily*, *Red Flag*, and *Liberation Army Daily*, January 1, 1972.

CHAPTER 8

1. Peking also bases claims in the East China Sea and in the South China Sea down to the Tsengmu reef off North Borneo on (a) the "Continental Shelf" theory which extends territorial waters from the coast to the point where the sea becomes more than 200 meters deep, and (b) the "Archipelagic Principle" that all the seas between the islands of an archipelago are part of its territorial waters, as well as on (c) the navigational landfalls made by Chinese fleets in the past, notably during the thirteenth and fifteenth centuries. All are disputed, however.

CHAPTER 10

1. On June 8, 1974, the *People's Daily* reported that 4,942 bamboo slips had been found in a tomb in Shantung, on which were inscribed two separate treatises—the thirteen chapters of Sun Wu's *Art of War*, and the hitherto lost *Art of War* of Sun Pin, thus establishing for the first time that they were separate works. Sun Pin lived from 380 to 320 B.C. and his defeat of Wei was accomplished in 341 B.C. See also page 48. The main difference between the two "Sun Tzu" is that Sun Pin recommended seizing towns where possible, if only briefly, as by his day they had developed more fully into the political and economic centers of the state, and the storehouses of its wealth.
2. This version of the jingle differs from the one in *The Chinese Looking Glass*. It is the official Communist translation, however, taken from the *Selected Military Writings of Mao Tse-tung* ("Problems of Strategy in China's Revolutionary War").
3. *Selected Works of Mao Tse-tung*, Vol. I.

CHAPTER 11

1. The capital of King Huai of Ch'u was at P'engch'eng, on the Ssu River. P'engch'eng was later known as Hsu Chou and was defended by Liu Pei during the "Three Kingdoms" period (page 155). It is modern Suchow in Kiangsu Province, where the Chinese Nationalists were decisively defeated by the Communists in December 1948.

CHAPTER 12

1. In modern terms the kingdom of Hanchung consisted of north and central Szechuan, northwest Hupei, and south Shensi provinces.
2. The secret road led through Ch'en Ts'ung, now Pao Chi County in Shensi Province. It was also successfully used by Chiang Kaishek's troops in the fighting against the Japanese.

CHAPTER 14

1. The Ta Yueh Chi, known by the Greeks as the Asii, who were defeated by the Huns in 165 B.C. and migrated westward to the region of the Oxus and Jaxartes.

CHAPTER 16

1. The oath in the peach garden was sworn by Liu Pei, Kuan Yu, and Chang Fei. Kuan Yu was to become "Kuan Ti," the Chinese god of war.
2. Hsu Chou (the capital) was the "P'engch'eng" of Hsiang Yu, the Hegemon of Western Chu. It is to be noted that formerly the capital city of an administrative *chou* was commonly known by the name of the *chou* itself, and if the capital was moved, the title moved with it. See also note 1, Chapter 11.

CHAPTER 19

1. Shu's commerce was with Chien Yeh, the Wu capital near modern Nanking on the Yangtse with which merchants of the Eastern Roman Empire are also said to have traded.
2. Quoted from *Ts'an Chia Chung Kung Wu Chuang Tou Cheng Chi Shih* (see Bibliography).

CHAPTER 20

1. *A History of China,* by Professor Wolfram Eberhard, page 125 (see Bibliography).

2. The Toba (Wei) Empire of Tartar tribes of Tungusic stock, 386–557.
3. From *T'ang Shu.*

CHAPTER 21

1. In his treatise of August 1937 "On Contradiction," Chairman Mao commended Wei Cheng for warning men: "Listen to both sides and you will be enlightened, heed only one side and you will be benighted." But in 1962 both the quotation and the context were of a different character.

CHAPTER 23

1. Quoted from the Ch'ing Confucians Yen Yuan and Li Kung.

CHAPTER 25

1. See note 2, Chapter 4.
2. Peking has been known by many names in history. The Kin called it Chungtu, the Mongols called it Khanbalik (Cambaluc), and it acquired its present name when the Chinese Ming Dynasty Emperor Yung Lo made it his capital early in the fifteenth century.

CHAPTER 26

1. See joint editorial in the *People's Daily, Red Flag,* and *Liberation Army Daily* dated January 1, 1973.
2. *Historia de la cosas mas notables, ritos y costumbres del Gran Reyno de la China,* by Juan Gonzales de Mendoza (Rome, 1585), translated into English 1588, quoted from *China in the Eyes of Europe* (see Bibliography).

CHAPTER 29

1. Successful open rebellion began with the Wuchang Uprising on October 10, 1911. For the Nationalists, the "Double Tenth" has since been China's National Day (for the Communists it is October 1).
2. Chang Tso-lin marched through the pass in 1921, 1923, and 1927. He gained control of North China, but was assassinated in 1928.
3. *Revolution in China,* page 38 (see Bibliography).

4. The Kuomintang had been founded as a union of revolutionary groups in 1912, after Sun Yat-sen had ceded the presidency to Yuan Shih-k'ai. Sun Yat-sen shared the leadership of the party with Huang Hsing and Sung Chian-jen (whom Yuan Shih-k'ai later had murdered), and it held most of the seats in the National Assembly.

CHAPTER 30

1. Quotations from Communist sources in this section are taken mainly from the following publications:
   Red Flag: No. 11, 1973, and Nos. 4, 5, 6, 7, and 9, 1974.
   Peking Review: May 3, mid-May, June, July, September 13, September 27, November 1, and November 15, 1974.
   China Pictorial: August and September 1974 and April 1975.
   China Reconstructs: September 1974.
   People's Daily: June 19, 1974.
   The above is only a sampling of the historical analyses published during the campaign against Confucius and Lin Piao. Chinese Communist newspapers and periodicals carried innumerable articles on the subject during 1974 in particular.
2. Professor Arnold Toynbee, in an article, "Inheritors of the Earth," published in *Horizon* in 1974.

CHAPTER 31

References to Machiavelli and Clausewitz and quotations from their works have been taken (with few exceptions) from the following:

Machiavelli: The Discourses, edited by Bernard Crick (translation of Father Leslie J. Walker), including notes on *The Art of War,* Penguin Classics, 1970.

Machiavelli: The Prince, translated by George Bull, Penguin Classics, 1972.

Clausewitz: On War, edited by Anatol Rapoport (translation of Colonel J. J. Graham of 1908), Penguin Classics, 1968.

1. "On the Chungking Negotiations," *Selected Works of Mao Tsetung,* Vol. IV.
2. "Problems of War and Strategy," *Selected Works of Mao Tsetung,* Vol. II.

The Order of Events

Note: Some of the dates listed in *The Chinese Looking Glass* have been amended here. Early Chinese chronology is the subject of much contention and revision, and new information has since come to light.

The Emperor Fu Hsi (legendary)

THE HSIA DYNASTY (apocryphal) 1990–1557 B.C.

THE SHANG DYNASTY 1557–1027 B.C.

THE CHOU DYNASTY 1027–221 B.C.

Spring and Autumn Period 722–481 B.C.
Kuan Chung 710–645 B.C.
Ts'ao Mo threatens the Duke of Ch'i with a dagger 682 B.C.
Confucius 551–479 B.C.
Confucius accompanies the Duke of Lu to Ch'i 500 B.C.
Lao Tzu 5th century B.C. (?)
Sun Wu executes the King of Wu's concubines 496 B.C. (?)
Wu Tzu-hsiu of Wu commits suicide ("Tear out my eyes . . .") c. 490 B.C.

The Warring States 481–221 B.C.
Mo Tzu 468–376 B.C. (disputed)
Chuang Tzu 4th century B.C. (?)
Shan Yang 390–338 B.C. (authorities vary)
Mencius 386–312 B.C. (Communist sources say 390–305 B.C.)
Shen Pu-hai (reputed author of *Shen Tzu*) 385–337 B.C.

Wu Ch'i executed 381 B.C.
Sun Pin 380–320 B.C.
Shan Yang arrives in Ch'in c. 361 B.C.
Sun Tzu's *Art of War* 350 B.C. (?)
Sun Pin defeats P'ang Chuan of Wei 341 B.C.
Kuei Ku-tzu 4th century B.C.
Chang I becomes the chief minister of Ch'in 322 B.C.
Tsou Yen of the Yin-Yang school of philosophy c. 340–260 B.C.
Chi-hsia Academy established by King Hsuan of Ch'i 342–324 B.C.
Hsun Tzu (c. 312–233 B.C.) joins the Chi-hsia Academy c. 264 B.C.
Han Fei 280–233 B.C.
Li Ssu 280–208 B.C.
King of Ch'in overruns the other six states 229–222 B.C.

THE CH'IN DYNASTY 221–207 B.C.

First Emperor (Ch'in Shih Huang-ti) of a united China 221–210 B.C.
Li Ssu memorializes the emperor on the burning of the books 213 B.C.
Second Emperor 210–208 B.C.
Ch'en She mounts an insurrection 209 B.C.
Liu Pang (future emperor Han Kao-tsu) takes Hsienyang and accepts the submission of the Third Emperor of Ch'in 207 B.C.
Liu Pang and Hsiang Yu duel for the dominion of all China 207–202 B.C.
Liu Pang leads his men out of Hanchung by the "secret path" 206–205 B.C.
Hsiang Yu kills himself 202 B.C.

THE HAN DYNASTY 202 B.C.–A.D. 220

Western Han 202 B.C.–A.D. 9
The Emperor Han Kao-tsu (206–195 B.C.)* invites scholars to help administer the empire 196 B.C.
Dowager Empress Lu 188–180 B.C.
Emperor Wen 179–157 B.C.
Han Wu-ti 141–86 B.C.
Ssu-ma Ch'ien, compiler of the *Historical Records* c. 145–86 B.C.

* King in 206 B.C., emperor in 202 B.C.

Chang Ch'ien's mission to the west 138 B.C.
Sang Hung-yang introduces his economic reforms 110 B.C.
King Hermaeus installed by the Chinese 48 B.C.

"Hsin Dynasty" of Wang Mang A.D. 9–23
Red Eyebrows insurrection begins 18
Wang Mang struck down 22
Restoration of the Han Dynasty 25

Eastern Han A.D. 25–220
Pan Ch'ao's mission to the west 73
Eunuchs imprison the empress regent, execute all leading scholars, and dominate the young emperor Han Huan 168
Yellow Turbans revolt 184
Emperor Han Ling dies without direct heir 189 Yuan Shao butchers the eunuchs and Tung Cho seizes power
Tung Cho assassinated 192 Ts'ao Ts'ao gains control of the new emperor
Liu Pei seeks out Chuko Liang c. 207
Ts'ao Ts'ao eliminates Yuan Shao and controls North China by 208
Battle of Ch'ih-pi 208
Kuan Yu defeated and killed 219
Ts'ao Ts'ao dies 220
Ts'ao P'ei usurps throne from Emperor Han Hsien and becomes first ruler of Wei (North China) 220
The masters of Wu and Shu follow suit, and China is divided into three kingdoms 220–222

THE THREE KINGDOMS 220–265
Chuko Liang dies 234
Shu falls to Wei 263
Ssu-ma Yen usurps the throne of Wei and founds the Tsin Dynasty 265
Wu falls to Wei 280

THE PERIOD OF DISUNION 280–589

Western Tsin Dynasty 265–317
Huns overrun North China 316 Tsin court withdraws south to Yangtse River, near modern Nanking

Eastern Tsin Dynasty 317–420
Tibetan Empire displaces the Huns and dominates North China 351–394

Fu Chien (357–385) invades Tsin China. Battle of Fei River 383

Toba (Wei) Empire becomes dominant power in North China 385–557

Toba Empire splits into Northern Ch'i (550–577) and Northern Chou (557–580)

Yang Chien assassinates the Northern Chou emperor and undertakes the reunification of China 581

THE SUI DYNASTY 589–618

THE T'ANG DYNASTY 618–906

Li Shih-min reigns as Emperor T'ang T'ai-tsung 627–649

Wu Chao (623–705) reigns as Empress Wu Tse-t'ien 690–705

Wu Tse-t'ien liquidates 3,000 families 688–691

Emperor T'ang Hsuan-tsung (Ming Huang: 712–756) takes Yang Kuei-fei as concubine 745

Chinese defeated by Arabs near Samarkand 751

An Lu-shan revolt 755

Tibetans sack Ch'ang An 763

Ch'ang An and Loyang sacked following popular uprising led by Huang Ch'ao 880–881

Final collapse of T'ang China (and subsequent division into a northern empire and ten independent states in the south) 906

THE FIVE DYNASTIES 906–960

THE SUNG DYNASTY 960–1127

Sung China begins paying tribute to the Kitan in the north 1004

Wang An-Shih introduces economic reforms 1068 Dies 1086

The Kin destroy the Kitan empire 1125

The Kin seize the Sung capital at Kaifeng 1126

Hangchow becomes the capital of the "Southern Sung" after 1127

PARTITION: NORTHERN KIN AND SOUTHERN SUNG 1127–1279

Chu Hsi, leading Neoconfucian 1129–1200

Yo Fei begins to recover territory from the Kin 1131

Yo Fei murdered 1141
Sung Chiang forms a "righteous assembly" of outlaws 12th century
Yelu Ch'u-ts'ai 1190–1244
Mongols annihilate Hsia 1224
Genghis Khan dies 1227
Mongols take Kaifeng from the Kin and invade Sung China 1233

THE MONGOL (YUAN) DYNASTY 1260–1368

Wen T'ien-hsiang 1236–1283
Hangchow surrenders to Mongols 1276
Last Sung emperor drowns at Yaishan 1279
Shih Nai-an, author of *Water Margin* 1296–1370
Lo Kuan-chung writes *The Romance of the Three Kingdoms* 1364 (?)
Chu Yuan-chang (1328–1398) captures Nanking from the Mongols 1356
Chu Yuan-chang enthroned at Nanking as Ming T'ai-tsu, first emperor of the Ming Dynasty 1368

THE MING DYNASTY 1368–1644

The rebel Prince of Yen (future Emperor Yung Lo: 1403–1424) takes Nanking (1402) and moves his capital to Peking
The seven expeditions of Admiral Cheng Ho 1405–1433
The eunuch Liu Chin falls from power 1510
Portuguese sail up the Pearl River to Canton 1517
Japanese pirates besiege Nanking 1555
Ch'i Chi-kuang in Chekiang 1555
Portuguese allowed to trade at Macao 1557
Father Matteo Ricci reaches the interior of China 1598
Tunglin College established 1604
Downfall of the eunuch Wei Chung-hsien 1627–1628
Captain John Weddell arrives off Canton 1637
Li Tzu-ch'eng marches on Peking, Wu San-kuei turns his coat, and the Manchus invade China 1644

THE CH'ING (MANCHU) DYNASTY 1644–1912

Shih K'o-fa defies the Manchus at Yangchow 1645
Koxinga at the walls of Nanking 1659 Retires to Formosa 1661

Emperor K'ang Hsi authorizes foreign ships to trade at Canton 1685
First British "factory" built at Canton 1715
Captain George Anson at Canton 1742
White Lotus sect rebellion 1775
Lord Amherst leads an embassy to China 1816
Opium War 1840–1842
Treaty of Nanking, Hong Kong ceded to the British 1842
Hung Hsiu-ch'uan leads the Taiping Rebellion 1850–1864
Tseng Kuo-fan 1811–1872
Sino-British hostilities 1857–1860
Treaty of Tientsin 1860
Sino-Japanese War, Japanese acquire Korea and Formosa 1894–1895
Emperor Kuang Hsu calls for reform and is incarcerated by the Dowager Empress Tzu Hsi 1898
Yuan Shih-k'ai organizes a modern force of 7,000 men 1898
Boxer Rebellion 1900
Dowager Empress Tzu Hsi dies 1908
Yuan Shih-k'ai relieved of office 1909
Wuchang Uprising October 10, 1911
Yuan Shih-k'ai recalled November 1911
Revolutionary government at Nanking elects Dr. Sun Yat-sen (1866–1925) first Provisional President

THE CHINESE REPUBLIC 1912–1949

The Ch'ing Dynasty abdicates power and declares a republic February 1912 Sun Yat-sen cedes presidency to Yuan Shih-k'ai
Yuan Shih-k'ai announces his reign title as future first emperor of a new dynasty 1915
Yuan Shih-k'ai dies 1916
Chang Tso-lin master of Manchuria: rising power of warlords 1916–1927
May 4 Movement 1919
Communist Party inaugurated in Shanghai with Ch'en Tu-hsiu as Chairman 1921
Kuomintang reorganized with Russian assistance 1923
Whampoa Military Academy opens 1924
Sun Yat-sen dies 1925
"Northern Expedition" mounted by Chiang Kai-shek to unify China 1926

Chiang Kai-shek suppresses his Communist allies in Shanghai during the march north 1927

Mao Tsetung sets up his first guerrilla base at Chingkangshan 1927 Ch'en Tu-hsiu loses leadership of the Party

Chiang Kai-shek takes Peking 1928 Chang Tso-lin assassinated by the Japanese

Japanese occupy Manchuria (1931) and create puppet state of Manchukuo 1932–1945

"Long March" of the Communists under Mao Tsetung 1934–1935

The "Sian incident" in which Chiang Kai-shek is kidnapped 1936

Sino-Japanese War 1937–1945

Communists and Kuomintang join forces against the Japanese 1937

Mao launches "rectification" campaign to sinify Communism 1942

Civil war breaks out between Communists and Kuomintang 1946

Chiang Kai-shek withdraws to Formosa 1949

THE PEOPLE'S REPUBLIC OF CHINA 1949–

The Great Leap Forward and the formation of "people's communes" 1958

The Soviet Union suspends all aid to China 1960

Lu Ting-yi commissions a biography of Wei Cheng 1962

First Chinese atomic explosion 1964

The Great Cultural Revolution: Red Guards unleashed against "old ideas" and "revisionist" party bureaucracy 1966

Lin Piao named as successor to Chairman Mao at Ninth Congress of the Chinese Communist Party 1969

China joins the United Nations 1971

Lin Piao disgraced and reported killed in an air accident 1971

President Nixon visits Peking 1972 China and Japan establish diplomatic relations

Cross-posting of powerful military regional commanders officially announced January 1974

Nationwide campaign against Confucius and Lin Piao 1973–1974

Bibliography

CHINESE SOURCES

The Four Books: *Ta Hsueh*
Chung Yung
Lun Yu
Meng Tzu

The Classics: *Li Chi*
Shu Ching
Ch'un Ch'iu
Tso Chuan

(The Book of) *Mo Tzu*
Chuang Tzu
Hsun Tzu
Han Fei Tzu

Tao Te Ching
Lu Shih Ch'un Ch'iu, of Lu Pu-wei
Chang Kuo Ts'e, of Liu Shang
Sun Tzu Ping Fa, of Sun Wu
Shih Chi, of Ssu-ma Ch'ien
Han Shu, of Pan Ku
San Kuo Chih, of Ch'en Shou
San Kuo Yen Yi, by Lo Kuan-chung
Shui Hu Chuan, by Shih Nai-an
Yu Lin Wai Shih, by Wu Ching-tzu
Tzu Chih T'ung Chien, of Ssu-ma Kuang
Sui Shu
T'ang Shu

Sung Shih
Ming Shih
Sun Chung-shan Hsuan Chi. Chung Hua Book Co., Hong Kong, 1966.
Mao Tse-tung Hsuan Chi. People's Publishing Co., Peking, 1966.
Ts'an Chia Chung Kung Wu Chuang Tou Cheng Chi Shih, by Kung Ch'u (former political commissar of the Red Army under Mao Tsetung)
Kuo Fang Lun, by Chiang Fang-chen
Kuo Hsueh 12 Chiang, by Ts'ao Chu-jen. San Yu Publishing Co., Hong Kong, 1972.

ENGLISH-LANGUAGE SOURCES

PHILOSOPHY

The Chinese Classics, translated by James Legge, D.D., LL.D. Oxford University Press:
Volume 1: *The Confucian Analects*
The Great Learning
The Doctrine of the Mean
Volume 2: *The Works of Mencius*
Volume 3: *The Book of Historical Documents* (*Book of History*)
Volume 4: *The Book of Poetry* (*Book of Odes*)
Volume 5: *The Ch'un Ts'ew. The Tso Chuen*
Sources of Chinese Tradition, edited by William Theodore de Bary. Columbia University Press, New York, 1960.
Chinese Thought, by H. G. Creel. Eyre and Spottiswoode, London, 1954.
Three Ways of Thought in Ancient China, by Arthur Waley. George Allen and Unwin, London, 1939.
The Philosophers of China, by Clarence Burton Day. The Citadel Press, New York, 1962.
Confucius and the Chinese Way, by H. G. Creel. Harper and Brothers, New York, 1960.
The Book of Lieh Tzu, translated by A. C. Graham. John Murray, London, 1960.
The Way and Its Power, by Arthur Waley. George Allen and Unwin, London, 1934.
Chuang Tzu, translated by Burton Watson. Columbia University Press, New York, 1964.

Mo Tzu, translated by Burton Watson. Columbia University Press, New York, 1963.

Hsun Tzu, translated by Burton Watson. Columbia University Press, New York, 1963.

Han Fei Tzu, translated by Burton Watson. Columbia University Press, New York, 1964.

HISTORICAL CHINA

Records of the Grand Historian of China, translated from the *Shih Chi* of Ssu-ma Ch'ien by Burton Watson, Volumes 1 and 2. Columbia University Press, New York, 1961.

Records of the Historian, translated from the *Shih Chi* of Ssu-ma Ch'ien, Volumes 1 and 2. Hong Kong Contemporary Library, 1967.

China: A Short Cultural History, by C. P. Fitzgerald. Cresset Press, London, 1935.

A History of China, by Wolfram Eberhard. Routledge and Kegan Paul, London, 1950.

A Short History of the Chinese People, by L. Carrington Goodrich. George Allen and Unwin, London, 1957.

East Asia: The Great Tradition, by Edwin O. Reischauer and John K. Fairbank. Harvard University Press, Cambridge, 1958.

Chinese Civilisation, by Marcel Granet. Alfred A. Knopf, New York, 1930.

Everyday Life in Early Imperial China, by Michael Loewe. B. T. Batsford, London, 1968.

Daily Life in China, by Jacques Gernet. George Allen and Unwin, London, 1962.

Lady Wu, by Lin Yutang. William Heinemann, London, 1957.

The Empress Wu, by C. P. Fitzgerald. F. W. Cheshire, Melbourne, 1955.

The Traditional Chinese State in Ming Times (1368–1644), by Charles O. Hucker. University of Arizona Press, Tucson, 1961.

Europe and China, by G. F. Hudson, M.A. Beacon Press, Boston, 1931.

The Travels of Marco Polo, translated by Ronald Latham. Penguin Books, London, 1958.

Foreign Mud, by Maurice Collis. Faber and Faber, London, 1946.

The Great Chinese Travellers, edited by Jeannette Mirsky. George Allen and Unwin, London, 1965.

East-West Passage, by Michael Edwardes. Cassell, London, 1971.

China in the Eyes of Europe, by Donald Lach. University of Chicago Press, Chicago and London, 1965.

Science and Civilisation in China, by Joseph Needham, F.R.S., Volumes 1, 2, 3, 4(1), and 4(2). Cambridge University Press, 1954–65.

The Legacy of China, edited by Raymond Dawson. Clarendon Press, Oxford, 1964.

MILITARY

The Art of War, by Sun Tzu, translated by Samuel B. Griffith. Clarendon Press, Oxford, 1963.

A Military History of Modern China, by F. F. Liu. Princeton University Press, 1956.

The Red Army of China, by Edgar O'Ballance. Faber and Faber, London, 1962.

Selected Military Writings of Mao Tse-tung. Foreign Languages Press, Peking, 1966.

MODERN HISTORY

Revolution in China, by C. P. Fitzgerald. Cresset Press, London, 1952.

Selected Works of Mao Tse-tung. Foreign Languages Press, Peking, 1965.

Mao Tse-tung, by Stuart Schram. Penguin Books, London, 1966.

Chiang Kai-shek, by Robert Payne. Weybright and Talley, New York, 1969.

A History of Modern China, by Kenneth Scott Latourette. Penguin Books, London, 1964.

FICTION

The Romance of the Three Kingdoms, by Lo Kuan-chung, translated by C. H. Brewitt-Taylor. Charles E. Tuttle, Rutland, Vermont, and Tokyo, 1959.

Water Margin, by Shih Nai-an, translated by J. H. Jackson. The Commercial Press, Hong Kong, 1963.

All Men Are Brothers, by Shih Nai-an, translated by Pearl Buck. Methuen, London, 1933.

Index